BELOVED BROTHER

(Amato Fratello)

A Past-Life Novel in
Seventh-Century Scotland

WILLIAM L. SHAFFER

BALBOA.PRESS

A DIVISION OF HAY HOUSE

Balboa Press books may be ordered through booksellers or by contacting:

Balboa Press
A Division of Hay House
1663 Liberty Drive
Bloomington, IN 47403
www.balboapress.co.uk
1 (877) 407-4847

Print information available on the last page.

ISBN: 978-1-9822-8103-8 (sc)
ISBN: 978-1-9822-8104-5 (e)

Balboa Press rev. date: 11/07/2019

"To love another person is to see the face of God."

– Lyric by Herbert Kretzmer
(From the finale of the musical play *Les Miserables*)

"To speak Italian is to make love."

– William Shaffer
(Speaking from personal experience
via his seventh-century lifetime in Scotland,
but at that time known as Alba – the country,
not William!)

This novel is dedicated
to my beloved parents,
Harry and Eugenia Shaffer.
Thank you for being my parents
and for all you taught me.

Also, a very special thanks to my life-partner,
Donald Johnson, for his expert editing and for all the
support he gave me during the writing of this novel.

Contents

Author's Foreword xiii

PART I

One.. 1
Two.. 3
Three 9
Four 23
Five 35
Six.. 43
Seven 57
Eight 69
Nine.. 81
Ten... 89

PART II

Eleven 117
Twelve 145
Thirteen... 173
Fourteen 193
Fifteen... 219
Sixteen 233
Seventeen 255

Author's Afterword 259

Author's Foreword

I have no concept of seventh-century Italian dialects. So join me as the readers of this past-life memory novel by simply accepting the twenty-first century Italian that I used, while you and I pretend *in spirit* that Richard of Venice is using whatever dialect of early Venetian Italian that he actually spoke back then.

Venice, or Venezia as the Venetians call their home, was already a city by the seventh century A.D. Historians can date it back to at least the fifth century as an established city by the year 421 A.D., although people had been living in the area as far back as at least 1000 B.C.

Scotland was called Alba by the Celts living there at the time this book takes place. So whenever you read Alba in this novel, you will know what the hell I am talking about – Alba = Scotland.

All events and circumstances in this novel are described exactly as I have "remembered" them according to my own personal past-life memory – with the exception, of course, of the dialogues between the two ravens or when there is one raven thinking to himself. These two ravens have been added to my originally written 1984 version of the novel to provide a Greek chorus (or, in this instance, a *Scottish* chorus) to add depth and a finer explanation to what was really happening during my past-life. Therefore, all raven dialogues are pure fiction, but please enjoy them for the deeper insights that they bring to this story.

In the few scenes where I as Brother Peter was not present, I feel I have been guided to be thoroughly accurate in depicting what was said in those scenes. How do I know? Because my inner being, which I refer to as my Higher Self, told me so. Look – you either believe in this spiritual process or else you can read the novel as a science fiction fantasy. The choice is yours.

In my present life, I am still working on some of the same emotional issues that surfaced during my seventh-century past-life. Otherwise, there would have been no point to my writing this novel. Fortunately, re-writing this novel in 2019 has enormously improved my understanding and emotional processing of these issues, leading to a deeper healing transformation within me. I am most grateful for that.

France was known as Gaul by the ancient Romans, but this name was discontinued in 494 A.D. when the Franks, a German-speaking tribe, invaded and conquered. This former Gaul was mostly known in the seventh century as Francia. But I figured, what the hell? I'll just call it France. Go with it, and *sei gesund!* (Be in good health!) The characters will go back and forth between saying Gaul or France because news travelled very slowly back in those pre-internet centuries. Some people were uninformed or just downright confused back then, just like now.

Next, not everybody used the term "Moslems" (or "Muslims") back in seventh-century Europe, even though that term had existed since Muhammed's life. In Chapter 13, when you come across "Muhammadans", they are Moslems (or Muslims). Also, there is no recorded history of referring to Jews as "Jews" before 1275 A.D. So in this novel, Jews are referred to as Hebrews.

Now for a few words about my lover Richard. I know who Richard is, reincarnated into this present lifetime, and I even know the city where he lives and what he does for a living. But no, I don't know his home address, phone number, mobile number or e-mail address. I am NOT going to try to meet him, and I am NOT stalking him!

The reincarnation of Richard looks today EXACTLY as he and I both looked 1,300 years ago (you will understand this more clearly later on in the book). This sort of thing happens sometimes. I had quite a shock when I saw him for the first time three years ago in 2016. A BIG shock! I even burst out crying. Past-life memories – what are you going to do?

But I don't know if today this reincarnated Richard will ever read *Beloved Brother.* Nor do I know if he remembers any of that particular past-life within himself, or if he has chosen in this lifetime to not believe in reincarnation at all. But as a religious Catholic cousin of my partner

Donald once said, "I don't believe in reincarnation, but maybe I will in my next life." You just have to love that.

Either way, I wish the reincarnated Richard a life full of happiness, love and passionate magic. I hope he achieves, in his own way, whatever learning, healing and transformation he needs in this life.

I also need to make one thing perfectly clear to the presently reincarnated Richard, in case he ever does read this novel and recognises himself and his past in it. There are NO karmic connections binding us together in any way. There is NOTHING we need to continue or complete between us this time. We have moved on to work through our own unresolved issues on our own. There are no obligations or responsibilities between us. Okay? So you do not need to contact me – unless you WISH to. That would be something else, and I would be delighted. Otherwise, this time around I expect that you and I will live our lives separately.

OH! Before you start reading this novel, I have to give you fair warning. I am occasionally very explicit in describing the physically intimate scenes between Richard and Peter (*c'est moi!*). Yes, there is SEX aplenty in this book. If I am going to remember and process my past lives, then I think it is only fair for me to feel and re-experience those goody scenes, not just mentally recall them. There has to be SOME fringe benefits to this deep processing! So don't be surprised if some people who read this book view it as spiritual pornography! What a lovely thought!

Okay – go! Read my book. Enjoy!

PART I

One

THE SOARING CIRCLING raven thrilled at the sensation of cold air blasting against his wings. Playing with swirls, nosedives, curlicues and flamboyant curves, the raven spread his wings to full capacity in order to enjoy every aspect of magical flight. Gusts of air danced across the shiny blue-back of his feathered wings, as the raven navigated himself along the foothills of the Alban {Scottish} Highlands.

Below him, the raven caught sight of his favourite dark-robed monk making his way towards the foothills.

"There he is again," the raven thought to himself. *"That lone human is headed once again towards the foothills, as he does almost every day. It is always about the same time as the day before and the day before that,"* the raven noted as he checked the position of the sun in the sky. *"This human is once more leaving the fellowship of that cacophony of monks whose minds are as endlessly noisy and empty as the sounds they utter from their faces. No wonder my monk seeks time away from them. But why he is with them to begin with is beyond my understanding."*

The raven knew this lonely man very well, observing the monk daily for over three years. Whether the raven was seeking food or a new mate or to just enjoy the loveliness of his flight, he could always spot the lone human monk who separated himself from his brethren to seek peace and union with the Earth in the foothills of the Highlands – on his own.

"This human is very interesting," the raven noted as he flew in circles a hundred metres above. *"There is an immense depth of sensitivity, compassion*

1

and intelligence, but so much of it is repressed by the heavy weight of his fears. I KNOW there is bubbling passion in this monk, buried beneath fear, doubt and a lack of trust in himself. This human is terrified of rejection, yet his actions provoke constant rejection from his fellow monks. He fears loneliness but lives a life filled with it. What he fears the most he relentlessly creates and draws to himself. Humans are most bizarre in their total ignorance of what they persistently create for themselves."

The raven made another circle around the walking monk before lowering one of his wings in greeting to the man. The monk waved his response, always looking for the raven's greeting as he eagerly returned the gesture with the wave of his arm.

"This human is indeed most peculiar. The energy of the aura around his body screams for love and connection, yet he does everything in his power to avoid that which he most seeks. He is terrified that getting what he wants will only result in giving him more pain. As intelligent as this man thinks he is, still he does not grasp that the more he holds on to that fearful belief, the more he will deny himself what he most desires. This human is in desperate need of a life experience that will throw open the gates of his self-inflicted imprisonment and give him what he most wants. But will he allow it? Or will his fears remain in control and dominate his life and soul, imposing eternal loneliness and separation?"

The raven felt hungry and decided to leave the walking man and hunt for food. The human would be there walking tomorrow and the day after that, so the raven dipped his wing in farewell and sped away.

Two

BROTHER PETER EAGERLY waved his greeting to the circling raven high above him who greeted the monk with the dip of a wing during every one of Peter's daily treks into the hills, regardless of the season.

Only these walks gave true balance to his soul. Only here, walking alone across the heather-covered foothills of the Alban Highlands, could the lonely monk recapture his inner peace. He sighed in gratitude as the blissful silence enveloped him like the monk's robe that draped over his body.

Brother Peter stepped with sure-footedness along the gentle slopes, the two ends of his rope belt bobbing like a meditative litany against his left thigh and in unison with his heartbeat. The hood of his dark brown robe was pulled up over his head, and his hands grasped the opposite wrists inside his long sleeves, to protect them from the cold lashes of the mid-September winds.

The hills were ablaze with the fiery reddish-gold of the early autumn heather, transformed a few weeks earlier from swaths of lush purple. Brother Peter loved equally the summer purple and the autumn reddish-gold, and he especially enjoyed the heather's spectacular transition of colours from one season into the next. It gave him the unique experience of walking the same Earth daily, but as if through different worlds of visual sensation.

Only here in these hills could Peter escape the daily monotony of his monk life, the endless stream of work, prayers and meditation – the drudgery of his sparse and self-denying life. After all these years, he dreaded the relentless clanging of that damned rusty bell summoning the brothers back to never-ending prayer.

First was Matins in the darkness of the middle of the night. Then cockcrow Lauds. Prime called forth the monks a mere hour later. Terce followed three hours after Prime. The bell clanging at noon called the monks to Sext. A mere three hours later was Nones. Another three hours later the bell announced Vespers. And, according to Peter, just one hour later added insult to injury with Compline. When all that daily routine was finished, it would start all over again.

Peter constantly fumed internally about all this. *"WHO or WHAT kind of God,"* he thought to himself, *"needs so much attention and prayer from monks that he has called forth to this duty so relentlessly and mercilessly?"*

The worst for Brother Peter, however, was that the food was boring, the monastery was boring, his tiny personal cell was boring, prayers were boring, meditation was boring and almost all the other monks were EXTREMELY boring. Even the never-ending boredom was boring.

"Stop it!" he muttered under his breath, briefly massaging both of his throbbing temples before resuming the wrist-clutch within his sleeves.

Once upon a time Peter used to take great delight in the choir chanting, the lit candles and the ringing bells. But it had all quickly faded into hollow boredom. Now one day was like the next – no variety, no spontaneity, no stimulation. Just the same, day after never-ending day.

Only the heathered hills offered Peter solace and escape from the maddening sameness of his life.

Brother Peter paused to catch his breath, enjoying the cool, crisp fresh air that filled his lungs. The sweet smell of the heather caressed his nostrils until he thought his heart would swell up and burst out of his chest.

"I'm so damned sick of *aves* and *paternosters*, of *glorias* and *psalms!*" he yelled at the heathered hills. "It is all so useless, meaningless and BORING!"

Then Brother Peter sighed as he had sighed hundreds of times each day, chasing the uncomfortable feelings away and recapturing the soothing peace of the Highlands. But his mind was as relentless as his life, and soon he was muttering out-loud to himself again.

"You are a poor son of a poor farmer. That life as a farmer would have been just as boring as this one. Thank God that my father recognised and appreciated my sharp mind and encouraged me to be a monk so I could at least put my mind to use, to learn to read and write and transcribe, instead of simply working myself to death tilling the land as he did."

Farmer or monk – those had been his only choices. The drudgery of a poor farmer's life or the drudgery of a monk. Such were the limitations of a soul born into late seventh century mid-Alba.

Or, Brother Peter had considered, there was a third choice. He could have become a soldier. To go into battle in order to kill or be killed fighting for other men's disputes, petty jealousies and revenges? To participate in slaughter, rape, pillaging, and drinking himself stupid every night?

"No thank you!" Brother Peter's mind responded to that.

The other monks had recognised Brother Peter's mental sharpness and had initially welcomed him into the monastery. So to the monk's world he had succumbed. Brother Peter had been taught to read and write and had quickly displayed an immense talent for copying the manuscripts of the Lord's holy words.

But for Brother Peter, manuscript-copying became just another way to escape from his hated emotions of loneliness and hopelessness. Peter's mind wandered inside the stylish sweeping curls of the Latin calligraphy, just as his feet wandered across the heathered foothills. But a monk's personality he did not really possess. Surrender, patience, devotion, discipline, compassion, and the hardest one of all – obedience. All these were alien to Brother Peter, if not downright abhorrent.

He was a loner, an individualist, and as stubborn and immovable as the stones beneath his feet. He was impatient of patience and intolerant of any sign of ignorance or slowness in others. Blind obedience was anathema. Humility was impractical, self-denying and nauseating to his temperament. He liked to do things his way and in his own particular time. Everyone else should stay out of his way. If anyone needed Brother

Peter to explain something more than once – run for the hills as fast as you can!

The other monks quickly had their hands full with Peter. "Arrogant, cold, selfish, impatient, intolerant and unfeeling," were the usual complaints. "God will strike him down one day!"

There were, however, a few monks who found Brother Peter sometimes amusing, while a mere handful could be patient with him because they could sense hidden passionate potentials buried deep under a mental mountain of loneliness and insecurity.

However, one young and naively idealistic monk found Peter fascinating, powerful, enticingly handsome, wonderfully mysterious and downright godlike. But that boyish monk, Brother Andrew, would never allow Brother Peter to know his true feelings for fear of both Peter's anticipated disgust-filled rejection and the terror of God's wrathful punishment for any man who had such 'evil' sexual feelings towards another man.

But Brother Peter was impatiently annoyed by all the monks – because it was easier that way. He kept to himself and intolerantly ignored the lot on grounds of their presumed stupidity. And this scorn only fuelled the debate about Brother Peter among his so-called brethren.

Back to Peter's walk in the Highland foothills. He knew that he had finally reached the point where he must turn around and return to the monastery – which was nearly an hour's walk away from the southern shore of the enormous lake that centuries later would be known as Loch Lomond. Peter longed to keep walking, heading due west into the heart of the Highlands. But he knew he must return to the monastery before *vespers* or catch hell for being late.

Father Abbot might forbid Peter to walk into the foothills again for a month or more. Peter also feared he might be condemned to endless weeks of floor-scrubbing, meditation and psalm-reading that would keep him away from his beloved hills for far too long. Full of self-righteous disdain, Peter grudgingly forced his feet to turn around and head back to the monastery – "this imprisoning hell of God," as he derisively called it.

Stressed by the need for speed, Peter hurried back – his mouth set in a frozen petulant frown. His feet stomped unforgivingly as he urged his stiff and tired body onward. Caught up in his self-pity, Peter was at first completely unaware of the cacophonous commotion emanating from the monastery, which was now some hundred paces ahead of him. In fact, it wasn't until Brother Peter approached the stone arch in the outer wall that the noise finally penetrated his morose brooding.

"Now what?" he complained aloud as he marched through the archway entrance.

A little more than a hundred metres behind Peter, a man on horseback arched an eyebrow as he sat quietly upon his horse and observed Peter's quickening form. The man was hoping that following the monk at a discreet distance had finally led him to what he was looking for.

Three

Noisy chaos flooded the monastery courtyard. All forty-eight monks were either huddled together in small frightened groups or were running helter-skelter as if escaping from a beehive some maddened bull had kicked.

Brother Peter's dark chocolate brown eyes (if they had known what chocolate was in seventh-century Alba) smouldered with anger as he spied the scattered robes, kitchen utensils, broken wine jars, unrolled manuscripts and various writing materials strewn across the courtyard amidst the huddled groups of quivering monks. Goats, pigs, chickens and a mule wandered aimlessly or stood motionless beside the monks and the dispersed debris, adding their animal noises to the cacophony of the monks.

"What a God-damned mess!" Brother Peter thought with fuming anger, more concerned about the disarray that would have to be cleaned up than the cause of the spectacle. He loathed messiness, uncleanliness and disorganisation above all things – except stupidity. The scene before him triggered all his "piss me off" issues, especially the stupidity box.

For one instant, however, Brother Peter allowed himself to be amused by the cries of the monks that sounded all too similar to the cackles, bleats and grunts of the monastery's animals.

"Chubby Brother Joseph squeals like our pig and *looks* like one too," Peter said aloud to no one in particular.

But his sense of being offended by the filthy disorder recaptured Peter's attention. With mounting impatient anger, he demanded to the chaos in his most booming voice, "What in God's name is going on here?"

Most of the monks jumped in fear as they turned to face the tall, broad-shouldered, narrow-waisted figure of Brother Peter who remained standing just inside the monastery's stone-entrance archway.

"Brother Peter, where have you been?" a whiny voice from one of the terrified monks asked. "Thank the Lord you have returned. It is sheer pandemonium here!"

The whining voice belonged to blond Brother Andrew, the twenty-year-old newest and youngest monk, six years Peter's junior in age but (according to Peter) always acting half that. Andrew's petite body raced towards Peter, hoping he would now be protected by the tall, handsome and smouldering monk. Andrew stared into Peter's exquisitely chiselled face, falling in love again with those dark eyes, the aquiline nose and two high-boned cheeks adorned by a neatly trimmed dark beard. Andrew hopelessly adored Peter.

However, Brother Peter's eyes bore impatiently into the young panic-stricken face of Andrew, neither admiring nor acknowledging Andrew's rumpled blond hair circling the head's small tonsure – or Andrew's blue eyes, clean-shaven rosy cheeks and narrow chin. Peter was impervious to any feelings or desire concerning Andrew – or any other human being, for that matter.

Andrew's hope for loving protection was instantly crushed as he pulled back in fear from Brother Peter's scornful expression. No compassion or comfort were offered here – only Peter's impatient anger.

"Will somebody please tell me what in the HELL is happening?" Peter demanded. "Who made this mess? Why are none of you cleaning up this utter chaos?"

Most of the other monks were still too stunned and frightened to reply, remaining in their terrified huddles and staring stupidly at Brother Peter. A few monks recovered enough from their panic to become angry at Peter's arrogant demeanour, but they remained unwilling to answer his questions.

Andrew, assuming as usual that Peter's annoyance had something to do specifically with *himself*, remained silent out of a guilt that said he was somehow the cause of all this trouble – whatever "this trouble" might be.

Finally, a middle-aged tall and thin Prior Thomas stepped forward from a huddled group and addressed Peter. "While you were out wandering the hillsides as you are always prone to do instead of remaining here to fulfil your duties to your brotherhood, some vermin highwaymen descended upon us like a plague of locusts, stealing our food, tearing the monastery to pieces and demanding we hand over the jewels and gold they imagined us to have hidden somewhere in the chapel. God only knows why they think we could possibly have such treasures here." Prior Thomas' tone was scathing. "Does that sufficiently answer your questions, BROTHER?"

Brother Peter ignored the sarcasm and glanced around the courtyard, spotting three saddled horses standing together in a corner as they calmly grazed the monastery's short grass, oblivious to the human commotion.

"Three horses, therefore three highwaymen," Peter announced in a cool voice. "I would hardly call that a plague of locusts. Am I to understand that nearly fifty monks cannot control these three useless rats?"

Fear transformed into outrage as several monks reacted with angry shouts. "We are MONKS, servants of God and Jesus Christ. We do not resort to violence!"

Brother Peter rolled his eyes in exasperation and exhaled yet another impatient breath, puffing out both cheeks and then briefly sticking out the tip of his tongue from between his clenched front teeth. This was his standard expression of annoyance, known irritably by all the other monks.

"Lord have mercy upon us ignorant, helpless sheep," Brother Peter prayed aloud with equal irony to match Prior Thomas. "Self-defence does not equate us with marauding thieves, you spineless nitwits! Where is Father Abbot?"

As if on cue, Father Abbot Paul emerged from the monastery chapel, taunted and jostled by the three ugliest, filthiest and most disgusting men Brother Peter had ever seen. Their clothes were nothing more than tattered rags, and their hair were dark mats glistening with sweat and oil.

Peter shuddered disapprovingly, imagining the lice proliferating among the three men. Seeing their blackened hands, swaggering movements and obscene loud ignorance forced Peter to consciously prevent himself from vomiting.

"Unhand Father Abbot at once and remove your offensive presence from our holy place!" Peter shouted as he stepped further into the monastery's courtyard.

Time froze in an ugly tableau of apprehension by the monks but violent glee from the three thieves.

"Well, well, well, lookie here, boys," one of the men said. "We finally meet a cock among the castrated chicklets."

Father Abbot was gruffly thrown to the ground as the three thugs leered hungrily at this "new meat" to play with. A few monks started to help Father Abbot Paul to stand up and move away to safety, but then they froze in mid-stride when all three highwaymen suddenly brandished their knives and swords.

"A monk with balls!" one of the three men called out.

"Are you sure about that?" another of the men taunted. "Perhaps we should investigate for ourselves."

Two of the thieves kicked Father Abbot in the ribs as the frightened monks winced in sympathetic pain. Then all three outlaws turned on Brother Peter as some of his fellow monks managed to drag Father Abbot back inside the monastery. Those monks remaining outside in the courtyard stood frozen while frenzied farm animals squawked among them all.

Brother Peter pushed a quivering young Andrew away and stood defiantly with arms crossed and feet planted firmly apart, his eyes pouring raw rage into the stupid leers of the three criminals.

"How dare you desecrate a house of God!" Peter spat as the three thieves stopped in front of him, swords and knives held loosely at their sides. "We have no gold or jewels here. We are simple monks living out our own lives, which does not include you. Leave us NOW!"

"Where is your humility and compassion, oh holy monk?" one of the men jeered as he traced a line with the tip of his sword from Peter's chest down his right leg.

Peter willed himself not to flinch a muscle, and then he spoke slowly, as if to idiots, and with increasing volume. "Remove yourselves and your stinking lice and leave us before your filth defiles us any further."

All three highwaymen reacted with murderous rage. "Perhaps this holier-than-thou rooster needs a lesson in divine humility," one of the men replied.

"I say we de-cock this arrogant rooster," said another, grinning.

"If there really is anything there to de-cock," the third man added.

Instantly, two of the men dropped their weapons and attacked Brother Peter with their bare hands. Peter was strong, but the rage he had provoked was too much for him to fend off. In seconds, the men had thrown a wildly kicking Brother Peter to the ground as the other monks remained too terrified to move.

The third highwayman knelt down at the feet of the pinned monk. "I have always wanted to know what you monks were hiding under your robes. Spread his legs," he ordered his two compatriots.

The other two highwaymen fiercely held Peter down as they first forced his legs apart and then held the legs down. Peter wanted to cry out from the searing pain of their cruel grips, but he willed himself to remain silent while gathering his wits and energy to free himself.

The highwayman kneeling at Peter's feet began to pull his robe above the monk's naked knees. When Peter tried to kick him away, the thief punched Peter just above his groin. Peter wheezed from the loss of air, the pain blinding him nearly senseless as he desperately tried to breathe.

"You just relax and be a good boy and this will not hurt a bit. Or maybe it will," the man laughed with a sinister hiss.

The kneeling man then thrust a filthy hand up Peter's robe and grabbed hold of the monk's penis and testicles.

"Ho-ho!" the highwayman laughed. "This monk is indeed a cock, and he wears no undies. How convenient of you!"

The other two highwaymen laughed as they tightened their grips.

All the other monks turned away in horror and shame, crossing themselves and praying for this unspeakable atrocity to end quickly. Not one of them attempted to overpower the three men and rescue Peter. Some of monks even suppressed the tiniest of smiles because finally, they thought, their arrogant, elitist brother was meeting his appropriate punishment from an avenging God.

Brother Andrew grew paler by the second, spots swirling before his eyes until he feared he would choke and pass out. His heart cried out to save Brother Peter from this horrifying violation, but Andrew also cursed himself for his cowardly immobility.

The highwayman mercilessly teased his victim by gently, almost lovingly, caressing Peter's penis and testicles. "There, there," he purred. "Be nice and cooperate."

Peter struggled to free himself so he could spit into the face of his molester. But for his efforts he was slapped several times, their grips twisting his arms tightly until Peter thought they would break off. Then Peter screamed hysterically as his penis was tugged and his testicles squeezed so hard he feared they would be crushed.

"Is he hard for you yet?" one of the men holding Peter in place asked the one grabbing the monk's genitals.

"Not yet, but I will get him there," the kneeling highwayman grinned.

"Then turn him over so all of us can take turns buggering him real good," the other man holding Peter down crudely suggested.

"Cut off his balls," the other man said.

"We can do both, boys," the molester replied, intensifying his grip on Peter's penis.

"Or," a rich, baritone voice with an odd, distinctly foreign accent suddenly offered, "let him go right now so I can slice you three into tiny, insignificant pieces of stinking turds."

Peter sighed with relief as the grip on his penis and testicles was finally released. The three men turned in surprised unison to face a knight atop a white steed. The visor on the dark circular metal helmet was down, concealing the knight's face.

"Where did YOU come from?" the man who had been gripping Peter's genitals asked angrily. "Did a fairy conjure you out of thin air? Go away and do not interfere in what is none of your business."

"I have just made it MY business, and you three stinking turds will get on your horses and leave now!" the knight commanded in his foreign accent as he drew his sword and leapt off his horse.

All the other monks froze, barely breathing. None of them had even noticed when the knight had mysteriously entered the courtyard on his white horse, as if a spectre had instantly materialised out of nothingness.

What followed next would always remain as a blurred memory to Peter as well as to the other monks. Peter would later recall being released and rolled over onto his side as he heard curses and clashes of steel. He would vaguely remember Brother Andrew helping him to stand, fussing and clucking over him like an over-protective mother hen. And Peter would not recall any other monks ever coming to his assistance.

The four men swirled around one another, swords striking, and intermittently the highwaymen's knives thrusting towards the knight. Their bodies moved in blurred lightning speed as pigs and chickens raced amok, shouts and curses abounded, and always the flashing and clashing of weapons. First one highwayman and then another were knocked down, only to rebound in a few moments. But the knight never fell.

Attacks, thrusts and counter-thrusts swirled everywhere, with the monks constantly running out of the way. The knight stepped with grace and speed, turning and twisting his sword to fend off his three foes, never once faltering.

At some point, Father Abbot re-emerged from the monastery with Prior Thomas and the healer monk, Brother Bartholomew. All three monks were visibly dismayed by the erupting violence.

Meanwhile, Peter felt sickened by the most intimate and disgusting invasion of his body. The violation of his private parts had made Peter feel horrifically humiliated. He was bruised and sore, but otherwise safe and unscathed. Peter's disgust at his personal invasion competed with his fascination towards his mysterious saviour.

Who was this shining knight, and how had he shown up at this remote monastery at such an opportune moment? Had the knight been pursuing the three highwaymen for some time? The speed and skill of the knight fighting the three thieves held Peter spellbound, and all the other monks too.

Peter then realised that one of the three highwaymen lay dead with his severed head rolling away from the still-twitching body, blood spurting from the dead thief's gashed neck like a jerking, spasmodic fountain.

"Fascinating," Peter thought with intellectual awe but void of any emotion. Andrew and several other monks turned away to retch violently. One monk passed out, was then scooped up and carried away by a few other monks.

"Well," Peter thought sullenly, *"at least some of the brothers have finally transformed themselves into active beings. My near-rape and probable murder certainly did not elicit any reaction from them."*

A second highwayman fell to his knees, holding his stunned head. Then the knight swiftly turned to the third man and thrust his sword deep into the villain's stomach. As the sword was pulled out, the highwayman's body crumpled to the ground, a narrow stream of blood oozing from his abdomen. Several more monks vomited or fainted, but a few cheered.

The knight turned and gave his audience a little bow, the blood-drenched sword held lightly at his side. But as the knight took a step towards Brother Peter, he suddenly halted – as if seeing Peter had given him an enormous shock.

Staring intently and closely into Peter's face for the first time, the knight muttered, ***"Cosa vedo? Tu chi sei?"*** {"What am I seeing? Who are you?"} The knight spoke in a language that Peter could not understand.

In the next split second, the highwayman who had been stunned leapt up from his kneeling position and thrust his sword into the knight's left side, the blade having penetrated through a gap in the knight's rusted chainmail.

"Dio porco!" {"God of a pig!"}

All the monks, including Peter, gasped in horror as the knight dropped his sword, swayed, and sank to his knees. Then the knight reached out an arm to Peter, who grabbed the knight's hand and stared at his helmet, frustrated that he could not see his rescuer's face through the slit.

Gasping for breath, the knight muttered, ***"Sei della mia anima."*** {"You are of my soul."} With another gasp, the knight fell forward and crashed upon the ground.

The remaining living highwayman held his sword as he rose and then stood over the fallen knight. As he grabbed his sword's hilt in both hands and prepared to plunge his sword into the knight, something immediately and irrevocably snapped in Brother Peter. The monk filled with blinding rage, unconscious of where he was or what he was doing. Before the highwayman could deliver his final strike, Peter snatched the knight's sword and in one swift movement, he bore down upon the shocked highwayman.

"My God, what is happening?" Father Abbot asked aghast as the other monks were seized anew by paralysing shock.

But Brother Peter was not finished, not by a long shot. Consumed by fury, Peter hacked again and again at the highwayman. Thick blood spurted everywhere as Peter kept stabbing at the long-dead body. No amount of thrusting was enough.

Pieces of hair and skin flew about. Sword striking bone created a horrendous cracking sound. Peter's hands, face and the front of his robe were covered in blood while the hacking and stabbing continued.

"Stop it!" Father Abbot finally managed to cry out. "Stop this madness at once!"

The highwayman's body had become nothing more than a mass of bloody pulp, but Peter kept hacking, completely deaf to Abbot Paul's command.

Finally, Brother Bartholomew, the monastery's healer, broke free of his terror-stricken paralysis and stumbled towards Peter. With some effort, the healer-monk managed to grab the hacking arm from behind as he spoke patiently and soothingly to Peter. It took a full minute for the tall, narrow-bodied and narrow-faced Brother Bartholomew to cease Peter's dreadful stabbing.

Peter stared blankly at the body he had so thoroughly destroyed as well as at the other two corpses, in that moment not knowing who he was or what had happened. He knelt down, sat back on his haunches against the also kneeling Brother Bartholomew and just continued to stare blankly.

Suddenly, prayers, cries and groans from the monks punctuated the shock-laden air while the animals remained stilled and silent from the horror. Brother Peter blinked and frowned, as if returning to consciousness from some far-away place.

"What happened?" Peter finally asked.

"Everything will be fine," Brother Bartholomew whispered soothingly, his hands delicately releasing their hold on Peter's arm while gently removing the sword from Peter's grasp. "It is over. The three men are dead. We are all safe now."

Brother Peter shook his head to free himself from his stupor. He slowly stood up, moved with jerky steps, then knelt beside the knight who was lying in a foetal position upon the ground. Peter turned the knight's body to face him and cradled the wounded warrior in his arms. Blood oozed from the knight's dirty blood-stained jerkin, between Peter's fingers and onto Peter's already blood-stained robe. The knight's helmet had not yet been removed, so Peter could still not see the face of the man who had saved his life.

Concern and gratitude for the valiant warrior filled Brother Peter, but only momentarily. He was not used to feeling anything for anyone else, and he was overwhelmed by the intensity of the events as well as by his alien emotions.

Peter's mind automatically took over with its controlling thoughts about focusing on what his mind determined were the crucial minute external details to be taken care of as soon as possible in order to protect himself against the invasion of his "dangerous" emotions. He therefore concerned himself solely with all the blood, dirt and chaos around him that needed (his mind told him) to be cleaned up.

While Peter remained focussed on the external chaos around him, Bartholomew knelt beside the wounded knight and quickly examined the stab wound through the knight's rusty chain mail. He gingerly felt around the wound as well as put his ear to the knight's chest to listen to the man's breathing and heartbeat. And then Bartholomew placed his fingers around one of the knight's wrists to check the pulse.

When Bartholomew completed his initial examination of the wounded knight, he joined Father Abbot, Prior Thomas and Brother Andrew as all four men approached the still shaking and stunned Peter.

"Help us move this knight inside immediately," Brother Bartholomew ordered several other monks. "He is hurt and may be dying. I must act quickly if there is any hope of saving him. And will one of you please see to the knight's horse, put him in the stables and make sure he is adequately fed."

A few traumatised monks slowly mobilised themselves to lift the knight from Peter's lap, while others took care of the horse.

"What about the other three horses, the ones that belonged to the highwaymen?" another monk asked.

"For heaven's sake," Prior Thomas cried out in condescending impatience. "Can none of you think for yourselves? Of course, tend to the other horses as well!"

"Gently, gently," Father Abbot admonished. "We are all in a state of shock. And let us not be the cause of this valiant knight's death. Be gentle."

As the knight was gently lifted up by four monks who then followed Brother Bartholomew to the monastery's infirmary, Brother Peter only had one question to ask.

"Who is going to clean up this courtyard mess?" Peter asked, louder than he had intended.

"Just like Brother Peter," Prior Thomas hissed, "to be more concerned with his obsessive need for tidiness than for the life of the man who just saved his life!"

"Still arrogant, even after facing his own near-death," another monk piped in.

"A castration might have done him good, the cold devil," a third monk added.

"Shame on all of you!" Andrew screamed as the unconscious knight disappeared with his four monk bearers inside the monastery. "You are all far worse than what you accuse Brother Peter of, you cowardly hypocrites!"

Brother Andrew blushed crimson at his own outburst. He rarely spoke up around others, much less in such an aggressive manner. His body shook with waves of guilt and also worrying about the penance he would have to pay for such a wanton outburst (in his own mind).

Monks shuffled away from an equally blushing Peter who struggled to suppress the memories of his public violation and the unbearable humiliation his mind refused to allow him to feel. Then Peter wobbled to his feet.

Other brothers dragged away the three dead highwaymen's bodies to prepare for burial, whimpering and gagging with each step. Gradually, in an aura of heavily numbed shock, the clean-up of the courtyard began.

Brother Peter vaguely heard scurrying feet and other human and animal sounds around him, but he remained emotionally frozen. If only he could escape back to his beloved hills and be rid of all this blood and filth and chaos. He could still feel the grasp of the highwayman's filthy hand on his genitals, and it sickened him beyond bearing. As the monks around him cleared away the chaos, Peter vaguely overheard some brothers gossiping.

"Did you see Brother Peter? He acted like a crazed madman."

"It was pure murder in his eyes."

"What you actually mean is, there was *nothing* in his eyes. Stone-cold and unfeeling. He was devil-possessed, I tell you."

"You would be too if you were nearly raped and murdered."

The monks collectively shuddered at that last statement.

"It was the Lord's revenge for Brother Peter's unfeeling arrogance."

"He is forever obsessed with dirt and disorder and cares nothing for his fellow brethren."

"He is rude."

"He is evil."

"He is mad."

"He is a child of God as we all are, so can you all just shut up now and do what needs to be done?"

Eyes glared testily towards the source of the last remark.

"Why do you defend him, Brother Clair?"

"I neither defend, criticise nor condemn," came the reply from the short, chubby monk. "And that is more than I can say for the lot of you — a pack of gossiping hens violating Brother Peter just as offensively with your words as what those men committed with their actions. So much for humility and compassion. Brother Andrew was right — you are all hypocrites. What was it our Lord said about 'casting the first stone'?"

The monks glared peevishly as the plump monk moved away from them.

"Hmph, Brother Clair of course," one of the gossiping brothers spat. "Leave it to one madman to stand up for another."

"Well said, Brother. Yes, consider the source."

"Are you ill?"

At first, Brother Peter jerked at Brother Andrew's intrusive question. Then Peter nodded slowly, frowned and mutely shook his head.

"Let me help you," Andrew pleaded, unmasked adoration towards Peter shining from his sky-blue eyes.

Peter shook his head, oblivious to anything masked or unmasked in Andrew's face.

"Please, Brother Peter, let me help you," Andrew insisted.

But when Andrew tried to grasp Peter's hand (with a hot tingling sensation exploding down the young monk's spine), Peter pushed Andrew away.

Two other monks, witnessing Peter's rebuke and Andrew's guilt-ridden face, shook their heads and glanced at each other with mutual knowing. "Typical," one whispered to the other.

"Brother Andrew is so damned annoying," Peter thought defensively to himself. *"He is too sensitive and over-reacts to everything. And his neediness gets on my nerves."*

Peter hated Andrew's "illogical and inefficient" emotions. Walking away, Peter gave his trademark deep exhaling of breath, with his cheeks puffing out and his tongue tip peeking from between his front teeth. He was relieved his own emotions were finally getting under control, or so his mind tried to convince Peter. But deep down, the humiliation of his physical violation twisted and stabbed inside Peter's stomach.

"I must not feel this anymore," Peter ordered himself. *"I have to get away and be alone. I will forget this invasion of my body. Stay in control. It is over. It is finished. I will feel nothing. I am in control."*

Peter moved unconsciously as he helped clean up the holocaust around him, his face remaining resolute. *"I will not allow any emotions to destroy my clarity and peace. I will feel nothing. I am in control."*

Two ravens sat on a monastery stone wall observing the human drama in the courtyard below.

"Which human do you pay so much attention to?" one raven asked the other.

"That one there, walking under the arch," the second raven replied.

"The one that was nearly raped and killed by the three intruders?"

"Yes, that is him."

"What a disgusting drama that was. Your monk is lucky it did not get any worse. It is a good thing that the knight showed up, and then look what happened to HIM. Humans are so damned disgusting. So tell me, what makes your monk so special from the other human idiots?"

"There is far more inside him. He is deeper in so many ways. More powerful. A profound emotional body, if we can just get him to open up to it and trust it. But he is horribly repressed and damaged by his many past-life self-denials and fears. He is going to need a lot of work."

"What human does NOT need a lot of work?" the first raven asked. *"The other humans, I must say, are all weak and complete idiots."*

"Mostly, I would agree with you, though there is a small handful of these monks who are also very interesting and filled with deeper thoughts, emotions and energies that are quite promising."

"You give far too much credit to humans. They are dumber than the shit I poop when I fly."

"Not all. Some are worth watching. This one they call Peter I am very interested in. I have known him for many centuries of his lifetimes by now, and I can tell you that he is not at all what he appears to be on the surface. There is far, far more inside him that I hope will soon come out into the open."

"You give far too much credit to humans," the first raven repeated.

"And you do not give enough."

"Hardly."

The ravens flew away to find their next meals, as the humans below continued clearing up the monastery courtyard.

Four

BROTHER PETER SAT impatiently in the monastery's meeting cell as he awaited Father Abbot's arrival. The plain wooden chair was uncomfortable, and Peter squirmed from the spasming lower back pain whenever he had to sit straighter in the chair.

The tiny grey stone cell was lonely in its stark and drab emptiness. For this meeting cell, Father Abbot insisted on minimal furniture and no wall decorations or floor coverings. He wanted only the chairs and the monks present in the room whenever there was a brother-to-brother meeting. Not even a simple table was allowed in the cell.

"How odd," Peter thought again as he did whenever he was called to this small meeting cell. *"Not even a crucifix on a wall. I understand that Father Abbot wants simplicity to convey clarity, but why the absence of the crucifix that is hung in every other cell of our monastery? What is he hoping to say that will not upset the other monks?"*

Peter had no time to answer his question as Paul, the Father Abbot, silently glided into the room. Closing the door, Paul stepped past Peter and sat down quickly, the hem of his dark robe swirling around his feet. Peter barely had time to rise, bow to Father Abbot with his palms pressed together, and then sit down again. The two men sat across from each other in a moment of silence as Father Abbot appraised Brother Peter and vice versa with sharply analytical eyes.

Paul was a full head shorter than Peter and mildly on the stout side. Thick and wavy silver hair adorned a round face with plump rosy cheeks, a slightly tilted pug nose and sparkling emerald eyes. Thick lips curved into a warm smile that revealed stumpy crooked teeth.

Peter felt genuine warmth and compassion from Father Abbott's kind face, but he also sensed an incisive mind probing deeply into Peter's own soul, excavating its layers of defensive walls. Although Peter trusted and respected Father Abbot, any penetration into his own defences was an excruciating personal violation, on an equal par as the physical violation he had endured the day before from the three highwaymen.

Violation! That grimy highwayman's hand squeezing Peter's genitals, causing horrible pain and indecent humiliation. Peter shuddered violently.

"Stop that at once!" Peter ordered himself. *"I will not allow emotions to take over and cause me any more pain. I am in control!"*

Peter was not aware of the increased intensity in his breathing and heartbeat, nor that his right knee was nervously shaking.

None of this, however, escaped Abbot Paul's notice. Maintaining his friendly smile, Father Abbot continued to scrutinize Brother Peter. The younger monk was an exceptionally handsome man, Father Abbot observed – tall, broad-shouldered, narrow-waisted. Thick curls of luxurious dark brown hair adorned an oval face with its perfectly proportioned nose and deep dark-brown eyes that masked depths upon depths of intelligence, insight, power, loneliness, sorrow, fear and denied passion.

Peter's eyes, Paul decided, were as luxurious as the younger monk's hair. But while his hair was soft and glowing, Peter's eyes were deep wells of darkness that cried out for companionship, while also warning against intrusion. Peter's incisive eyes stripped away all masks in everyone else, while defending his own shrouded mysteries. Abbot Paul quickly observed the younger monk's narrow, closely cropped bearded chin, with lips that were full and red, although usually (as they were in this moment) pursed in tight, impatient tension.

Father Abbot noted that Peter always showed him proper respect, along with sharp intelligence, clarity, organisation and leadership. But Paul had never once witnessed Peter's face expressing any love, compassion, warmth or happiness. There was only cold respect, cold intelligence, cold clarity. But warmth and vulnerability, the pain of loneliness and alienation, any glimpse of potential passion were all forever locked away, buried in the depths of Peter's shrouded eyes. Paul could sense hidden somewhere in Peter a great pool of love, warmth and compassion mentally interred in an inner cavern of a heart heavily armoured with thick mental walls of defence and denial.

"How are you today, my son?" Paul asked, finally breaking the prolonged silence of mutual scrutiny.

"Fine, Father Abbot. Thank you."

"Fine my ass," Father Abbot thought. "I am most distressed by your unfortunate experience of yesterday –"

"I am fine, Father Abbot," Peter interrupted, his face betraying no emotions.

"Brother Peter," Father Abbot tried again, "I am here if you need any –"

"No need, Father Abbot, thank you," Peter interrupted again, his voice revealing the tiniest strain of tension.

"Brother Peter, there is no shame –"

"I am FINE," Peter interrupted for the third time. His voice implied that this conversation was over, with nothing more to be said. But Father Abbot was equally stubborn and kept chipping away at Peter's defensive armour.

"Brother Peter, please do not run away and attempt to hide inside some impenetrable masked prison. Let me in to help you. The shame and trauma from yesterday must be overwhelming. It is evident on your face."

Peter arched an eyebrow. He knew his face showed absolutely nothing of the kind. His emotions were successfully locked away, and no amount of spiritual seduction by Father Abbot would be allowed to unleash them.

"My son," Paul persisted, "yesterday you were nearly killed. If not for our Lord's divine intervention in sending our valiant wounded guest to save you, things would have ended up tragically different. Please do not be afraid. I beseech you, face the experience and allow yourself to feel, accept and move through the pain. Allow the light of Christ into your heart to heal and comfort you in this difficult time."

Brother Peter might as well have been a stone statue or even the dead chair itself, for all the feeling being totally denied and buried deep within him.

"I would like to slap your face!" Paul thought angrily, *"in order to knock some human emotions out of you!"* Father Abbot momentarily shut his eyes, then blinked with tearful determination. *"Forgive my thoughts, Lord. He tries my patience like no other, truly he does. You know this. I must show patience and compassion to this tormented soul so lost in some inner hell that he allows no one to be close to him. But I MUST be patient, or how else will I ever manage to get through to him?"*

A deep exasperated sigh escaped from Father Abbot's lips. "I am most concerned with your action immediately following your rescuer's stabbing. Your face was void of any feeling or awareness." *"As always,"* Paul added to himself. "Yet your body moved with demonic frenzy when you kept stabbing at the already dead body of that highwayman. We were all astounded by your actions."

"I do not remember," Peter stared blankly.

"Er – what?"

"I do not remember stabbing the attacker." Peter's face remained cold and blank, his voice a tightly controlled whisper.

"You do not remember?"

"I do not remember stabbing anyone," the young monk repeated.

"This is even more distressing. But –"

"I am sorry for what happened," Peter said distantly. "I ask your forgiveness for whatever incorrect action I may have taken. I ask for God's forgiveness. Whatever punishment –"

"PUNISHMENT?" Paul interrupted in a frustrated wail, waving his hands as if trying to clear away a thickening fog. "Wait, wait, this is NOT the point I was trying to make at all. Er, I mean, that is not what I intended." He cut himself off in sheer exasperation. "I am concerned for your mental and emotional – and yes, your SPIRITUAL – welfare. You were attacked. Those three men intended to brutally rape and kill you. Then a man suddenly shows up out of nowhere and saves your life, and he himself is nearly fatally wounded. There was such – such total ABANDONMENT in your reaction to all this. Your stabbing that dead body – you were practically unstoppable. And you were so, so PERSISTENT in such a – a – oh! What do I mean to say? A faraway not-present way. Do you understand?"

Peter merely re-arched an eyebrow.

This infuriated Paul. *"He is impatient with me, the arrogant little shit!"* the Father Abbot realised. *"I really SHOULD slap his face!"*

"I am very sorry, Father Abbot," Peter said calmly, "but I do not remember any of this. Thank you for your concern, but I assure you that I am doing well."

"LIAR!" Father Abbot screamed inside his head.

"Thank you for your concern," Peter repeated. "However, I am apparently guilty of the most heinous crime of taking another man's life, even though he threatened the life of myself and of our wounded knight. I am ready to do whatever penance is required of me as punishment for this undeniable and unforgiveable sin."

"You are NOT doing well!" Paul screamed in helpless frustration, "And you are insufferably hiding behind this mock *mea culpa* performance of yours!"

"He has done it again!" Father Abbot complained inside his head. *"He has taken away my control and instead now has me totally in HIS control! You are so unbelievably stubborn, my stubborn Brother Peter. In so much pain, yet you will not open up one-tenth of an inch to me. And you wonder why you are so rejected and resented by the other brothers. The more you fear rejection,"* Paul thought as he stared incredulously at Brother Peter, *"the more you attract it from others. So hungry for companionship and love, yet so terrified of getting it because you think love will cause you even more pain. How do I teach you that love and happiness do not automatically bring pain? How do I teach you it is the FEAR and EXPECTATION of pain that brings you the very pain you think you can avoid but instead continue to recreate?"*

The two men sat in prolonged silence, Peter in protective defence and Paul in ever-deepening frustration.

"He is so busy trying to protect himself against his fear and vulnerability, that he does not even think to ask about the fate of the knight who saved his life."

"The knight," Father Abbot now said aloud, "still lives."

Peter made no comment nor gave any indication that he had heard what was said to him or that he even cared.

"You are not making this easy, Brother Peter. So I must force you to face it yourself."

Peter lifted both eyebrows at that statement and stared with blossoming panic.

The abbot continued. "We are very grateful for Brother Bartholomew's excellent medical skills for this knight. It took many hours to stop the bleeding and mend the wound, but Brother Bartholomew did a remarkable job in repairing the knight's side and cleaning it out completely. Our guest has lost much blood, and there is always the threat of infection or other complications. Though he has not yet awakened since his injury, he breathes deeply and regularly. We can only wait and pray."

"Yes, Father Abbot. Of course."

"Oh no, you think that your response ends this conversation? Hardly! I am in control here, not you."

Peter flickered his eyes, pretending he didn't understand what Paul had just said.

"Our unconscious guest will need constant attention to monitor his progress. Someone must be present at all times to take care of any emergency and to notify us when the knight finally awakens."

Peter tensed. *"No, God! He does not mean to —"*

"As of this moment, I am assigning that role to YOU."

"No!" Peter blurted as he shot up from his chair. Then seeing Paul's enraged expression, Peter sat back down. "I mean, no thank you, Father Abbot. I could not —"

"You can and you will."

"But —"

Father Abbot silenced the monk with a raised hand. "This man risked his own life to save yours, for God's sake! You owe it to him. Where is your gratitude, your compassion, any sense of love or even the most remote consideration? WHAT IS GOING ON INSIDE YOU?"

Peter slumped forward, staring at his still nervously bobbing right knee.

"What reason could you possibly have to NOT care for the man who saved your life?" Paul demanded angrily.

"Father Abbot, I know nothing about caring for another person – I mean medically."

"Interesting slip you just made there. You really meant far more than just medically. Therefore, Brother Peter, it is time for you to LEARN!"

"But –"

"No 'buts'," Paul interrupted with a raised voice that was stripped of any patience he thought himself capable of regarding Brother Peter. "You are now in charge of our guest's well-being and recovery. Brother Bartholomew will be on hand whenever you need assistance – medically speaking, of course."

"But –"

"Brother Peter, you exasperate me!" Paul yelled. If there had been a table or a desk, the abbot would have slammed a hand forcefully upon it. In this moment, he was angry with himself that he had made the decision to not have any other furniture in the meeting cell.

"Whatever happened to your vow of obedience?" Paul demanded. "Remember that word – OBEDIENCE? You asked for appropriate 'punishment' for your 'undeniable and unforgiveable action.' Your words. Well, there you go. Your so-called punishment, since you are determined to see it that way, is to learn how to take care of another human being and feel and express gratitude, compassion and love for others. And you will learn both obedience and love if I have to BEAT it into you!"

"But Father Abbot, this means I cannot walk into the Highland hills whenever I want to."

"Tough shit!" Paul thought with full exasperation. "EXACTLY!" he said loudly. Again, this is your so-called punishment, as you insist on seeing it. You will do as I say and there will be no argument!"

"But those walks are a spiritual NEED for me!"

"So is the ability to feel and express gratitude, compassion, caring and love FOR OTHERS. Right now you need to develop those human qualities far more than walking in the hills."

"Which you do to ESCAPE us!" Paul added to himself.

"Have I made myself PERFECTLY CLEAR to you?"

Peter stared at the floor feeling defeated, trapped and lost. But after a long pause, he slowly nodded his assent.

Father Abbot felt deeply relieved that he had finally gained control over this rebellious monk – for his own good.

"I have spoken. You will be obedient to my words. You will experience gratitude and loving compassion for someone outside of yourself. Report at once to Brother Bartholomew in the infirmary. Help the knight, take care of him, and when he awakens, you must get to know him. Learn to take care of someone else rather than just your own personal needs."

"Now I will never get back to my beloved hills," Peter mourned within. *"I will be trapped inside this monastery forever."*

"That is all. You may leave." *"Please go,"* Paul thought, feeling completely exhausted, *"so I can have some rest and avoid you giving me a heart attack!"*

Peter stood up, bowed with his hands momentarily pressed together, and then left the monastery's small meeting cell to make his way to the infirmary.

Turning a corner on the way there, Peter stopped abruptly when he saw Brother Clair sitting on a long wooden bench against a corridor wall. Brother Clair was the greatest enigma of all to Peter. Clair was also the shortest and plumpest of the monks, a cookie-jar figure (had Peter known what a cookie jar was) with robust apple-coloured cheeks and the merriest eyes Peter had ever seen. Clair's bald head glistened, his body jiggled with laughter, and his bright face shone with joy at the sight of Peter.

"He is always smiling and laughing," Peter thought irritably. *"No one can be THAT happy all the time and still be SANE! He is either crazy or utterly diabolical."*

"Brother Peter!" Brother Clair said cheerfully. "Good day. How nice to see you doing well now."

"Brother Clair," Peter responded coolly with a minimal nod.

"Dear Brother Peter, where did you go off to so imperiously this morning – not long before our huge drama in the courtyard?"

Peter cocked an eyebrow, a sure sign of annoyance. "I do not walk imperiously."

"Do not worry about it. It comes naturally to you."

"Is he being rude?" Peter wondered. "I am in a hurry. Father Abbot has ordered me to care for the injured knight."

"A splendid idea! Someone should do it, so why not you?"

"What?"

"Nothing, nothing. Glad to hear it. I am delighted you shall care for our brave guest. What a splendid way to show gratitude to the man who saved your life and liberated the monastery from those ruffians. The knight will be in very good hands."

"What do you mean by that?" Peter asked suspiciously.

"What do I mean?" Clair asked with confusion. "Exactly what I said. Please, dear Brother, relax and enjoy your assignment. You have been given a marvellous task, and the knight will be grateful to have you caring for him. But please do try to relax, Brother Peter. You often take yourself far too seriously. That HAS to hurt."

"What do you mean by that?" Peter demanded. "I am competent and efficient."

"Okay."

"And I certainly cannot waste time talking with you."

"That IS a pity. Oh well, someone has to sit here, and apparently that is me."

Peter wondered how quickly he could escape Brother Clair and not have to endure another minute of this inane conversation.

"Enjoy this glorious day," Brother Clair continued. "And please ENJOY caring for the knight."

"Enjoy?" Peter asked with exasperation. "Duties are to be carried out, not ENJOYED. And anyway, how can I enjoy being stuck inside the infirmary all day staring at an unconscious invalid?"

"An interesting question, Brother Peter. Any situation is enjoyable if you know how to make it feel that way. When you cannot be outside, then bring the outside inside – into yourself, I mean. Whatever situation you are in, managing it well is a matter of ATTITUDE, Brother Peter. That is the key. And try to think of all the fun you will have learning about that."

Although Peter wanted to feel impatient and get as far away from this rotund monk as possible, simultaneously he couldn't help but feel himself somewhat surrendering to Brother Clair's inspiring words — while simultaneously wanting to smack one of Clair's rosy cheeks.

"And as to our valiant guest being unconscious," Clair continued happily, "hopefully he will soon wake up. Just think about all the wonderful fun you will have getting to know him and sharing your two lives together. It will be tremendous! Perhaps I can look in on you two now and then to see how things are progressing? That would be nice. Have a beautiful day, Brother Peter. May the sun forever shine from your heart, and may your beloved hills with their sweet smell of heather embrace and comfort your soul wherever you are and wherever you go."

Peter shook his head as if awakening from an alien dream. *"What the hell is that crazy monk talking about?"* Peter wondered with frustrated anger.

Peter quickly left Brother Clair smiling happily on the bench and resumed his hurried steps towards the infirmary. Shaking with fury, Peter wondered if the knight would indeed ever wake up — and if so, what would that mean for himself.

"You see," one of the ravens said to his feathery companion as they perched on one of the monastery's walls, telepathically listening to the conversation below between Clair and Peter. *"All your precious little Peter cares about is himself and how everything relates just to HIM. He showed no concern for the human who saved his life. As far as I am concerned, your monk is a moron."*

"Give him time," said the other raven who acted as Peter's animal spirit guide. *"He is just beginning a great adventure. I predict a major breakthrough for my human very soon."*

"You give humans more credit than they deserve."

"That again? And you give them nothing, which makes you a constant pain in the ass."

"Say that if you want. But it does not change anything about human behaviour."

"Has any other raven ever told you how compassionate, loving, uplifting and knowledgeable you are?"

"What? Um, no."

"And they NEVER will! Now fly off before I poop all over you."

"You only talk to me like that because you know I am right, and it galls you to admit it."

As usual, the two ravens bickered back and forth for hours.

Five

BROTHER ANDREW SAT in the infirmary as he awaited Peter's arrival. The young, delicately built monk with an unruly mop of blond hair (minus the small tonsure) above a beardless and angelically pale face with light blue eyes, sat beside the bed staring at the unconscious man. The long, slumbering knight lay unmoving under a grey wool blanket. On the nightstand beside the bed, Andrew had placed a large wooden bowl filled with water, and alongside the bowl was a short pile of neatly folded cloths.

"Brother Peter, you have come," Andrew whispered in an excited tone, his face alight as Peter finally entered the infirmary. Andrew prayed fervently that his adoration for Brother Peter was sufficiently concealed – but Andrew didn't realise he had nothing to fear. Brother Peter never noticed any feelings towards him from anyone. Andrew desperately loved the older, handsome monk but was constantly wracked with guilt for the "sin" of having such "evil feelings" towards another man. And if Brother Peter ever found out (Andrew thought with terror), the wrath from Peter would surpass anything God Himself could ever generate.

Peter arched an eyebrow, the reliable clue that he was already annoyed and impatient.

"What are you doing here?" Peter asked coldly.

"Father Abbot sent me in case you needed any help with the knight."

"He told me nothing about this."

"Maybe he forgot or was focussed on something else. But I –"

"You can go, Brother Andrew. I will not need your services."

"But I —"

"I do not need you," Peter said harshly. "In fact, I am quite sure you are needed elsewhere. You may go."

Peter's dismissal bitterly stung star-struck Andrew. Yet another rejection from the handsome monk. *"Surely,"* Andrew thought guiltily, *"this is my deserved punishment for having sinful feelings towards Brother Peter."*

"There is the most extraordinary thing about the knight —" Andrew began, hoping to gain more time to be with Peter.

"Whatever it is, Brother Bartholomew can tell me," Peter interrupted.

"No, really, it is extraordinary. You will not believe this but the knight —"

"Yes, yes, I am sure Brother Bartholomew will give me the details."

"This does not require Brother Bartholomew —"

"I will ascertain whatever it is on my own," Peter interrupted angrily. "Thank you, Brother Andrew, for your time here. But you can go now."

Andrew wanted to disappear deep into the Earth. He felt thoroughly rejected, and the rejection made Andrew feel utterly useless and unworthy. Punishment for his sinful feelings, he reminded himself again.

"As you wish." With tears in his eyes, Andrew left the infirmary.

But before Peter could approach the bed, Brother Bartholomew appeared.

The healer monk was as tall as Peter but narrower in shoulder and thinner. Neatly combed thick black hair adorned a long and narrow face. The monk also had a long and narrow nose and dark eyes slightly slanted, giving him an Oriental look (if seventh-century people in Alba had been aware of the Orient). Peter always felt that "narrow" was the theme for the healer monk, except never narrow in his wisdom. In that aspect, Bartholomew was quite expansive.

"Welcome to your new assignment, Brother Peter. I hope you will derive much pleasure from helping our wounded but recovering hero."

Peter rolled his eyes. Pleasure? Was Brother Bartholomew serious?

"Do you know where Brother Andrew is?" Bartholomew asked.

"I told him to find something else to do."

"You what?" Bartholomew exclaimed.

"I let him go."

"What do you mean by YOU let him go? That was not for you to do, Brother Peter. That is for ME to decide."

"He is unnecessary here. Whatever needs to be done, I am sure that you and I can manage. I do not need the assistance of Brother Andrew."

"And that is ALL it is about?"

"What do you mean," Peter asked, genuinely perplexed.

"What I am hearing from you is that it is all about what YOU need. Must I remind you that it is the KNIGHT who is the patient here, not you? It was not for you to decide whether or not Andrew could be helpful. You never stopped to think, for example, that it might be good for ANDREW to be assisting us?"

"What? But you just now said it is about the knight and not me. So, if it is not about me, then it certainly is also not about Andrew."

"Sometimes, Brother Peter, I would like to slap you until Jesus comes back, and then continue slapping you anyway!"

"Whatever for?"

Bartholomew sighed deeply. "Never mind. This is a waste of time. Pearls and swine. Let us meet the patient, shall we?"

"Pearls and swine," Peter wondered to himself. *"Whatever is he talking about?"* But aloud, Peter asked, "Yes. How is he doing?"

"So far, no change," Bartholomew spoke in a whisper. "There has been no sign of awakening or any movement at all, but he breathes deeply and steadily. His wound was cleansed thoroughly and sewn up."

As Bartholomew spoke, he quickly ran his hand over the knight's bandaged side and then felt the patient's forehead and temples. The healer nodded with approval.

"Still no fever, good," Bartholomew whispered again.

"Why are you whispering?" Peter asked with confusion.

"Excuse me?"

"I mean, we were not whispering at the beginning, and now suddenly you begin to whisper. Is the knight asleep or unconscious?"

"He is unconscious, of course."

"Then why the need to whisper?"

"*Now I really want to slap the life out of him!*" Bartholomew screamed inside his head. "You are right," the medic brother said aloud. "Whisper, scream at the top of your voice, do whatever the hell you want!"

"Well, I was only saying –" Brother Peter stopped mid-sentence and stared down in shock at the unconscious knight.

"Oh, yes, by the way, Brother Peter," Bartholomew said in an almost sneering tone, enjoying every second of the impact upon Peter. "Surprise!"

Peter continued to stare at the unconscious knight in complete shock. This was the first time Peter was seeing his rescuer without his helmet. The man in the bed could be himself – almost. The knight was nearly identical in appearance to Brother Peter. The differences were subtle. The knight appeared slightly older, five to seven years perhaps. The sleeping face was handsome beyond description, the image of Peter but somehow even more handsome. But still, it was practically Peter's face.

"Why did you not tell me before of his physical similarity to me?" Peter demanded.

"Similarity is putting it mildly," Bartholomew replied with a grin. "And miss this exquisite moment of seeing the shock on your face? No way."

"We could be brothers – twins, in fact. Except, as I see now, I can tell he is slightly older than I am."

"Do you have any brothers who are knights?" Bartholomew asked.

"I am an only child."

"I am not surprised."

"What?"

"Nothing, nothing. He does look remarkably like you, Brother Peter. And yet, you two are not related. Most extraordinary, do you not think?"

Peter ignored the healer monk's question and stared for several minutes, trying to overcome the shock of the knight's incredible resemblance to himself.

"So, what am I to do here?" Peter asked, unable to take his eyes off the knight's face.

"Just sit with him and be there for him. If he moves or wakes up, come and get me immediately."

"That is it? THAT is what I am needed here for?"

"For now, yes," Bartholomew replied with mounting irritation. "Once the knight is conscious, there will be much more for you to do. But for now, just be here for him."

"For this I have to sacrifice my beloved hills!" Peter fumed. *"I feel SO TRAPPED and furious!"*

Bartholomew could easily sense Peter's inner thoughts. "Think of all the meditation and reflection you can do while sitting here with the knight. It would do you a world of good."

"I am thrilled," Peter grunted in the most un-thrilled tone.

"If only you were," Bartholomew sighed.

Bartholomew began to leave but then turned back to face Peter. "If you truly wish to be helpful and also more active, take a cloth, soak it in water and wipe the knight's face."

"Oh, very well," Peter muttered irritably.

Peter stepped around Bartholomew and approached the nightstand next to the bed. In a hesitant gesture of sheer clumsiness, Peter's right hand grabbed a cloth and threw it into the wooden bowl of water, drenching his robe's sleeve and splattering water everywhere. Then, removing the cloth from the bowl but without squeezing out the excess water, he plopped the dripping cloth onto the knight's forehead, sending rivulets of water all over the patient's face.

"I think something is wrong," Peter said.

"I think you might be right," Bartholomew replied, astonished at Peter's stupidity.

Bartholomew quickly grabbed the drenched cloth, threw it onto the nightstand and then immediately selected a fresh cloth to roughly pat the knight's dripping face dry. "Obviously," Bartholomew commented with impatient irritation, "you have never had to care for another human being before."

"What happened?" Peter asked in confusion.

Bartholomew took a deep breath, then decided it was best to take two more slower and deeper breaths.

"Squeeze out the excess water BEFORE you place the cloth onto the patient!" Bartholomew explained with no patience whatsoever. "And the point is to not just PLOP it somewhere, but rather to use the cloth in gently wiping motions to remove sweat or dirt from the skin and give a sensation of CARING for the patient. Can you possibly grasp that?"

"Yes, certainly," Peter replied uncertainly.

"So try again, and THIS time more carefully and with some self-awareness, if you please."

Peter took another cloth, dipped it more carefully into the bowl (no water splashed this time onto his sleeve), squeezed it out thoroughly, and then used the cloth to very gently wipe the knight's forehead, temples, nose and bearded cheeks.

"Congratulations. We may, with a LOT of hard work, make you a professional care-giver worthy of calling himself a monk. Call me if you need anything or if the knight moves or awakens."

"What, already? Well, right – yes, Brother," Peter answered.

Bartholomew left, leaving Peter on his own. Peter stared down at the unconscious knight, still amazed by their similar appearance.

"What the hell is this all about?" Peter wondered, unable to fully grasp the nearness of appearance between the knight and himself. But receiving no reply, he pulled up the chair to be closer to the knight as he began his vigil.

The two ravens stood on the sill of an open window in the infirmary, observing all the human activity.

"Is it just me," one raven asked the other, *"or do those two humans look remarkably alike?"*

"The human in the bed," the second raven replied, *"does look very much like my human. And do not even attempt to tell me that ALL humans look alike, because you know that is sheer nonsense."*

"They may not all look alike, but too many of them ACT alike, and not in a good way."

"They have a different Akashic process from us. Their lessons are more difficult as a result."

"Their lessons are harder only because humans ignorantly choose to believe in a God externalised and separate from themselves – an external God who to them can only be angry and jealous, possessive and vengeful, not helped in any way by their added belief that they have to suffer to grow. Hideous stuff. Far too many of these humans have brains like rotten squash."

"Regardless of what YOU might think," the other raven retorted, *"that kind of thinking is the primary karmic issue humans are working on. It is their lot. They have to go through what they have to go through to learn,"* the second raven continued to explain. *"It is not just being stupid. It is a continuous process of learning and self-discovery."*

"Self-discovery process my feathered butt," the first raven retorted. *"Mother Earth and all who live on Her have to suffer because of this continuously rampant human idiocy."*

"So you are saying that you are a victim – a victim of humans?"

"Absolutely."

"Then you are no more intelligent than they are."

Incensed, the first raven flew away, while the other bird remained and continued to telepathically sense the unfolding drama between Peter and the knight.

"My dear, dear human," the remaining raven addressed Peter. *"You have so much to understand, to see, to feel. Stay with it. I will help you all I can."*

<hr />

Peter sat down in a chair near the bed and observed the handsome unconscious knight.

"He IS beautiful," Peter spoke aloud, not realising that he was therefore stating how beautiful he himself was as well. Although his mind understood that he and the unconscious knight looked alike, Peter could not make the connection that he was therefore just as handsome. The monk was totally cut off from relating to himself as a physical being.

Gradually, while staring at the knight, a new sensation completely alien to the monk began to unfold. Peter could feel trickles of a painful loneliness, an aching for something more in his life, a desire to touch and be touched, and deeper still – a trembling fear that to open up to these new and alien feelings would somehow inevitably result in crushing hurt and pain.

Peter shifted in his chair as he kept staring at the sleeping image of himself in the knight, and he began the long vigil.

Six

BROTHER PETER AWOKE with a start. *"What happened?"* he wondered. *"Where am I?"*

He had fallen asleep in a chair. Chair? *"Oh, yes,"* he finally remembered. *"I fell asleep in the chair. I am in the infirmary, and I am looking after the knight."* Peter slapped his right cheek. "Wake up, Peter," he ordered himself out loud. "Be conscious and remember what you are doing."

The monk had slumped forward, nearly spilling out of his seat which had caused him to awaken. Peter wearily straightened himself, wincing at the pains running down his spine, at the base of his neck and across his broad shoulders.

"God, I ache everywhere!" Peter complained bitterly to himself. *"I am more tired now than before I dozed off."*

Rolling his head in a futile attempt to ease various throbbing pains, he pouted aloud, "Now I will never see my hills again."

Peter's fingers had just begun to massage the merciless pounding at his temples when he suddenly stopped and listened. All his senses sharpened immediately. What was that? He dropped his hands and listened, acutely aware that he was not alone with the knight.

Peter heard humming and felt movement near him. Slowly turning, he stared in utter shock.

Brother Clair was sitting in another chair next to the knight's bed that must have been brought in at some point while Peter had been slumbering. The blanket draped over the patient had been thrown aside, and the knight was completely – naked! Brother Clair was wiping down the knight's body with a damp cloth while he hummed merrily to himself. Working his way down the knight's chest and abdomen, the rotund monk next began to work on – the knight's genitals!

Peter blinked several times, unsure he was observing reality. He looked again. Clair held the knight's long and hefty penis in one hand while gingerly wiping it with a cloth. Peter was mortified.

"Brother Clair, what ARE you doing?" a horrified Peter asked.

"Oh, welcome back to the world of the living, Brother Peter. I hope you slept well." Clair continued cleaning the knight's penis as he spoke. "I thought it would be a good idea to give the knight a nice, thorough bathing, but I did not want to disturb you while you slept. I hope I did not awaken you."

"Would you please let it go!" Peter ordered in a shrill voice.

"Let what go?"

"What do you mean 'what'? The man's – his – private parts!"

"Private parts? Oh, you mean his penis. But I am still washing it."

"How much washing does it need?"

"Until it is thoroughly clean."

"I think you have gone beyond THOROUGHLY cleaned by now! It is not THAT necessary to be so – thorough."

"Are you kidding?" Brother Clair asked incredulously. "Are you not as thorough with yourself and your own penis when you wash?"

"That is different," Peter insisted.

"In what way?"

"I am washing MYSELF and my own – private parts. I am not handling someone else's."

"One must be thorough in all things in all situations to all involved in order to achieve the very best," Clair intoned teasingly.

"I think you are more than done."

"If you say so. Lovely, is it not?"

"Is WHAT lovely?" Peter asked.

"His penis, of course. Well, ALL of him, for that matter. It is magnificent, like the rest of him. In fact, I would go so far as to say his penis is a finely crafted work of art, do you not agree? God certainly knew what He was doing when He created THIS man!"

"LET GO OF THE MAN'S PENIS!"

"Why are you so obsessed with me releasing the man's penis, Brother Peter? I – oh, oh, NOW I understand. YOU want to take over for me. Here you go," Brother Clair said, lifting the hefty penis towards Peter.

"NO THANK YOU!" Peter shrieked, suddenly realising he had better calm down before he had a heart attack. "That is NOT what I meant. You are done. PUT IT BACK!"

"My heart attack is on its way, any second now!" Peter thought dismally.

"Well, well, okay." Clair laid the penis down, gave it a few cleaning swirls around the testicles (which drove Peter completely crazy) and began to wash the knight's legs and feet.

"Brother Clair is forever smiling, happy and laughing," Peter thought with irritation. *"Anyone who smiles and laughs that much cannot possibly have his mind in proper working order."*

Clair finished washing the knight's legs and feet, then ran the damp cloth one more time across the knight's abdomen and chest. Fine, dark brown hair rose like a tree trunk from the knight's bushy groin, rising past the navel to spread up and across his well-rounded breasts like a blossoming tree.

"There, now I am done," Clair announced. "Magnificent body. He has the prettiest nipples I have ever seen."

"WHAT?" Peter asked.

"Nipples. His nipples, Brother Peter. They are so luscious and pert. Very, VERY pretty nipples indeed."

"Nipples are not meant to be pretty."

"Where is THAT written? And anyway, you are SO utterly wrong, Brother Peter. Nipples, like every other part of the human body, are meant to be pretty and enjoyed, not just functional. And look at the hair on his body – how it delicately stems up from the groin like a great tree trunk, branching out to curve around his gorgeous breasts – with his two scrumptious nipples like ripe, luscious fruits ready to be plucked. Breathtakingly lovely, do you not agree?"

"If you say so," Peter grunted.

"Oh, I do. I absolutely do. You must admit that he is an extremely beautiful man, Brother Peter. And he looks so remarkably like you as well. Which can only mean, therefore, that you are an extremely beautiful man as well."

Peter could not see that at all because he was so completely cut off from identifying himself as a physical being.

"Imagine that!" Clair continued. "You two look like twins. I wonder if you two are long-lost brothers?" After a moment's hesitation, Brother Clair added, "And that also makes me wonder something else."

"I am afraid to ask."

"Well, he is so similar to you in the face," Clair smiled. "And you two seem to be of similar body shape and build. That makes me wonder if you have nipples as pretty as his."

Peter closed his eyes and took several deep breaths. *"Will this nightmare conversation ever end?"*

"I am sure I would not know the answer to that."

"Really?" Clair asked. "Why on Earth not? You have seen his nipples, and certainly you know what your nipples look like. So you MUST know if your nipples are as pretty as his!"

Peter closed his eyes again, hoping that would help him escape this most uncomfortable conversation.

"Can we move on, please, to something else?"

By the time Peter opened his eyes, Clair had replaced the previously discarded robe upon the knight and laid the blanket back across the unconscious knight's body.

"That finishes me here," Clair announced with effusive glee. "Brother Peter, I envy your opportunity to continue caring for the knight – physically, emotionally and perhaps spiritually as well. I hope you will take full advantage of this glorious opportunity. Enjoy every second of it and give all you can to help bring this beautiful man back to full health. And remember – it is always a great gift to serve another person."

Peter rolled his eyes. "Gift? Are you serious?"

Ignoring Peter's last question, Clair waddled out of the infirmary with a merry bounce. A deeply rattled Peter exhaled heavily several times, trying to shake off both Clair's bizarre conversation and the chubby monk's intimate "handling" of the knight's nakedness.

"When will this ever end?" Peter asked himself dramatically. *"Pretty nipples indeed!"*

The monk collapsed back into the chair in which he had been earlier sleeping, completely exhausted from Brother Clair. *"Will I ever see my hills again?"*

In the next instant, Peter noticed movement from the knight for the first time. There were some small moans, the head jerked first left then right, and then the whole body appeared to spasm. Slight rasping breaths escaped from the knight's lips.

Immediately, Peter leapt to his feet with renewed focus and concern. "God, something is happening," he said aloud without realising it. Peter's mind clicked into a high gear of panic.

"Thank God this man is awakening!" he uttered out loud, again without realising he did so. "Maybe I can go to my hills soon, after all! But what if something is wrong here? What if I am supposed to DO something? Do? What should I DO?"

A big rumbling moan emerged from the knight. Within seconds, the skin on his beautifully chiselled, bearded face paled and started glistening with sweat. Another moan followed, filled with reverberating anguish from the depths of the knight's bowels.

Peter stood tensely with his long, narrow hands clenching and unclenching at his sides. He stared helplessly at the knight.

"Now what do I do?" he thought to himself. *"Do I go and get Father Abbot or Brother Bartholomew? No. I probably should not leave his side. Perhaps a passing brother will hear and can go fetch Brother Bartholomew and Father Abbot."*

There followed more movement from the knight. His head jerked again left then right, and spasms shook his body.

"Do something, you idiot!" Peter chastised himself out loud. "Do not just stand there like a blooming fool!"

Peter was about to go to the door and call for help when he noticed increasing sweat on the knight's face. Peter paused. Doubt seared his thoughts. Finally, he willed himself into action.

"He might be feverish. I will wipe the sweat from his face first and see if that soothes him."

After dunking a cloth into the large wooden bowl of herbal water,

Peter was about to place the dripping cloth on the knight's face when he angrily turned back to the bowl.

"Squeeze out the excess water from the damn cloth FIRST, you pea-brain!" Peter hissed.

After twisting the cloth tightly over the bowl, Peter began wiping his patient's sweat-drenched face. By this time, the knight's spasmodic movements had thrown off the blanket and most of the knight's robe, revealing again his magnificent chest and muscular arms.

Remembering Brother Clair's words, Peter surprised himself by agreeing that the knight was indeed remarkably handsome. Even though Peter knew the two of them were extremely similar in appearance, he still could not realise that to see the knight as beautiful would be to see himself as beautiful as well. More gently than before, Peter continued wiping his patient's face, chest and arms.

Peter's more sensitive actions immediately triggered a new response from the knight, who now began to jerk more violently while his mouth suddenly shrieked in agony.

Peter jumped backwards, knocking the chair over. The thud of his chair hitting the stone floor and a new scream from the knight jarred Peter's nerves and sent his stomach into somersaults of panicked frenzy. Now Peter was sweating as heavily as the knight.

"Good God, what should I do? Is he dying? Is that the death rattle?"

Peter's shaking hands re-applied the damp cloth to wiping the knight's pale brow. Instantly, the screams ceased, but the knight's body continued to tremble and jerk all over as if the knight were experiencing an epileptic fit.

"I am killing him!" Peter cried out. "Why can I not tear myself away to get help? I am as useless as the other brothers. Idiot! DO something!"

The knight's arms had remained limp at his side, even during the spasms. Now, suddenly they flew into the air as if warding off the blows of some unseen assailant.

The knight's flailing arms sent Peter crashing into the nightstand, which in turn sent waves of water over the bowl's rim to splash Peter's backside and pour onto the floor. The monk's heart was racing so fast and hard, he was sure it would burst out of his chest. Desperately, Peter tried to capture the knight's arms.

What unfolded next happened too quickly for Peter's overwhelmed mind to perceive. But somehow, the knight was now sitting up, eyes opened wide with terror and yet simultaneously unseeing. One hand of the knight gripped Peter's left shoulder while the other hand grasped the monk's nape.

"It is all right," Peter whispered, not feeling at all that it was all right. "Lie down. You are safe, and you will be fine. I am here for you, and I will help you any way I can. Just lie down."

He spoke thusly to the knight for several minutes, repeating the same sentences over and over – to calm himself as much as to calm the knight. Peter had never said in his entire life that he was here for someone else or would do anything to help another person. He was barely aware of what he was saying.

Slowly the knight laid back down, but he refused to relinquish his holds on the monk's shoulder and nape. This forced Peter to uncomfortably lean forward as the knight sank back upon the bed. The knight's dark, penetrating eyes stared with a crazed blankness into Peter's eyes, but the monk was too dazed and shaking to see that the knight's eyes were an almost exact mirror of his own.

Peter was now intensely aware of the moaning knight's well-developed bare chest as the monk's nose was pressed firmly against the knight's left nipple. Struggling to breathe, Peter smelled a musky scent from the skin beneath the fine soft brown hair that spread across the knight's chest like the blossoming tree Brother Clair had described. The knight's shoulders and arms were taut with strong muscles, and the powerful hands gripped the uncomfortably bent-over Peter into a most awkward position.

"Let go of me, please!" Peter cried. "You are safe, I assure you. I am here. Please let go!"

Between sighs and grunts of pain, the knight suddenly whispered in a barely audible tone, *"Dio aiutami. Dove sono?"* {"God help me. Where am I?"}

The intensity of the knight's stare was as gripping as his hands' hold on Peter's shoulder and nape. Lips attempted to form more words, and the forehead creased with desperate frustration. Somehow Peter was now embracing the knight, his hands drenched with sweat from the knight's back – hard yet smooth like marble.

After a few guttural attempts, the knight was suddenly sapped of all energy. He collapsed against his pillows, eyes closed, his arms finally releasing the monk to lie limply again at his sides.

Peter painfully lifted himself up and staggered backwards into the already once-beleaguered nightstand. His monk's robe was soaked with sweat, his own as well as the knight's. Peter's robe was also wet with the spilled water that had poured out of the previously disturbed nightstand bowl. He panted in rapid breaths that matched his still-pounding heart.

The knight, meanwhile, appeared to sleep peacefully, his brow smooth, his breaths slow and deep. Peter wiped his forehead with a shaking hand and finally managed to drag himself to the infirmary door to call for help.

———————◆◆◆———————

"Remarkable recovery," Brother Bartholomew said with a warm smile to Peter who assisted the healer monk as he finished his examination of the now-awakened knight.

Brother Bartholomew was a tall, narrow-faced and narrow-bodied figure. Thick, dark curly hair adorned a narrow head with a long, narrow nose and a closely cropped dark beard. Bartholomew's eyes were also dark and penetrating, but they sparkled with an exuberant lustre that exuded a joy of life and bountiful warmth, love and compassion.

"Truly a miracle," Bartholomew continued. "Praise the Lord!"

"Thank you, Brother," the knight mouthed imperceptibly. His face appeared relaxed, although pale from weakness.

"Your accent is quite unusual," Peter stated, "but also very beautiful. I assume you were not born in this country. Where, may I ask, are you originally from?"

"The Italian peninsula," the knight muttered.

"How extraordinary!" Bartholomew said. "What brought you to this land of ours?"

The knight looked down, hesitant to reply. "I am very tired," he finally managed.

"Of course, of course," Bartholomew reprimanded himself. "Do not speak any more, my friend. Save your strength to mend. I will look in on you again later today and every day to check on the progress of your wound which I have just re-dressed. Meanwhile, I will leave you in the capable hands of Brother Peter, who will soon bring you a nourishing herbal broth that I have prepared especially for you. Eat as much as you can. And afterwards, get as much rest as you can."

The knight nodded and tried to speak again when Brother Bartholomew held up a halting hand.

"No, friend. Do not speak any more. Conserve your strength. I will leave you now, and Brother Peter will return shortly with the broth. Eat and sleep well."

The knight suddenly held out an arm and desperately pawed at Brother Peter.

"Yes, what is it?" Peter asked as the knight weakly tugged the monk down closer to him.

"Dov'è il mio cavallo?" {"Where is my horse?"}

"I am sorry, sir," Peter said, "but I cannot understand you."

The knight grabbed Peter's left arm. *"Per favore,"* he pleaded in a barely audible whisper, *"abbi cura del mio cavallo."* {"Please take care of my horse."}

"What is he saying?" Bartholomew asked Peter.

Peter turned away from the knight and faced the healer monk. "I have no idea. This is very frustrating." Peter again leaned forward to speak to the knight. "I apologise, sir. I cannot understand the language you speak. Can you try again in my language?"

The knight nodded and took a moment to shift out of his native tongue. "Orion," the knight whispered.

"What?"

"Orion," the knight repeated feebly.

"Orion? The constellation?"

"No," the knight replied, shaking his head while attempting a weak laugh. "My horse."

"Ah, your beautiful white steed!" Peter exclaimed with

understanding. "Orion is your horse's name. Rest assured, sir, your horse is being well taken care of. Orion is brushed, walked, watered and fed every day. He is fine and is in our stables being well looked after by some of the other monks."

"Thank you."

"Of course. Now rest, as Brother Bartholomew advised. I will be back soon with your herbal broth."

The knight nodded his gratitude and closed his eyes in sheer exhaustion.

———————•◆•———————

Bartholomew and Peter exited the infirmary together. Outside a motley group of monks awaited Brother Bartholomew's news. An enthusiastic Andrew darted some occasional adoring glances at Peter. A grinning Clair and a calm Father Abbot radiated all patience and love. Prior Thomas, on the other hand, just stared – tall, pinched-mouth and as gloomy-eyed as ever.

Bartholomew quietly closed the infirmary door behind him and faced the circle of expectant monks

"His recovery is truly remarkable. Whatever Brother Peter has been doing has worked well. The wound in our guest's side is healing cleanly, and I do not anticipate any infection or complications. However," Bartholomew added with a more serious tone, "the healing will nevertheless take a long period of time, and we will need to watch our friend closely and patiently."

"How lovely!" Brother Clair exclaimed with a rapturous smile. But then instantly, his eyes blinked, and he stopped celebrating. "What I mean is, not lovely that his recovery will take a long time, but how lovely that such a brave man is well on the road to such a wonderful recovery." Relieved he had clarified himself, Clair's natural radiance immediately returned.

Most of the monks glowed in the shared celebration of Bartholomew's news. Except, that is, for Peter and Thomas who were absorbed in their mutual dislike for one another.

Father Abbot observed the two rival monks and thought to himself,

"They look like they both sat on the same spiky pinecone and are blaming each other for placing that pinecone wherever it was when they both sat on it."

"This is such joyous news," Clair continued happily, "that I shall go immediately to the chapel and give thanks to our Lord. Feel free to join me. I wish a glorious day to all of you, my beloved brothers."

As Clair waddled away to the chapel, even Peter and sour-faced Thomas could not suppress their smiles of amusement. Then suddenly Peter broke the mood.

"I suppose this means I am now released from this nursing obligation to resume my real duties."

"REAL DUTIES!" echoed everyone in the circle except Andrew. This sudden group outburst shocked Peter.

"On the contrary," Brother Bartholomew replied in a curt but carefully controlled voice. "Your 'OBLIGATION' – as you call it – must continue. Your knight has a long recovery ahead of him, so you must ensure that he certainly maintains all his strength for his healing. You have even MORE responsibility now, Brother Peter."

"WHAT? But –"

"Brother Bartholomew is correct," Father Abbot interrupted. "I insist that you remain with our guest until he is completely recovered, as long as that process takes. Brother Peter, your manuscript work can wait. A human soul is far more important than copying words onto parchment. Besides, you need to get away from that constant bookwork of yours and spend more time working together with other people. And your hills, of course, can also wait. They are not going anywhere."

"But –"

Prior Thomas rolled his eyes. "So typical of Brother Peter to put his own desires first. I do not understand –"

"That is correct," Father Abbot interrupted again. "Prior Thomas, you definitely do not understand. So please keep quiet and do not issue judgements about what is not your understanding."

Brother Thomas was appalled by Father Abbot's strict reaction, so he glared at Paul with fierce anger. However, Thomas had been trained to give obedience and respect to his superiors – so he shut himself down externally while he kept fuming internally.

Peter's reaction to this duel was to wonder why Prior Thomas forever bore the expression of someone smelling fresh pig shit.

"I can help Brother Peter so that he is not so tied up with our guest all the time," Andrew eagerly volunteered, his sparkling eyes aglow with puppy love.

Peter almost thanked Andrew, but wise Paul intervened a third time.

"Thank you for your generous offer, Brother Andrew — but this is a task for Brother Peter to complete alone. We must not interfere with his obligation — or rob our brother of his divine opportunity to serve. We must leave Brother Peter to his duty — for the good of everyone involved. This, of course, applies to ALL of us."

Andrew nodded in immediate submission, though his faced showed crushed disappointment. He had been hoping for opportunities to spend more time with Peter.

Thomas eyed Andrew with inner fury. He refused to understand why the young monk forever needed to be associated with Brother Peter. It sent pure rage up his spine.

"There is an herbal broth I have prepared for our guest," Bartholomew reminded an infuriated Peter. "Please feed him as much as he can take."

Peter nodded silently.

"You will serve with willingness and love," Paul instructed Peter. "Learn when it is necessary to surrender and accept what is."

"Yes, Father Abbot," Peter answered quietly.

As the other monks departed, Peter left in the opposite direction to fetch the healing herbal broth to feed to the wounded knight.

------◆◆◆------

"You still think your human is so wonderful?" one raven asked the second.

"What is your problem this time?" the other raven asked.

"Did you not see how eager he was to get away from the wounded knight who saved his life? Not very grateful, is he? Cold, selfish, unfeeling — so typical of the species."

"Give him time, for Heaven's sake. Let him live the experience and grow

from it. And keep in mind, what you are describing about him comes from fear, from self-doubt and lack of inner trust. How can he show anything loving towards another person before he learns to do so for himself?"

"I will repeat to you a thousand times," the first raven repeated for the thousandth time, *"you give far too much credit to humans."*

"You are blinder than they say bats are. Look at Father Abbot, that clever healing monk and certainly that chubby little monk. They all show enormous wisdom, compassion, patience, tolerance and love. Great spiritual qualities being expressed by HUMANS who you say are incapable of such qualities."

"They are the ex—"

"Stop it!" the second raven cawed angrily. *"You speak once again from bigoted ignorance. Remember that ancient HUMAN proverb that says, 'Physician, heal thyself.'"*

"Whatever."

"My human is being put into a situation to teach him some very valuable emotional lessons. You do not learn any truth until you fully act it out and thereby LIVE that truth. Just leave my human alone and let him experience what he needs."

"I still say —"

"I am SO not interested," the second raven interrupted.

"That prune-faced prior is far more typical of humans," the first raven insisted.

"Only in your rotting mind."

The two ravens flew away in opposite directions.

Seven

"Sorry, I did it again," Brother Peter apologised for the tenth time as he wiped spilled broth from the knight's beard and bare chest, while the recovering patient sat weakly upright in his bed. "I am so clumsy today. I do not know why."

The knight watched the anxious monk with amused eyes.

"This poor man is so afraid – of me? But why?" the knight wondered as he continued to watch Peter's shaky attempts to feed him. *"I am not THAT frightening, am I? And yet, there is something so endearingly sweet about him. I simply cannot take my eyes off him. He captivates me, and NOT because he looks like me. However, that similarity DOES make me wonder if I have a bastard brother my father kept hidden from the family."*

Nervously, Peter tried spooning another portion of the broth towards the knight's lips, then sighed with relief that at least one of his attempts had finally reached its mark.

Weak as he was, the knight enjoyed watching this beautiful clumsy monk in his desperate attempts to feed him. *"I thought monks did this sort of thing all the time,"* the knight continued to muse. *"But this one acts as if he has never helped anyone in his entire life."*

The invalid guest was also fascinated by Peter's unconscious habit of puffing his cheeks and then sticking out his tongue every time he spooned out some broth to the knight.

"Cute," the knight whispered feebly.

"What?" Peter leaned forward earnestly, wondering what could be wrong this time.

"Cute," the knight repeated hoarsely, raising a trembling right finger to Peter's face and tracing a line down the monk's bearded left cheek with his fingernail. Then the hand collapsed suddenly back onto the bed.

Peter pulled back sharply, taken completely off guard by the knight's touch.

"Have I done something wrong?" the knight whispered.

"What? Oh! Not at all. I, uh – I was just taken by surprise."

What Peter was not saying, because he could barely understand it himself, was that the gliding touch of the knight's fingernail was not just a surprise. It had triggered an explosion of energy throughout Peter's body. Instantly, the monk felt he wanted to melt into that finger, but he could not fathom where this feeling was coming from or what it could possibly mean.

"By the Cosmos, is your human monk genuinely that naïve?" one raven asked the other as they perched on the roof of the monastery, telepathically observing the scene in the infirmary.

"Be quiet!" the other raven ordered angrily. *"Give him a chance. Things are just getting started."*

"No, really! Is he so stupid that he does not understand what he is feeling or what his emotions could possibly mean?"

"I said, NO! Now be quiet and let things unfold and see what happens."

The first raven shook his head in despair. *"Humans!"*

Normally, Peter hated being touched by anyone without his permission, which he NEVER gave. But the slightest touch from this knight sent quivers up and down Peter's spine. Suddenly, he wanted to cry out and merge completely into the knight's body. Peter had never been this aroused before and it terrified him – not because it was towards a man but because the feeling was there at all.

Apprehensively, Peter lifted the next spoonful of broth, but he was shaking so much from the electrifying reaction of the knight's touch that he spilled the broth again all over the knight's exposed chest.

The knight giggled weakly. "Boom again," he whispered.

Deeply embarrassed, Peter repeatedly wiped a wet cloth across the knight's chest.

"That feels nice," the knight whispered, his face beaming.

"Oh, well, I am glad – I think. Please forgive my clumsiness, sir."

"Rich—ard."

"What?"

"I have not yet – told you – my name," the knight struggled hoarsely. "My name is – Richard."

"I am very glad to meet you, Sir Richard. I am Brother Peter."

"I was born Riccardo – Riccardo *figlio di* Alfonso – where I am from. But in your language, I am called Richard, son of Alfonso."

"Riccardo, or Richard, it is still a beautiful name. Your accent is also quite beautiful, so that must mean your entire language as well as where you are from are beautiful as well."

"Thank you. I believe so."

"I am afraid my language is rather gruff, but it serves its purpose."

"Do I call you – Brother Peter or – just Peter?"

"Oh, well, I have not really thought about that." Peter paused a moment to think it through. "Here in the monastery we add 'Brother' or 'Father Abbot' or 'Prior' at all times, but it IS rather formal, is it not? I will leave it up to you, Sir Richard. If you prefer to call me Peter, that is fine with me. I am not sure, however, that the other brothers will feel the same way concerning themselves. You will have to ask each one individually."

"Thank you – Peter. And please stop – the 'sir' and – call me just Richard."

"Yes, I will, just Richard," Peter teased, something Peter had NEVER been known to do before.

The knight grinned. "I see humour is something else cute about you."

Peter smiled and blushed.

"Why am I blushing?" Peter wondered irritably. *"What is wrong with me?"*

Richard gave a reassuring nod then tilted his head to one side and looked at the monk with an amused expression. "I like it when – you smile – with or without the blush. It makes you – very pretty."

Peter flushed anew and stared blankly. He had never been praised before in his entire life. He hadn't a clue how to handle a compliment.

Richard's eyes widened in surprise. "Should I – not have said that?"

"Oh, um, no, er – I mean, it is fine. I, uh –" The monk paused to clear his head. "I mean, thank you." Peter was visibly stunned and didn't know what was going on. A man complimenting HIM? Why? He had no answer for that.

In Peter's next attempt to feed Richard, he once again spilled the broth on the knight's chest.

"It feels warm and nice," Richard sighed with a smile.

"Damn, damn, damn, damn, damn, damn, DAMN!"

"A cursing monk," Richard spluttered between laughs and cries of pain. "It makes you – even MORE beautiful."

Peter didn't hear Richard's last statement as he grabbed the cloth and wiped the knight's chest for the umpteenth time.

Poor Peter's next attempt to spoon-feed Richard was even worse. He dropped the bowl of soup held in his left hand, while simultaneously dropping the spoon held in his right hand. The wooden bowl crashed on the floor, broth spilling everywhere, while the spoon clinked and clanked until it ended up under the bed.

"I am utterly useless!" Peter cried out.

The knight's shaking hand grasped his bandaged side as he both laughed and cried from the pain caused by his laughter. "Damn!" he barked in support of Peter's previous long string of damnations.

Peter quickly retrieved the bowl and plopped it on the nearby nightstand. Then he got down on his hands and knees, even down onto his stomach, as he pushed himself under the bed to retrieve the errant spoon.

Richard held his breath in curious anticipation. Within seconds, he felt a thump underneath him as Peter banged his head against the bottom of the bed. Whomp! Whomp! Then another whomp! Peter repeatedly hit his head against the bed's bottom as he chased after the spoon. Finally capturing the renegade utensil, Peter next had to crawl out backwards, his back and head banging repeatedly against the bed's bottom, jolting Richard several more times. Peter held the spoon tightly and cursed so extravagantly, it would have made any soldier blush with shame.

Richard loved the whole comic scene, even though the constant bumps under the bed caused by Peter's ungraceful movements resulted in the knight occasionally screaming in agony.

"Horsey, horsey, ride 'em horsey!" Richard called out weakly with each thump under the bed. ***"Grazie Dio!"*** the knight prayed silently. ***"Questa è la migliore medicina curativa che Tu abbia mai potuto darmi."*** {*"Thank You, God! This is the best healing medicine You could have possibly given me."*}

Aloud, Richard said, ***"Mi fai ridere digioia, anchese provo anche dolore. Ma la amo!"***

"What did you say?" Peter asked while still attempting to extract himself from beneath Richard's bed.

"Excuse me. When I am most happy or excited, I slip back into my own language." Richard needed several deep breaths before he could continue talking. "I said that you make me laugh with joy – even when I am also in pain. But – I love it so much!"

"I am glad to oblige you."

"Please, understand – I laugh WITH you, never AT you."

"Yes, I get that," Peter muttered irritably.

After much clamouring and head-banging, Peter finally emerged from under the knight's bed, his dark robe, beard and hair covered in old dust. He threw the offending spoon onto the nightstand, emitted several more choice curses to Richard's delight and then rubbed his pounding head.

"Peter, now you need someone – to take care of YOU!" Richard said with glee. Then he crooked a forefinger at Peter. "Come here."

"What? Why?"

"Please come here." Richard patted the bed space next to him and motioned again with his forefinger.

"What is it?" Peter asked suspiciously.

"Please, Peter, come to me."

Peter guardedly sat down on the edge of the bed. "What?"

Richard reached out with his right hand and grasped Peter's shaking left hand. Then the knight tenderly kissed each of the monk's fingers. "I like you. I like you very much. You give me so much joy."

Emotions rushed up into Peter's tearing eyes, and then Richard's trembling finger caressed the monk's falling tears.

Peter felt that his whole chest was ripping open and that a crashing weight on his neck and shoulders was being cast aside.

"This knight makes me cry, and I do not understand why," Peter thought.

The monk partly wanted to run away, while another part of him wanted to melt completely into Richard. Peter had never before felt so open and vulnerable with another human being. It terrified him – but at the same time, he didn't want it to stop. He wanted to somehow merge completely and utterly with this magnificent man.

Peter stared into Richard's face for several minutes, unaware he was doing so. Richard raised an eyebrow, wondering what would happen next. Then suddenly, Peter realised he had been mutely staring for a long time.

"I am so sorry," the monk finally said. "I have been very rude staring at you like that. I apologise."

Richard shrugged. "There is no need to apologise. Stare at me all you want. It makes me feel cozy and warm. Maybe you find me interesting?"

Peter blinked several times and blushed again with embarrassment.

"It is fine," Richard said. "I like looking at you, and I find you – VERY interesting."

Peter's blush turned an even deeper crimson. "Um, I do actually find you very interesting."

Peter hesitated a moment, wondering if he should say next what he truly wanted to say. As the knight watched him expectantly, Peter decided to go for it.

"Actually, I have so many questions I would like to ask you."

"Then please, ask." But to himself, Richard wondered, ***"Mi chiedo che gusto hai."*** {"I wonder what you taste like."}

"I do not want to seem nosy and ask about what is not my business. And I also know you are very tired, and I do not wish to overly exhaust you."

Richard smiled. "I will let you know — if I am too tired to speak," the knight said in a hesitant and tired voice. "Please ask."

"You mentioned before that you were from the Italian peninsula."

"That is correct. I am from a city called Venezia."

"Whatever made you leave your home and come to this big faraway island of all places?"

Richard grinned. "Do you not love — this big faraway island?"

"Yes, I do. What I have seen of it, anyway. But I was just curious as to what made you leave your home to come here."

Richard nodded with a look that spoke of many painful memories. "The cruelty of politics."

Peter raised both his eyebrows, not thoroughly understanding Richard's point. But he watched Richard closely as the knight continued his tale.

Richard had to take several gasping breaths between each sentence, but he managed to maintain his speaking.

"My family was one of the twelve original ruling families in Venezia — or Venice as it is pronounced in your language. We of the original twelve families are descended from the senatorial aristocracy of ancient Rome." Richard had to pause a moment to catch his breath. "There were constant political games and intrigues going on among these families as they competed for power in Venezia."

"And your family got trapped in someone else's intrigues?"

"That is it exactly," Richard agreed.

"What happened to your family?" Peter asked.

"They were all assassinated," Richard said simply in a hushed tone. "Everyone was killed but me."

"Oh, Richard! I am so sorry! That is horrible!" Peter exclaimed aghast. Your parents and — did you have any brothers or sisters?"

"Both my parents were killed. And I had an older brother, Marco, and his wife and two small children."

"Lord have mercy! Even children were killed! That is so terrible. Richard, I am so, SO sorry!"

The knight shrugged. "I have been through many years of grief and loss. I live with this grief because I must. Versions of this story come up so many times in Venezia and anywhere else in the world, for that matter." Again, Richard had to pause to catch his breath. "It is always politics and the fight for control, power and money. Families are forever being destroyed."

"I am so sorry," Peter repeated in anguish. "How did YOU escape?"

"I was not in Venezia at that time. I was on business in nearby Verona and heard what had happened to my family."

"That had to be so dreadful for you! Your whole family obliterated and you not there to help them." Tears welled in Peter's eyes. "You are all alone and homeless. I am so, so sorry."

Richard eyes also began to well with tears, deeply moved by Peter's caring about his family as well as his present wounded state.

"Did you feel your life was in such danger that you had to leave not only your beloved Venezia but the entire Italian peninsula as well?"

"Essattamente."

"Pardon?"

"Excuse me. I was back into my own language again. I said exactly. I gradually realised that remaining in the Italian peninsula was too dangerous. I had to leave, as far away as possible for my protection."

"I am so sorry, Richard."

"For what, Peter? Life does what life does. My family was murdered, and I would have been next if they had found me. So I fled. But here I am now, safe with you."

Richard attempted a small smile.

"For good? I mean, will you ever be able to return to Venezia or to the Italian peninsula?"

Richard shrugged again. "That I do not know, Peter. Perhaps many years from now when I am old and grey and most of the original old players involved have died, I may be able to return, possibly in disguise, and see my home again."

Peter shook his head. "I am so, so sorry. I know I keep saying that, but I do not know what else to say."

Richard grasped one of Peter's hands and held it. "Thank you. That is very kind of you."

"Now I understand why you left your homeland. But what brought you to this big, faraway island?"

"Everywhere I went it was the same. Always the same conspiracies and power struggles. Always the same greed, jealousies, revenges and intrigues. Every place was the same." Richard took several deep breaths so he could continue. "I wandered from place to place feeling dissatisfied, disillusioned, frustrated and always very unhappy." Again Richard paused to catch his breath. "Then I had the silly idea that coming here to the edge of the world would be different – but of course, it is not. It is the same everywhere. But now I have nowhere left to run to, and I might as well stay here on your island."

"Of course, I am horrified for what happened to you and your family. But I must honestly tell you that I am also very grateful that you came into my life. If you had not shown up when you did, I would have been brutally raped by those vile men and then tortured and killed."

Tears welled up again in the monk's eyes. Richard leaned forward and gently wiped the tears from Peter's face.

"I am very happy to meet you, Peter. And I am glad I came when you were in need and I could help."

"But it nearly got you killed! Now you are badly wounded and will need a great deal of time to heal."

Richard smiled and caressed one of Peter's bearded cheeks. This immediately sent the monk into an inner battle between fearful confusion and aroused exhilaration. "I came when you needed me. And now you are here when I need you. How did that manage to work out as it has, I wonder?"

Peter nodded, for the very first time truly grateful for Father Abbot's wisdom in assigning him to this brave knight. Peter's hills could wait. This wounded and recovering man was far more important.

This was the first time in Peter's life that another person took precedence over anything he wanted for himself. The monk's gratitude to Richard was deep and genuine.

"Please, Peter," Richard suddenly said, "I need to ask you something."

"Of course, Richard. Anything at all."

"Come sta il mio cavallo?"

Peter blinked and stared blankly.

"I am so sorry," Richard said. "I am continually falling back into my own language. I guess it is the fact that I am wounded, exhausted and trying to recover. I asked you how my horse is."

Peter smiled. "I assure you, Richard, your horse is very well taken care of. He is fed, watered, his stall cleaned, he is brushed and walked every day. Perhaps soon you will be able to visit and see him for yourself. I hope this sets your mind at ease."

"Thank you so much, Peter. It does, and I appreciate it."

"Many of the monks are volunteering to help take care of your horse. I even manage to look in on him myself from time to time. He is beautiful and a delight to care for. You rest and heal, and know your horse is being well taken care of."

Richard smiled and gave Peter's cheek another loving stroke. "And now I am indeed very tired and need to rest."

"Of course, Richard. Thank you."

"For what?"

Peter blinked. *"Why DID I just say that?"* he wondered. There were several things he could have said in reply to Richard's question, but Peter thoroughly shocked himself again by simply saying, "For you."

Richard smiled warmly at the monk before closing his eyes and instantly falling asleep.

While he slept, Richard dreamed he stood in the courtyard of the monastery with Peter standing in front of him. They both smiled at one another as Richard took Peter's hands in his. In the dream the knight thought clearly, ***"Penso che potrei innamorami di te."*** {"I think I may fall in love with you."}

Peter sat on the bed beside Richard for a long time, staring into the slumbering knight's face. The monk's heartbeat pounded wildly, yet at the same time he also felt an inner peace he had never experienced before – except when he wandered across his beloved Highland hills.

"It has begun, and I am very pleased," said the raven listening to the humans' conversation while once again perched on a windowsill of the infirmary. *"This is my human's best opportunity to open up to his emotions*

and heal so many fears and self-destructive patterns. This is wonderful, do you not agree?"

But there was no response to the raven's question. He looked around and discovered he was alone. Where had his companion raven disappeared to? He swore the other bird had been next to him moments before. Apparently not.

The raven made a movement that was the closest possible to a bird's shrug.

"Oh well. In that case, I will not have to listen to any of your nasty complaints and negative predictions about humans. The gateway has opened, and now hope is ripe. Go for it, my human, and reach for the stars! Let yourself finally experience your deepest, truest love."

The raven cawed his own version of the human *"woo-hoo!"* as he flapped his wings and flew away.

Eight

"READY FOR SOME more wonderful stew, Richard?" Peter asked. "Did I remember to tell you it was just made today?"

"Yes, and I would very much enjoy some more of it, please. But let us see if any more of the stew actually goes INTO my mouth," Richard added with a gleeful smirk, "instead of down my front. Although, I must admit," the knight added playfully, "when that happens, it does feel rather nice."

"Very funny," Peter said with a pretended pout. "I cannot help it if I am so clumsy." Peter paused, then reconsidered his last words as he saw Richard about to speak. "Okay, okay, I really CAN help myself and not be so clumsy. I just need to focus."

"And ENJOY yourself as well," Richard added.

"Right – enjoy. Well, let us try the next mouthful."

Sighing with relief, Peter successfully hit the target.

"So far today no disasters!" Peter thought to himself. *"But, can I keep it up?"*

"You have gotten so much better at this the past few days than when you first began," Richard commented. "So far today you have hit the mark every time. ***BRAVISSIMO!"***

Peter gave a little bow before delivering the next successful mouthful. Richard applauded warmly and smiled his thanks.

The knight lay in a semi-sitting position in his bed, several pillows propped behind him and the wool blanket folded across his stomach. Richard's bare shoulders were broad and straight, his upper arms exquisitely muscled. The skin was golden smooth and clear. The dark fine hair spreading across Richard's chest again reminded Peter of Brother Clair's analogy of a blossoming tree with the two dark and prominent nipples like ripe fruits.

"What are you staring at?" Peter asked, suddenly unnerved by Richard's stare while simultaneously aware he had himself been staring at the knight and all too often at that magnificent chest.

"I still wonder if maybe we are long lost brothers."

"I doubt it."

"Or maybe we are simply soulmates."

Peter smiled. "I do not think soulmates are always automatically lookalikes."

Richard shrugged. "Oh well."

As Peter fed Richard another mouthful, the knight stared wonderingly at the monk and thought to himself, ***"Mi chiedo che sapore abbia questo uomo glorioso."*** {"I wonder what this glorious man tastes like."}

There was a slight pause after another spoonful of stew before the knight added, "I have been wondering about something else."

"What is that?"

"Do you know anything about astrology?"

Peter's eyes widened in surprise. Tilting his head sideways, Peter asked the knight, "Where did THAT come from?"

"I just wondered."

"Really? How odd. But why?"

Richard tilted his head as well. "Why not?"

Peter chuckled. "Why not indeed? Yes, I know something about astrology. But again, why?"

Richard shrugged and then smiled as he gazed admiringly at Peter. "You are always so efficient and orderly," Richard said after a moment. "You perform like the classic Virgo. Are you – a Virgo?"

"Actually," Peter answered, "I am not born a Virgo. But shhhh," he hissed, looking around with a fake expression of fearful conspiracy. "This kind of conversation we must keep to ourselves, truly. Monks are not supposed to talk about this, much less believe in astrology. In truth, my sun sign is Sagittarius. But my moon is in Virgo. And by the way, how do YOU know so much about astrology?"

"I learned here and there," Richard replied. "Both my parents were very, how you say, liberal – advanced in their thinking. Neither of them liked the rigid limitation, greed, narrow-mindedness and political control of the Church. They felt there was far more to life, and they did not like how the Church taught love with so much fear, ignorance, blame and hate."

"Yes, I understand that," Peter said, nodding.

"My parents encouraged me to seek knowledge from as many sources as possible, especially from within myself. That is exactly what I did."

"Wonderful."

"How about you and learning about astrology?" Richard asked.

"Ah," Peter said, shaking his head. "That is complicated."

"You prefer not to tell me?"

"Not that at all, but it really IS a bit involved. I have to explain some things about a few of us here, but it will take time. I want to tell you, really. But it is honestly better to discuss this another time."

"As you wish," Richard said with a shrug. "I look forward to our future discussions, then. Anyway, your Virgo moon explains to me your EMOTIONAL need to do things in such an orderly and efficient manner all the time. Sometimes, you know, the moon sign can be stronger than the sun sign."

"So I have been told. But remember, Richard, whenever we discuss this, it must be in secret."

"Of course," agreed the knight. After swallowing a few more spoonfuls of stew, Richard playfully mimicked Peter's looking around to be sure no one was listening before he spoke again. "Guess MY sun sign."

Smiling, Peter tilted his head again and studied the knight for a few moments. *"God, he is gorgeous,"* Peter thought. *"Concentrate, you fool! Richard just asked you a question that you need to answer!"*

As usual, Peter knew he and Richard looked alike. But because Peter remained in such deep denial of his own physicality, he only recognised Richard's beauty and could not connect to the truth that

71

their identical appearance meant that he was just as handsome. His brain simply refused to make the connection.

Aloud, Peter finally said, "On the one hand, you have the charisma of Sagittarius and the dynamic energy of Leo. But on the other hand, for some reason I feel your sun sign is Aries."

Richard was very impressed. "That is extraordinary. Yes, I AM an Aries, and my moon is in Sagittarius with my ascendant in Leo. You tuned in to all three of my main astrological signs!"

"My goodness!" Peter exclaimed. "That makes you TRIPLE fire."

"Meaning what?" Richard asked.

"Hot, hot, hot!" Peter joked. *"Did I just say that?"* Peter thought as he blushed scarlet.

Richard arched an eyebrow and grinned with a secret knowing and a challenging glint in his eyes. The expression on Richard's face caused Peter to suddenly break out in a sweat as a massive shiver raced down his spine.

"Um," Peter could barely speak as he tried to regain control by returning to the astrological discussion. "Your moon is conjunct my sun."

"Yes, my moon is on top of your sun. That is a position I always find rather appealing." This comment caused Peter to blush anew. "That creates a very strong emotional bond between us," Richard continued matter-of-factly. "You see, it is yet ANOTHER sign that you and I are soulmates."

"You may be right," the flustered and still blushing monk said, having difficulty regaining any sense of control within himself.

"Change the subject fast!" Peter ordered himself. "Just a little bit more stew, Richard, and you will have finished it all."

"And a very tasty stew it is! Please be sure to thank the brother who prepared it. But Peter, I feel I have had enough for now. Thank you."

"That is fine, and you are most welcome."

Richard's eyes bore into Peter's, always unnerving the monk but at the same time filling him with a dazzling warmth. Somehow, Peter managed to clumsily set the bowl and spoon down on the nearby nightstand.

"Please give me your hand, Peter," the knight requested suddenly.

"My hand? Why?"

Richard laughed with a small shake of his head. *"Dio mio!* MUST you answer every question or request with a 'why'?" Richard asked. "You do not always need to understand everything. Sometimes, just let things go and be in the moment. Then let the next moment unfold and so on. Okay? So – your hand, please," Richard stated as he held out his hand to receive Peter's.

Peter blinked with a perplexed look, but then he relented and placed his hand in Richard's. The knight then covered Peter's hand with his other hand. The firm silkiness of the skin and the warmth of the knight's hands sent thrills throughout the monk's body. Peter wanted to laugh and cry, his whole body feeling the knight's hands with an intense sense of – joy?

"But what exactly IS joy," Peter thought, *"and would I even know how to recognise it?"*

Peter was extremely confused. Normally he didn't like to be touched by anyone. But the touch of Richard's hands filled him with an overflowing happiness that he had never felt before. Peter simultaneously felt safe but also utterly lost at sea.

With his penetrating eyes, Richard observed the conflicting emotions in Peter's face.

"What now?" Peter asked nervously after Richard had held his hand for several minutes.

"Relax, my beloved brother," Richard whispered softly. "Just be in the moment with me right now – with me holding your hand. Enjoy it. Feel my hands holding your hand and savour the moment."

Richard continued to smile as he held Peter's hand. Peter wanted to relax, but his mind was overworking, attempting to understand what was happening, what Richard was really saying to him. The feel of Richard's hands was warm and breathtakingly wonderful. But what else was going on?

"Honestly," the first raven said to the other as they were once more perched upon the monastery roof, telepathically tuning in to the

ongoing scene in the infirmary, *"your monk is dumber than mouldy nut cake!"*

"Leave it alone, will you? It is happening. Things are beginning to open up with my monk. This is all very new to him. Let it unfold at its own pace!"

"But how can he be so stupid that he does not understand what is developing between them?"

"Back off or bugger off!"

--------◆·◆·◆--------

Richard emitted a slight laugh. "Peter, you think too much. I can hear and FEEL your mind's activity as if it were stampeding horses escaping from buzzing, over-excited hornets! Please ask your mind to be calm and quiet. Just BE here with me and enjoy our hands touching. Share this moment with me and be nowhere else. You do not need to understand anything at all. Just BE here with ME."

Peter tried – he REALLY tried. But the monk's mind would not stop bombarding him with endless questions. His eyes began to glaze over.

"Now you are trying TOO hard," Richard stated with a mirthful giggle. "RELAX! Be at peace, and be with ME."

Peter's hand trembled and now felt sweaty, but slowly he relaxed a bit by taking deeper breaths, and he finally managed to get his mind to quiet down – if only a little bit. The touch of Richard's hands remained comforting, soothing and exquisite to feel. At last Peter managed a hint of a smile.

"MUCH better, beloved brother. Just continue breathing and feel our hands touching."

Still feeling primarily uncomfortable and self-conscious, Peter focussed on the knight's two hands holding his left one. Richard's hands were large and powerful, the fingers long and elegantly beautiful. The nails were large and perfectly manicured, exactly like Peter's own hands.

"What are you thinking about?" Richard suddenly asked the monk.

Peter gave a slight jerk as he shifted his stare from their hands to Richard's face. Feeling hot and blushing a deep red, Peter replied. "Oh, nothing really."

Richard smiled warmly, and his eyes sparkled. "It doesn't look like nothing to me."

"Your hands," Peter finally admitted. "I was admiring your hands. They are very beautiful."

"Thank you." Richard glanced downwards before returning his gaze to Peter's face. "As are yours."

Peter shook his head. "Not really. Your hands are far nicer."

Richard shook his head. "I am sorry, Peter, but I do not agree." The knight's two hands held up Peter's hand closer to the monk's face. "Take a good look, Peter. Our hands, like everything else about us, are identical. If you see my hands as beautiful, then you cannot escape from seeing your hands are beautiful as well. They look the same."

Peter shook his head again. "Not to me."

"Well, to me your hands are beautiful."

Peter didn't answer, but he felt himself becoming increasingly warmer as his blush deepened. "What do we do now?"

Richard smiled. "I would like to continue holding your hand if I may. It gives me great pleasure and makes me feel so much better."

Peter smiled awkwardly at the knight, thinking that if he felt any hotter, he would end up as a massive heap of ashes. Feeling that Richard was expecting an answer, the monk meekly nodded.

Richard grinned with pleasure as his hands slightly tightened their grip on Peter's left hand. Richard then gracefully returned their hands to rest atop the knight's upper right thigh. They sat quietly with one another in the ensuing silence.

A quarter of an hour later, when the healer monk Bartholomew looked in on Peter and Richard, he found the two of them still holding hands and silently gazing into one another's eyes. Bartholomew backed away quietly, a large grin on his face as he sent a silent song of gratitude toward Heaven.

It was working. Peter was steadily awakening his heart and opening up to his long-buried emotions. There was finally a ray of hope. Richard was God-sent.

———•◦●◦•———

Several days later Peter gave Richard another bath. The monk first focussed on carefully wiping Richard's shoulders, arms and hands – then on cleansing the chest and stomach.

"You are very organised and thorough, Peter," Richard observed.

"Thank you. I try to be in everything I do."

When Peter had said this same sentence the day before, Richard had offered, "Have you ever considered being less intense about your thoroughness and relaxing more so you can actually ENJOY what you are doing?"

"What?" Peter had responded. "What do you mean? Chores are not something to enjoy but to get done – correctly and thoroughly."

"Oh dear," Richard had lamented with a smile, once again tracing a line with his forefinger down the left side of Peter's face. The knight's touch had caused Peter to shudder uncontrollably. Then Peter had become lightheaded and wondered if he was going to faint.

"What do you mean by oh dear?" Peter had asked, maintaining his efficiency over any thought of enjoyment.

"Nothing, my beloved brother. Never mind. Do as you do."

But from yesterday to today, Richard could already see a marked improvement in Peter. Richard now observed that the monk was more relaxed and appeared to be actually beginning to enjoy what he was doing, not just getting a chore completed.

In the next moment, bubbly Brother Clair entered the infirmary. To Richard's amusement, the portly little monk's fat belly seemed to *dance* into the room.

"Good day to you both," Clair announced cheerily. "Brother Peter, I see you are giving our wonderful guest another washing. My goodness, but you have learned quickly and well how to care for our glorious saviour knight."

"Yes, he does a very thorough job," Richard agreed.

"Welcome, Brother Clair," Peter said as he continued to wipe across the knight's sumptuous chest.

"Be sure to thoroughly cleanse his –"

"Done. All taken care of. Thank you!" Peter interrupted before Clair could mention the knight's genitals.

Clair noticed the wool blanket was still draped across the knight's legs, just below his navel – therefore, Clair knew that Peter had just lied.

"But Brother Peter, you really must remember to –"

"It is taken care of. Finished. Done."

"Are you certain?"

"Absolutely, Brother."

"God!" Peter thought anxiously to himself, *"Please do not mention Richard's genitals. Please, please, please do NOT say the word 'penis' in front of the knight!"*

"I just wondered because I can see that –"

"Honestly. Do not worry about it. It is all taken care of."

"Well, I –"

"Done. Taken care of. Thank you."

"If you say –"

"I do. Thank you."

Richard's head swivelled back and forth between the two monks as this rapid-fire conversation shot between them like a fast-paced tennis match (if tennis had existed in the seventh century).

"What the hell is going on between these two?" the knight wondered curiously.

"All finished," Peter announced as he threw the cloth onto the nightstand.

"Lord," Clair thought, *"he is so terrified to touch or clean Sir Richard's penis, he is even skipping washing the man's legs! Brother Peter needs more work than I realised."*

To Richard instead, Clair said aloud, "I must tell you, Sir Richard –"

"Please, just call me Richard."

"As you wish. Thank you. I must tell you, Richard, when I had the pleasure of washing you, I discovered that you have the prettiest nipples I have ever seen. Sumptuous beyond description."

"Thank you. I appreciate that," Richard responded with a huge grin, glancing momentarily at Peter and then winking.

Peter closed his eyes and exhaled heavily. What was Brother Clair going to say next to totally embarrass him? The answer to Peter's internal question came immediately.

"And it got me wondering, Richard," Clair continued, pretending to not notice Peter's mounting discomfort, "since you and Brother Peter look so closely alike in both face and physique, does that mean that Brother Peter also has sumptuously pretty nipples like you do?"

Peter gagged.

Richard grinned broadly and stared curiously at Peter's robed chest. "You know, Brother Clair, you ask a very interesting question, and you might be right. Perhaps one day we will find out for certain."

Richard continued to grin while Peter felt so giddy, he was certain he was going to faint.

"Please, just call me Clair."

"Thank you, Clair."

Clair beamed as if consciously trying to compete with the sun.

"My work here is done," Brother Clair announced suddenly as he turned and left the infirmary, leaving Richard smiling at Peter and Peter looking as if he desperately needed to sit down for a very long time.

"What is it with Brother Clair and nipples?" Peter wondered as his hands momentarily covered his own nipples so that Richard couldn't somehow see them through the robe's fabric. *"I need to lie down and take a nap,"* the monk decided.

Richard continued his grin that was filled with seductiveness, hilarity, mischievousness, challenge and utter delight.

———◆•◆•◆———

Another few days passed by.

An improved Richard was sitting upright in the bed, with several pillows supporting his back, waiting for Peter to return with his next meal. Peter had also informed Richard that he would look in on the knight's horse, Orion, to be sure the majestic steed was doing well and being well taken care of. Richard was deeply grateful to all the monks who were taking care of his beloved steed while he was incapacitated during his recovery.

Richard felt exhausted but held a smile on his lips as he silently mused to himself.

"I feel I have you all figured out, my beloved brother. You are a very lonely man terrified of your own compassion, your obviously deep emotions, your need

for love and your capacity TO love. But WHY are you so afraid, Peter? Why do you hide behind a monastery and monk's robes, pretending to believe in words of a faith you obviously do not truly believe? Why are you so afraid of love, beloved brother? Why do you hide so intensely behind impatience, efficiency and orderliness?

"They are all nothing but layers within layers of defensive walls. Is your capacity to love and your need to be loved so strong that you fear their power will result in your being crushed by them? Do you fear rejection, or do you fear actually GETTING what you want and need? And if so, why?

"You can deny until the Second Coming, my friend. You can hide behind all your self-created walls. But I see through them. I see YOU. I hear your loneliness. I feel your true compassion, no matter how often you try to conceal it. There is something about you that has grabbed me and will not let me go.

"I am not afraid of that. If anything, I am stimulated by it. I glimpse your true soul through the undetected cracks in your self-defensive walls, and I see your true Light and feel an exciting, exhilarating chance to share love deeply with you."

Richard was neither shocked nor afraid of his feelings towards another man, even though he had never experienced nor pursued this before. Instead, he felt peace as well as a fresh hope about what these new feelings promised him.

"I recognise that this wound in my side is only symbolic, a physical symptom of another wound buried somewhere deep in my heart. And Peter, my soul-wound is somehow connected to YOUR soul-wound.

"I feel drawn to you like a moth to a flame. But you will not burn me, beloved brother. Instead, I know you will lead me to a new and deeper enlightenment that will heal the wound of loneliness I bear in my heart. Compared to this heart-pain, my physical wound is inconsequential.

"Peter, I promise that I will not burn you either. Let me guide you to your true Inner Light as you guide me to my own. Let us meet our mutual pain and discover true happiness and healing through one another. Please let me in. We can give so much healing love to one another."

Richard suddenly began to sweat profusely as he fell into an exhausted sleep. He awakened with a start twenty minutes later as Peter entered the infirmary bearing the next meal for Richard. The knight quickly attempted to straighten himself upwards against the pillows while wincing in pain.

Seeing the pain-ridden stress on Richard's face, Peter immediately set the plate of food on the nightstand and rushed to help set the knight into a more comfortable upright position. Richard's body was stone hard yet silkily warm in a way that triggered sparkling thrills within Peter.

The two men stared at each other's mirror images, Richard glowing radiant charm and openness, while Peter's face looked confused and yet in some way also beseeching.

Peter quickly helped Richard into a more comfortable position, then fetched the plate and sat down on the edge of the bed to feed his beautiful knight.

This time Peter did not spill one drop or morsel anywhere. Richard stared lovingly at Peter, which made Peter very self-conscious. Peter felt that Richard's gaze completely penetrated into him, making Peter feel disrobed, nervous and vulnerable. But at the same time, Richard's insistently observing eyes filled Peter with a warm glow and excitement that he did not fully understand or know what to do with it.

Peter felt afraid, yet also protected, appreciated and liked by Richard. The monk didn't know what to do with any of these qualities he had never before allowed himself to experience with anyone else. He remained imprisoned by his own inner fears and self-denial. Therefore, Peter could not yet recognise the pure LOVE expressed to him by Richard, nor the responsive emotions brewing steadily within himself.

The healing days marched on.

Nine

"WHY DO YOU insist on making such a big deal out of all this?" one raven asked the other.

The two birds were perched on branches of a maple tree close to the monastery.

"What do you mean?" the second raven enquired.

"What do you mean, what do I mean? My question was clear enough and very straightforward."

"Excuse me that I do not grasp your ignorance. This IS a big deal – a major human breakthrough. Can you not see that?"

"Actually, no. Just because two MEN are falling in love? They are not the first, you know. Human love within the same sex has existed since the dawn of time. Even for animals and birds. So why the big deal?"

"Cosmos give me patience! It is not about sex or love between two males at all. It just HAPPENS to be that way between these two humans. The POINT, you nitwit, is that the monk has been emotionally shut down for most of his incarnations on Earth due to his extreme fears and negative expectations about love, which are the end result of being in such constant fear of his fears and therefore lacking self-love. Got it now?"

"Again, big deal," the first raven retorted. *"Fear and negative expectations are the building blocks of humankind."*

"Yes, but not in the judgemental way that you mean. Humans have much to learn about what love actually is, how it works and what it can accomplish. They first have to learn how and why they reject and distort love through fear – which is caused by a lack of self-love. They must learn to transform and HEAL their

fears in order to create true love. They need to recognise and release their false beliefs about love, all based on fears that create denial and pain. This leads them AWAY from the love that they desperately want and seek. But it is especially their fear of fear itself that sabotages everything."

"You make me dizzy with your words," the first raven complained. *"Humans are too stupid to achieve this level of awareness. Their brains are too tiny and limited. In fact, humans are incapable of understanding truest love at all."* The first raven spoke as if his theories were the most obvious truth.

"That is such total crap!" the second raven cawed angrily. *"You speak from YOUR ignorance and stupidity which you do not own as yours but instead project onto humans. They ARE capable, and that gift is the primary reason for their physical incarnations, you dolt!"*

"That is YOUR belief."

"That is the TRUTH."

"Have it your way," the first raven acquiesced, although not entirely convinced. *"So according to you, the human monk is, and let us be totally honest here, emotionally constipated. As if that is big news when talking about humans, especially humans living on THIS island. But what is the knight's issue? He seems to be too lovey-dovey, touchy-feely and full of way too much passion. What is wrong with him?"*

"There is nothing 'wrong' with the monk, the knight or even YOU, for that matter."

"Now I am totally confused."

"I am not surprised. Again, it is not about 'right' or 'wrong' or 'good' or 'bad'. It is about the state of a soul's energy and consciousness – what needs to be learned, healed and transformed to bring the soul to its highest development, fulfilment and happiness – for the good of all Creation."

"Okay," the first raven said. *"Tell me more."*

The second raven continued with his explanation.

"Untransformed fear is the primary blockage to love and happiness among humans. Fear is caused by lack of self-love. When you do not value yourself for who you really are, but instead seek value, acceptance, approval and validation through people or situations outside of yourself, this results in feelings of doubt, insecurity, anger, loneliness, self-hatred, jealousy and despair. Humans consistently forget that they are their own creators and masters.

"So, because humans do not generally love and trust themselves, they create

external gods to blame for their pain and problems. But then humans also think they can be SAVED by these external gods just by believing in them.

"And by the way, feeling fear is not a so-called 'bad' thing. Instead, feeling your fears is a great opportunity to start transforming your uncomfortable emotions into healing, creativity and personal growth. But to achieve this, humans must learn to feel their fears without always BELIEVING in them, so they can grow from the process instead of remaining imprisoned in it. Humans need to learn that everything they feel is real, but everything they feel is not necessarily true."

"Give me an example so I am certain I am following you."

"Sure. If I feel unlovable, that is a very real emotion indeed — but that does not automatically mean it is also TRUE. I need to fully FEEL the fear of not being lovable in order to embrace its deeper lesson that I do not sufficiently love myself. So then I need to consciously create new soul experiences that will help me choose to feel more lovable within myself. That way I am LEARNING from my fear instead of being IMPRISONED by it, and then I no longer need to believe the fear of unlovability whenever I feel it. Instead, whenever the fear comes up again, it is simply reminding me whether or not I emotionally trust my lovability that does not need to be earned or proven or validated by someone else. Does that example help?"

"Yes. I understand now. Go on."

"When you can feel all your fears and emotions but choose what is genuinely true for you and what is not, then you more quickly and more easily learn the deeper lessons that each emotion and fear are really there to teach you. This is how you liberate yourself from the imprisonment of believing everything you feel and fear. And so long as you remember that there is always a deeper learning and healing opportunity behind every emotion and fear, you eventually do not fear any emotions and fears but work WITH them and THROUGH them to achieve the highest healing and transformational growth."

"Right. I am actually following you now. But let me get this straight. You GENUINELY think humans are CAPABLE of achieving all of this? Really?" The first raven shook his head. *"I am amazed by your idealistic naivety in humans. But never mind. Getting back to the knight, what is wrong — oops, sorry about that — what is, uh, his limitation or ISSUE, as the humans say?"*

"Although he is more open to his emotions than the monk, the knight often creates life experiences to keep people at a distance. He fears intimate relationships and lifelong commitments, which he sees as threats to his independence and

individuality. He has used the role of a travelling knight as an excuse to alienate himself from people or to keep them, as humans say, at arm's length."

"But I do not see this knight holding back with the monk at all," the first raven insisted. *"In fact, quite the contrary."*

"Woo-hoo!" the second raven cheered.

"What was that?" the first raven asked with alarm.

"Oh, that is a joyful expression that I have heard humans utter when they are extremely happy about something. Woo-hoo!"

"Right." The first raven shook himself vigorously to get as much of the "woo-hoo" energy as possible free from his feathers. *"So back to the knight."*

"The knight, or Richard as he is called, has often manipulated people with his charm and constant work assignments to keep them at a 'safe' distance. But it is not happening this time. The knight IMMEDIATELY made the soul-connection with my monk, plus he is allowing himself to be in a vulnerable position when being a knight is no longer a reason to keep someone at a distance. He is allowing himself to dare to embrace his vulnerability and then let the soul-attraction work its magic.

"And in choosing to not fend off intimacy," the second raven continued, *"Richard is also awakening emotions in the MONK who for centuries has been starved for acceptance and love. So these two humans are creating a momentous opportunity for themselves to achieve the deepest levels of emotional expansion and transformative healing. This is to be supported and celebrated by all of Creation – including us. So WOO –HOO to you!"*

"But the knight has no choice in any of this," the first raven insisted. *"He is wounded and therefore really IS vulnerable and must rely on others."*

"What is your point?" the second raven asked. *"That he is a victim?"*

"Absolutely!"

"Wrong!"

"How so?"

"You MUST be pretending to be this naïve! I cannot believe you have ascended to the sacred level of Ravenhood and yet do not understand how the Universe functions!"

If a raven could have looked pissed off, the first raven would have done so.

"You know very well," the second raven resumed, *"that at the knight's*

highest soul-level, he has CHOSEN to co-create this experience with everyone involved — in order to finally teach himself to be safe with vulnerability and intimacy and also to open up to the power of this kind of opportunity. Richard is learning to no longer use his knight role — or any other role, for that matter — as an excuse to avoid deep and lasting relationships with other humans."

The first raven flicked a wing at the other bird to ward off the irritating exuberance of the second raven's excitement.

"Okay," said the first raven, *"you are excited for these two humans. Good for you. I hope you get even more happiness from the tragedy that is unfolding."*

"It is NOT a tragedy."

"Wait and see."

"Che barba," the second raven cawed.

"What did you say?"

*"Oh, sorry, for a moment I switched into the knight's language. I said, how boring. I find your negativity **che barba** — so boring. And anyway, why did you not understand me?"*

"Because, you idiot, you switched languages on me!" the first raven complained.

"So? We are telepathic. Therefore, we understand ALL languages."

"We do?"

"You did not know that?"

The first raven shook his head.

"How did you manage to incarnate as a raven? And anyway, why am I not surprised by your ignorance?"

"Well, now that you mention it," the first raven commented drily, *"I am getting **che barba** with you AND your humans. No matter what they do, they will always end up at the bottom of the shit heap."*

"Has any other raven ever told you how comforting, compassionate and loving you are?"

"What? Well, no actually."

"AND NO ONE EVER WILL!"

"You know what you can do with yourself."

"As one who does it to yourself on a regular basis, I am sure you can tell me all about it."

"Bitch! And I STILL do not see the importance in this grand spiritual awakening for them being two males."

"*There IS NO importance whatsoever, you moron who apparently never listens to a word I say! This is not about homosexual OR heterosexual attraction. It has nothing to do with any kind of sexual attraction or with them as physical beings at all. They are drawn to each other on the deepest SOUL level, and their physical sex has nothing to do with it. Yes, most times the physical sex is an issue with human souls but sometimes it makes no difference whatsoever to the healing and transformational growth that urgently need to happen.*"

"*If you say so.*"

"**Mazel tov.**"

"*What? Is that another term in the knight's language?*"

"*No, that is a term used by humans known as 'Hebrews'. They live in other areas of planet Earth, and I have spent time with them in some of my past-lives. It literally means 'good luck', but they also use the term to mean 'congratulations'.*"

"*So you were telling me congratulations?*"

"**Mazel tov.** *You got it.*"

"*All your incessant jabbering has made me quite hungry now. And I am tired of watching the humans. So I am leaving to hunt for food.*"

"*Hold on. I am feeling hungry as well, so I will join you.*"

The two ravens flew away from the maple tree in search of prey. But the one raven who was most sympathetic to humans and specifically watching over the monk sent a farewell blessing of hope, support and love to both the monk and the knight.

———◆•◆•◆———

Father Abbot Paul and Brother Clair sat side by side on the herb garden bench.

"How do you think it is going?" Paul asked.

Clair pondered the question for a few moments while gazing out at the garden. "I feel our Brother Peter is opening up and responding to Richard's eloquent advances."

Paul smiled. "I hope it works this time. Peter's soul has been shut down for centuries. He desperately needs someone as miraculous as Richard to help him make a breakthrough."

"Give them time, Paul. Peter is responding."

"In past lives, you and I always said to give him more time," Paul reminded his companion. "And every time we said that, something would then happen to stop the process. Every other time it ended disastrously. Just remember how horrific everything fell apart at Camelot."

"We can never force it," Clair reminded Father Abbot. "We have done what we can, and the rest is up to Brother Peter and Richard. And anyway, Paul, you know very well that it is only our mental perception that things ended badly in the past. We are judging those past events and not considering the larger picture of this epic learning and healing process. We do not really know if those past events were really disastrous simply because they felt and looked that way to us or if they were simply what was needed for them to occur as the next steps in their long-term healing process."

"Yes, yes, I know. It has always depended on the reincarnating souls of Peter and Richard, whether they were man and woman or man and man – and once, remember, when they were woman and woman. Yet every time it ended up the same."

Clair shrugged. "We cannot do more than we have. You know the laws of Karma. We cannot judge events by their surface appearances. We do not know the full extent of their learning process, and we certainly cannot do it for them."

Paul turned and suddenly ran his fingertips down Clair's chubby cheek. "God knows we have tried."

Clair momentarily placed his hand on Paul's. "Lord, how we have enjoyed doing that!"

Both men chuckled simultaneously, then quickly returned their attention to the herb garden in front of them.

"Have we missed anything?" Paul wondered.

"It does not matter if we have," Clair answered. "Whatever will be, will be. There is nothing more that we can do."

"It is so frustrating," Paul lamented.

Clair nodded. "Downright exasperating!"

"I wonder why they are man and man again this time."

Clair gave Paul a playful nudge. "Maybe for no other reason than to remind them that their physical sex has nothing to do with the deeper emotional and spiritual issues. For that matter, why are you and I man and man again this time, and as MONKS!"

Paul nodded and returned the nudge. The two men spent the next few minutes staring wistfully at their beautiful herb garden.

"I only want the most fulfilling and joyful love for them," Paul sighed.

"Of course."

"On the same level as us," Paul added.

Clair laughed. "On OUR level? Paul, my love, I think they passed us a while back."

Paul turned his gaze to Clair. "Not in my heart."

"Thank you, my love." Then Clair looked into Paul's serene eyes and decided to add, "By the way, dearest, your nipples are just as pretty as Richard's and I am sure as Peter's, once we find out about his."

Paul laughed heartily. "You and your nipples!"

"Oh no," Clair corrected Paul. "You and YOUR nipples!"

The two monks hugged, shared a heartfelt kiss and then returned their gazes to meditate once more on the beauty of their monastery's nurturing herb garden.

Ten

"BROTHER PETER, A moment if you will."

Peter stopped outside the door to the infirmary while holding a plate with Richard's next meal. Brother Bartholomew had waited several minutes for Peter's arrival, wanting to have a word with his fellow monk.

"I know you are eager to serve that meal to our guest, but this will only take a few moments."

"Certainly, Brother Bartholomew." But inside himself Peter immediately wondered, *"NOW what have I done wrong?"*

Peter had met Brother Bartholomew over three years earlier when Peter first joined the monastery. At the beginning, Peter had often referred to this tall, thin healer-monk with the narrow head, long narrow nose and narrow stature as "Brother-Lean-and-Narrow." But now Peter saw Bartholomew as warm, sincere, helpful, compassionate and intelligent. Bartholomew may be narrow in face and body, but NOT in mind or spirit.

"How is our patient doing?" Bartholomew asked, eyeing Peter closely to see what he could learn from Peter's body language as well as his words.

"Quite well, Brother Bartholomew. Richard is getting stronger every day."

"Good. What is his mood, do you think?"

"Hmmm," Peter mused cautiously before answering. "Our knight is in good spirits, I think. At the moment he has less physical pain and appears to be slowly but steadily increasing his energy."

"Good," Bartholomew repeated. "And how do YOU experience him?"

"I am sorry, but I do not understand your question."

Bartholomew scratched his head and thought a moment. "Let me see. Um, how do I reword this – what is your experience of Richard AS A PERSON? I mean, what do you FEEL about him intuitively?"

Peter remained confused. *"Exactly what information is Brother Bartholomew trying to get from me?"* Peter wondered. The monk couldn't yet differentiate his intuition from his butt. *"What is he looking for that I have so far not told him?"*

Aloud, Peter said, "Well, he is very friendly, warm and easy to talk to. Does that answer your question?"

Peter was NOT going to talk about the shivers that went up and down his spine every time Richard touched the monk's face. But this was exactly what Bartholomew could already sense from Peter's voice and slightly trembling body language.

"For now, that is fine, Brother Peter," Bartholomew replied. Then the healer monk decided on another tactic. "Richard's native language is quite beautiful to listen to, and his accent with our language is also lovely to hear," Bartholomew said as he maintained his scrutiny of Peter's non-verbal reactions.

"That is true," Peter agreed with a nod.

"What do you pick up about Richard when he speaks his language?"

Peter frowned. "That is a most unusual question."

"Humour me, please. I am very interested in your insights."

"Well," Peter ventured after several seconds of struggled, concentrated thought, "the language is warm and beautiful, very inviting and somehow lulling in a safe and pleasant way."

But Peter did NOT say that listening to Richard speaking in his native tongue made the monk want to ejaculate on the spot. Listening to Richard's rolling baritone voice either in the knight's Venetian or the monk's Gaelic tongues made Peter want to drop everything and leap immediately into Richard's arms (which, of course, Peter did not ever dare to do). But Peter could not reveal any of these inner reactions to either Richard or Bartholomew, and he wondered how long he could maintain his emotionally suppressive control.

Again, Bartholomew could sense all of Peter's unspoken thoughts, which could easily be interpreted through Peter's often tear-glistened eyes, his trembling hands, the strained posture of his body and the stressed tone of his voice.

Bartholomew celebrated inwardly, *"Go get him, Richard! Brother Peter truly WANTS you!"*

But aloud, Bartholomew said, "I have always believed that how a language is spoken indicates the character of the people who were born into that language."

"Really?" Peter replied. "What an interesting thought."

"Listen to our own rough Gaelic, for example," Bartholomew ventured. "On the surface, we sound very gruff and tough. But underneath, there is a definite lyrical and poetic quality to our native language. We Celts try to ACT very tough so much of the time, yet there is poetry, music and magic at the root of who we are as a people and, I believe, in the motives behind our actions."

Peter thought about that a moment, while simultaneously worrying that he was standing holding Richard's dinner that would soon turn cold if he couldn't get away from the healer monk in the next few minutes. "Yes, I agree with you about that," Peter said, sincerely impressed and intrigued by Bartholomew's enlightening theory. "That is very observant of you."

Bartholomew nodded his thanks, having never before ever heard Peter praise any other monk for ANYTHING. "Then there are the Anglo-Saxons to the south. Their Germanic language sounds like they are constantly throwing up on each other. They too sound rough and tough, but without any lyrical or poetic qualities as we have. To me they just sound mean and emotionally constipated."

Peter laughed. "That is so true. My father used to say the Anglo-Saxons always sounded like they were gagging on dinners they despised."

"You see! We humans act like the sound of our language."

"Fascinating."

"Well, Brother Peter, I will not keep you from your work. Richard is waiting for his dinner, and you are doing a very good job. Keep it up, my friend."

"Thank you, Brother Bartholomew," Peter said gratefully, sensing the meal becoming increasing cooler.

Then Peter entered the infirmary with Richard's meal, while Bartholomew remained outside, watching Peter approvingly.

"How much you are changing, Brother Peter," Bartholomew thought with satisfaction. *"You never used to share anything with anyone. But you have just shared more with me in this one conversation than you have done during the entire three years that I have known you. And with a compliment, to boot! Bravo, Peter! And bravo Richard too!"*

Two weeks passed.

Brother Bartholomew now allowed Richard to get out of bed three times a day and walk around the monastery grounds a bit. But the healer monk also warned Richard to not do too much too soon and thereby create unwanted complications.

Richard was daily led slowly and carefully by Peter to visit Orion, the knight's horse lodged in the monastery stables. The joy of watching Richard reunite with his powerful steed always filled Peter with happy tears. The monk loved horses and enjoyed seeing the special bond between animal and knight. Richard's daily visits with Orion were the most powerful healing experiences of the knight's recovery – except, of course, for his blossoming friendship with Peter.

One morning Peter was helping the knight walk around the monastery's herb garden just outside the infirmary. Richard was dressed in a monk's robe, and the appearance of Peter and Richard walking together was very disconcerting to the other monks since the two men looked identical. As a result, the other monks nicknamed Peter and Richard as 'The Twin Monks'.

"The knight is a very handsome man," one of the monks had commented on seeing Richard for the first time, and the other monks had all agreed.

Even though the monks saw that Peter and Richard looked

startlingly similar, none of the monks (except Andrew) ever said that Peter was equally handsome – nor had they ever commented on Peter's handsomeness in the years he had been living with them in the monastery. Because Peter would not make the reflective connection himself, therefore the monks didn't either. As a result, Peter, like all his fellow monks, saw beauty only in the look-alike Richard but never in himself.

"Let us hope the knight is not the same in PERSONALITY as Brother Peter," several monks said between one another. "We certainly do not need another Brother Peter among us in THAT way."

Some monks had taken a few moments to greet and speak to the knight and quickly related how warm, friendly and incredibly nice Richard was. "Not at all like Brother Peter."

"The knight is having a very positive effect on Brother Peter," some monks pointed out as the monastery gossip continued.

"He is in love with the knight," some suggested.

"What can the knight possibly see in him?" others sniggered.

"Something WE do not see," was often the reply.

"They look so much alike. Yet they are so different in personality. It is so strange," others said.

"Could we perhaps channel this energy in another way that will be more productive to us all as a group?" was the usual response from Brothers Clair and Bartholomew as well as from Father Abbot Paul.

Brother Andrew, meanwhile, observed Peter and Richard with enormous sadness. "I am obviously not good enough for Brother Peter, and he would, of course, only be drawn to someone as magnificent and as equal as Sir Richard. I am so obviously inferior," the young monk lamented.

Dour Prior Thomas watched Brother Andrew's love-sick sadness with mounting anger. "Must that young boy forever be moaning about Brother Peter?" he complained. The prior also observed Peter and Richard with ever-increasing rage and disgust. Whenever he saw them, he would march away in a dramatic huff, treating everyone else with disdain.

"What has gotten into Prior Thomas?" some of the monks wondered. "He makes Brother Peter look charming."

Father Abbot and Brothers Clair and Bartholomew, the leaders of the hidden inner spiritual circle, watched Peter and Richard with ever-growing joy and hope, seeing in the monk's caring of the knight the promise that the monk might finally drop his guard, let his walls down, and open up to his emotional potentials.

These three monks, however, totally ignored Brother Andrew and Prior Thomas. Unbeknownst to them, this choice to not give more attention to the prior and the youngest monk would trigger repercussions that would take centuries to heal.

———◆•◆•◆———

In the monastery's herb garden, Richard walked on Peter's left side, holding on with both hands to the monk's left arm just above his bent elbow. The knight was thrilled with his new opportunities to stand, walk, visit Orion and once more be outside in the fresh air, despite it getting colder each day.

It was now mid-November and the days were consistently icier. Richard felt a sharp chill from the cold breeze blowing across the garden. But his need to be outside was far more important to him than wanting to feel warm.

Weeks ago, the leaves had begun to change colour and fall from their tree branches. Both Peter and Richard could feel the land settling into a hibernating slumber. But today the sun was shining brightly, and both men endured the cold to enjoy being in the outdoors together.

"Peter, do you know anything about these herbs? Which is which, and what they are used for?"

"Actually, I know nothing about herbs – except that they are very healthy. Sorry."

"No problem."

"I could ask Brother Isaac who manages the herb garden or Brother Bartholomew who uses most of the herbs in his healing. They could answer all your questions."

"Perhaps another time," Richard said with a gentle smile. "Thank you."

Along one edge of the garden where they were slowly walking, the knight and the monk approached a sturdy wooden bench that was just wide enough to support the two of them.

"Richard, shall we take a rest and sit on this bench for a while?" Peter suggested.

"Good idea. Thank you."

Peter carefully guided Richard to settling down upon the bench, and then Peter sat down alongside him. Their bodies fit snuggly on the bench, with their hips pressed tightly together. Normally Peter never wanted his body to be in such close contact with another person. But when it came to Richard, this closeness instead created a kind of soothing warmth for Peter – and thrilling emotions as well. Peter remained too shy and self-unaware to understand the deeper meaning of the soothing warmth he experienced from the physical closeness of Richard.

———————◆•◆•◆———————

One raven shook his head at his companion raven as they observed the two men sitting together.

"Really? Still that blind and stupid?"

"Shut up, will you? Let my monk move at his own pace."

"Are you kidding? At this rate, three civilisations will have emerged and fallen by the time he wakes up."

"Do be quiet! It is unfolding as it needs to. So seal your beak!"

———————◆•◆•◆———————

The two relaxing men gazed pleasantly at the herb garden, both of them still trembling from the cold as they sat.

"It is quite cold this morning," Peter observed, still shivering.

Richard turned to look into Peter's eyes. "Then we must find ways to keep each other warm."

———————◆•◆•◆———————

"Hint, hint – you ignorant ignoramus!"

The other raven swiped his companion across the beak with his wing. *"One more telepathic word out of you, and I swear I will cause serious harm that you will never recover from!"*

———•◆•———

Richard's last statement made Peter feel giddy, and he was too nervous and self-conscious to understand the source of his giddiness, much less know what to do with it. Instead, he escaped the issue entirely by changing the subject.

"I have been wondering," Peter began but then stopped.

"Yes?"

"Several times you have mentioned where you come from."

"Yes."

"But you always call it the Italian peninsula. Is this peninsula not its own country? I mean, if it is the Italian peninsula, why is it not also a country called something like – Italy?"

"Good question," Richard replied. "Our peninsula is a huge collection of distinct regions and independent city states, all with quite different races, cultures and languages. Not just different dialects, but sometimes quite different languages."

"I did not know that. But do these diverse peoples have no desire or momentum to unify their peninsula into one great nation?"

Richard chuckled. "Completely impossible for now and probably for many centuries to come. The people are far too different in so many ways. Plus, there are mountain ranges running both north and south and sometimes east to west that severely fragment the peninsula, making travel very difficult and time-consuming. This further isolates the regions and city states from one another. So, Peter, I do not see a unified country on that peninsula for a very long time to come, if ever."

"I see. I did not realise that this level of human diversity there is so extreme and the geography so divisive."

Richard smiled warmly and leaned over to stroke the monk's right cheek. At first Peter was startled by Richard's public display, but then he felt even more warmth stirring deep inside his cold body. Nervous and self-conscious, Peter felt a need to keep talking to avoid his confusing and intensifying emotions.

"I am sorry if I am being too nosy."

Richard again stroked Peter's cheek. "Please, you never need to feel that way. I appreciate your interest, and you should always pursue what interests you. So tell me, Peter, what interests you so much about my homeland?"

Peter thought a moment. "Maybe it is that I have never set foot out of my own country and have seen nothing more, whereas you have travelled so extensively and have seen so many other countries. Maybe it is because your Venezia sounds so wonderful – so exciting."

"Or maybe all those things," Richard suggested. "But please never apologise for your interest. Pursue them. It is important."

Peter nodded, and the two men gazed deeply into one another's eyes for a few moments. But it was Peter's self-conscious insecurity that once more forced him to look away and stare ahead at the garden.

After a brief moment, however, Peter asked.

"Where on your Italian peninsula is this Venezia that you come from?"

"In the northeast."

"Is it a coastal city?"

"Well, yes and no."

"What?"

Venezia is near the mouth of the Po River, one of the largest rivers in the peninsula. Actually, there are four rivers which pour into our Venezian bay. Besides the Po are the Piave, the Brenta and the Sile."

"But why yes AND no to Venezia being a coastal city?"

"These four rivers empty into a bay, and Venezia lies IN the bay as a series of islands connected by bridges."

"Oh. I had not realised that. How marvellous!" Peter pondered this information for a moment. "When was Venezia founded?"

"That is hazy, even for us Venezians. We think that Venezia, is named after a race of ancient people known as the Veneti who first inhabited the region perhaps a thousand years before the birth of Christ."

"Oh!" Peter said. "That is very old indeed."

"My city is beautifully unique. It is made up of over a hundred islands surrounded by lagoons that in the beginning were very marshy and filled with the constant threat of malaria. In some places today, there are still islands that need to be cleared of the marshes and the threat of malaria. But back to what I was saying, besides the Veneti, there were also fishermen living on the Lido, a long narrow island running south of the main central area of the city. They were called **incolae lacunae** – the lagoon dwellers.

"Our most important church," Richard continued, "is dedicated to San Giacomo on the small central island of Rialto, a name which derives its meaning from **'rivoalto'** and means 'high shore'. I know that this church was dedicated in March of the year 421, so Venezia – or Venice in your language – has been a city at least since then. But how much older Venezia is as a city BEFORE that date, no one really knows for sure."

"San Giacomo? What saint is that in my language, do you know?" Peter asked.

"Let me think a moment." Richard mused deeply for a while, searching for the name. Finally, it came to him. "Ah yes – Saint James."

Peter felt he should mention something about that, but he couldn't remember what it was. He thought it was important, and it disturbed him not to be able to remember what it was.

"What is wrong with me?" Peter wondered helplessly. Instead Peter said aloud, "I see. It is all so fascinating. What else can you share with me about your Venezia?"

"Well," Richard continued with a slight shrug, "Venezia grew the most when the Roman Empire reached its final fall in the fifth century. As Germanic hordes, the Goths and later Atilla and his Huns invaded the peninsula, many people attempted to escape these invasions by seeking refuge in Venezia. They came mostly from surrounding towns such as Padua, Aquileia, Verona, oh, from many towns and villages in the area as well as many people escaping from the unprotected countryside."

"Why did the people think that going to Venice – um, I mean Venezia – would enable them to escape the invaders?"

"Remember, Venezia is on an archipelago of islands a few miles out in the sea."

"And?" Peter asked.

"And what, Peter?"

"What was to stop the invaders conquering those people by sailing out to sea?"

"On what?"

"On what? On boats!"

"What boats?"

"What? Oh, now I see."

"All these different invading peoples had in common that none of them were seamen. They were all conquering inlanders who had no boats and probably would not have known how to use them. So the people knew they would be safe from the invaders on the Venezian islands."

"I see."

"The year 452 was when the largest number of refugees came to our city. In fact, because of this, the very first name for Venezia was in Latin, called **Refugium in Periculus**, which means 'Refuge in Peril'. This referred to those people fleeing the invaders from the north and west. But I think there was a cosmic joke in that original name for Venezia."

"How so?" Peter asked, enthralled by all these exotic details about faraway places.

"Well, Venezia was supposed to be a safe haven from the invaders."

"Was it not so?"

"Yes, BUT – Venezia sits in a huge bay where those four rivers flowing into that bay. Plus, there is the wide and long Adriatic Sea that pushes infrom the east and south with its constantly surging waters. So, Venezia is etarnally at the mercy of the four rivers flowing in from the north and west which then never-endingly collide with the constant tempestuous sea pounding in from the south and east."

Peter nodded in understanding, totally awed by the exotic drama of it all.

"What else can I share with you, Peter? We are governed by the descendants of the original twelve so-called 'apostolic families' who could trace their lineage to the ancient patrician Romans who escaped to Venezia. I am descended from one of those families."

"Hence, you being a knight."

"Hence? What is the term 'hence'?"

"Oh, uh, thus, therefore."

"I see. Then, yes. Hence, I became a travelling and fighting Venetian knight."

"Your Venezia sounds amazing. And your life as well."

"Since you feel that way, I shall continue. Venezia is made up of one hundred and eighteen islands connected by several hundred bridges."

"Good Lord! That is extraordinary!"

"Yes, I quite agree. We do not walk on roads between our islands but instead travel in boats from place to place or walk across the many hundreds of bridges. Therefore, the canals are the 'blood veins' of our city."

"Someday I want to visit your wondrous Venezia."

"Peter, you will fall in love with it."

"I feel as if I already have! You said Venezia was named after an ancient tribe called the Veneti. But does 'Venezia' have any other meanings?"

"That," Richard replied with a warm smile, "has been under debate by the citizens of Venezia for generations."

"How so?"

"Everyone pretends to know, and no one ever agrees, which is common among the people of Venezia," Richard added with a laugh. "The debate goes on and on. Some suggest **'venetus'**, meaning the colour sea-blue. There are those who insist **'Venetia'** is associated with the Latin word **'venire,'** which means 'to come'. Because when the original twelve patrician Roman families, descendants of escaping Roman senators, first arrived at the lagoon, they cried, **'veni etiam'**, which in Latin means 'I have come.' The list goes on and on."

"Amazing."

"Wherever three Venezians meet, there will always be five or six theories or explanations on anything!" Richard chortled.

Peter joined in the laughter. "I think it is no different among my Celtic people."

The two men fell silent and stared blankly once more out across the garden.

"Now, may I ask YOU something?" Richard asked.

"Of course."

Richard suddenly turned and ran his hand through the thick, dark masses of Peter's hair. The monk was initially surprised, but then thoroughly enjoyed every loving touch of the knight's hand.

"Peter, you have a full head of black hair. But I thought that Christian monks must always shave off a portion of their hair, leaving a small bald circle at the top, called – um, called –"

Peter nodded. "A tonsure."

"Yes, a tonsure. But Peter, you do not have this tonsure. Nor does Brother Bartholomew or several other monks that I have seen. In fact, I have only seen a few monks with a tonsure, such as young Brother Andrew. Why is this?"

"Ah, yes," Peter said with a smile. "We have now come to THAT."

"And what is this 'THAT'?"

"Richard, I will now share with you a big secret."

Richard nodded with curious anticipation.

"Most of the monks here do not know this, and in the wrong hands this information could be very dangerous."

Richard put his face right up against Peter's so they were literally nose-to-nose. "Any secrets of yours are completely safe with me. *YOU* are completely safe with me."

Peter stared gratefully into Richard's eyes for a few moments. Feeling satisfied, he nodded.

"The majority of our monks here are true Christians – but some of us here are not exactly that."

Richard blinked several times. "Meaning?"

"Some of us walk a different spiritual path. We view life and the Universe quite differently than Christians. We choose to experience a Oneness – a belief that opposes most of what Christianity preaches. We few I am talking about live among these truly Christian monks to avoid being recognised as non-believers by those who would persecute us – even possibly kill us."

Richard paused momentarily to consider Peter's words, but then he ventured forth fully like the courageous knight that he was.

"God is everything, and everything is God," Richard stated clearly.

"Divinity is neither above us nor separate from us. Divinity is the totality of everything."

Peter was stunned with relieved amazement – then spoke in a flood of ideas and feelings.

"Yes, that is it exactly! Some of us here do not believe in externalising the All That Is. No external god saves us just because we believe in him or her. All humans – and all of creation as well – are purposeful manifestations of The One. And each of us is fully responsible for discovering our own unique truth within The One and also to grow from that inner process. We here in our secret group seek a truth and healing far beyond Christianity's fear-based limitations and narrow rules and bigoted judgements."

"I understand," Richard replied. "It is how I believe as well."

Peter's eyes teared as he smiled broadly. "I am extremely surprised but also grateful that you and I share these same beliefs. How did all this happen for us?"

"You are not alone in your beliefs, Peter. And this must also be how YOU learned so much about astrology."

Peter nodded. "We few also believe in reincarnation. All humans – and animals as well for that matter – live many lifetimes on Earth in order to learn lessons about loving, healing and creating. In other words, embracing the magic of spiritual transformation."

"I share this with you as well, my beloved brother. I was quite serious when I said I felt you and I were soulmates. When I first saw your face close up, I instantly recognised you, and not just because we physically look so much alike. I felt this 'knowing' that is far deeper than our mere physical similarity. I feel we look alike because we are soulmates meeting up again in this lifetime to ensure we recover our connection to one another."

Peter smiled. "That is a beautiful thought."

"I understand your hurt about very religious people quite often being blind to anything but the security of their narrow limiting beliefs. But I want to say to you again that your secret is safe with me and is also SHARED by me. You are never truly alone, Peter. Nobody ever really is."

Richard's last statement moved Peter profoundly, and he felt himself opening up to the knight more than ever before. In fact, it was precisely in THIS MOMENT that Peter finally understood he had been falling in love with this magnificent man for some time, and in this precise second Peter had actually crossed the border to being IN LOVE with him.

"WOO-HOO!" one raven cried in jubilation.

"Yeah, yeah. Let us just get on with it," the cynical raven muttered.

"Now there is something else I wonder about."

"Yes, Richard?"

"How do you get around your Father Abbot?"

"Get around him?" Suddenly Peter laughed. "That's right – I have not yet told you. Father Abbot is the leader of those of us who believe this way."

An enormous laugh exploded from Richard. "That is priceless! I love this place more and more! But how do the true Christians deal with those of you who do not have a tonsure?"

"Father Abbot came up with an excuse, claiming something or other as an explanation. The real, very religious Christians are not big on thinking for themselves. They see what they want to see, hear what they want to hear and believe whatever they are told to believe."

"Very religious people are often like that."

Peter nodded his agreement.

The two men gazed across the herb garden again for several minutes, until Richard spoke again.

"To change the subject entirely," Richard said, "we are in mid-November, which means we are soon entering the sun sign of Sagittarius. You told me you were a Sagittarian by birth. So your birthday will be coming up soon."

"The first of December."

"Really?" the knight laughed again. "My birthday is the first of April. Both of us are born on the first day of our birth months. Yet another sign we are soulmates," Richard added with a laugh. "What will you do to celebrate?"

"We do not celebrate birthdays here."

"What?" Richard asked incredulously. "Why not?"

"Monks do not do such things."

"But not all of you are genuine Christian monks. Surely you must do SOMETHING to celebrate your birthday, even in secret?"

"No, none of us do that. Even in our secret group, a birthday is just like any other day here."

"Not this time!" Richard announced loudly. "I will think of something. You and I will find a way to celebrate your birthday with fun and joy."

Peter watched Richard with a loving smile. "That would be nice. I look forward to it. Thank you."

"My pleasure. Um, out of curiosity, Peter, what do you call the month of your birth in your language?"

"Well, we name our months after trees, our ancestors being so closely tied to nature. Trees were always very important to the ancient Celts who saw trees as divine messengers and instruments of healing."

"I like that," Richard said. "So what tree is your birth month?"

"I was born on the thirteenth day of the yew tree, just before the beginning of the full moon."

"Yew? I don't know that word. What kind of tree is it?"

"Oh dear, um," Peter struggled. "It is an evergreen tree, and I have heard that in many places the Christians plant yew trees in church cemeteries as some sort of protection for the dead from evil spirits."

"Ah yes, I think I know what tree you are talking about. Would you know what tree is my Celtic birth month?"

"Let me see," Peter considered. "You are the first of April. So most likely your birth month tree would be the willow."

"I am afraid I am not familiar with these names for trees."

Peter scratched his head absently, trying to visualise the willow. "It is tall with long slender branches that curve forward and droop and flutter easily in the breeze."

"Yes, I think I know which tree you are talking about. Thank you for that, Peter."

After a few moments of warm silence, Richard spoke again. "Soon I want to walk my horse. I know it will be quite a while before I can ride Orion again, but he needs a longer walk than just around the monastery's courtyard."

"I will ask Brother Bartholomew how soon you and Orion can walk together."

"Thank you, Peter."

"Oh! I just had the most brilliant idea!" Peter said with a sudden spark of excitement.

"Yes?"

"I often walk to the Highland hills."

"I had heard that. I am sorry to have caused that practice to be stopped."

"Oh no, Richard, please do not feel bad about that at all. Everything is fine as it is, really. I understand that now. But my point is, I could ask Brother Bartholomew if sometime soon you and I could walk Orion together so I could show you my special Highland hills."

"Ottimo!" Richard exclaimed with joy.

"What?"

"Great!" Richard translated. "That sounds wonderful! Thank you, Peter."

"I will look into this for you. Just leave it with me."

"Thank you so very much. You take such good care of me and think about so many things to help me. I want you to know how much I appreciate that – how much I appreciate YOU."

Peter smiled self-consciously and looked away. He was still very uncomfortable with compliments, partially because he had hardly ever heard any compliments directed towards himself and partially because he lacked self-love. Peter had no idea how to act or what to say.

Richard observed Peter's discomfort. *"This poor man,"* he thought silently to himself. *"He is so desperate for love, and I want so much to give him that love. But I must move ever so slowly so as to not frighten him away."*

When Peter turned back to face the knight, Richard casually traced the backs of his fingers as a long and gentle caress down the right side of Peter's face. The feel of Richard's fingers down his face sent shivers exploding throughout Peter's body, and the monk feared that he might have an orgasm right then and there.

———————•◆•———————

A few days later Richard limped carefully with a wooden staff to check on his horse, Orion, in the monastery's small stables area. Brother Bartholomew was gradually allowing Richard more free movement so long as he did not over-exert himself.

As Richard approached the stables, he stopped suddenly and observed with great tenderness what he witnessed before him in a stall very near the entrance. Peter was grooming Orion with a long brush as he spoke quietly and lovingly to the horse.

"Here you go," Peter spoke soothingly. "Just a few more brush strokes for your back and sides. You are such a beautiful horse, Orion. I hope we have fed you right, treated you well and walked you enough. You are such a delightful visitor to have here with us isolated monks."

Tears welled in Richard's eyes as he watched Peter tend his horse and speak so lovingly to Orion.

"What he cannot express directly to fellow humans," Richard silently observed, *"he finds much easier to communicate to animals. How often that is the case!"*

"And I hope I am taking as good a care of your owner as well," Peter continued as he administered sweeping brush strokes across the horse's back. "Your Richard is a very special man, you know, Orion. You are very lucky to be with him, and I am enjoying my time taking care of him very much."

Peter suddenly realised that he was sharing some deep truths with Orion. He DID enjoy caring for Richard. It was genuinely no longer a problem that he had not been to his hills in quite a while. Peter was successfully accepting and managing some deep emotions that he had never before allowed himself to experience – and as a result, these feelings were no longer quite so painful or threatening. The monk now consciously understood that he was in love with the knight, and he was extremely grateful for it, even though he did not know what to do about it.

Richard quietly backed away a few steps from the stables entrance, giving Peter a few moments alone and then made an exaggerated noise so Peter would not realise that Richard had heard the monk's conversation with Orion.

Peter jerked and turned as Richard made his entrance.

"Richard! Does Brother Bartholomew know you have walked on your own to the stables?"

Richard gave a little bow. "Yes, Peter, I am here with his full approval."

"Are you in any pain?" Peter asked with deep concern. "Is it alright walking with that stick? Do you need any assistance, or to sit down?"

Richard chuckled at Peter's loving over-concern. "The pain is honestly very slight and not all the time. I am fine walking with this stick. I do not require help or to sit. Thank you for your wonderful concern."

"You are sure?"

Richard approached Peter and slid his forefinger down the side of Peter's face. The monk feared he would have to stand with his legs tightly crossed to avoid ejaculating just from the touch of the knight's gesture – a gesture Peter had now come to love exceedingly.

"I am sure," Richard replied. His eyes bored into the monk's face until Peter thought he would faint from the strength of it. "You take such wonderful care of Orion."

"It is a joy, Richard, believe me," Peter said. "He is a wonderful horse, and I love him very much."

Richard stared rapturously at the monk. *"He can love an animal and say so,"* Richard mused to himself, *"far easier than he can love a human and say so, especially to own loving himself. How I wish I were Orion in this moment. My beloved Orion, let us see if we can help this wondrous man feel and express the same for himself and to another human."*

Aloud, Richard said to Peter, "Thank you so much for taking care of my horse."

"My pleasure and my honour."

"And thank you for taking such good care of me."

Peter smiled self-consciously, unable to respond in words.

Richard turned towards Orion, the knight's eyes welling with tears.

Holding on to his walking stick, Richard gave broad strokes to Orion's side with his other hand.

"Sono così felice di vederti!" Richard addressed his horse lovingly.

"I assume Orion understands your language."

"He is fluent in my language. And actually, I believe all animals can understand every human language because they are all telepathic."

"I had not thought of that. I must say, that is very handy. But just out of curiosity, what did you say to Orion?"

"I told him I am so happy to see him."

Peter nodded. "As he must be to see you."

Richard smiled at Peter and gave a few more loving strokes to Orion.

"I think I need to return to the infirmary and rest awhile in bed. I am suddenly feeling extremely tired. Can you help me return to the infirmary please, Peter?"

"Of course. Take my arm and lean on me if that will help you."

"Thank you, I will."

The two men petted and kissed Orion before walking together back to the infirmary, Richard indeed taking hold of Peter's arm and leaning heavily against him.

As Peter led Richard back to his room, the knight thought with a deep sense of love, *"Ho bisogno di te più che mai."* {"I need you more than ever."}

As the two men headed back towards the infirmary, Peter hesitantly asked Richard, "I know you are tired, but I was wondering something."

"And that is?"

"I know you are very tired, so I do not want to tire you even more with questions."

Richard smiled. "Peter, trust me to tell you if anything you want to ask or do is too tiring. As tired as I feel physically, I am quite capable of answering questions as we walk. Please believe me when I say how much I enjoy it."

"If you are sure."

"I am very sure."

"In that case, you speak my Gaelic language very well. How and when did you learn to speak it?"

Richard continued to lean heavily against the support of Peter's strong body as they moved forward. "I have had to pick up many languages as I made my way across Europe trying to find a home for myself. Yours is simply one of the many languages I have picked up along the way."

"You must know a dozen languages by now," Peter wondered with genuine amazement.

"I know some better than others," Richard agreed. "I am glad to hear I am speaking your language well enough. And I have next to no problems understanding you or the other brothers. Perhaps I was born with a natural gift for learning languages. I have had to rely on that so much in my life."

"Well, you speak it very well. I think my Gaelic language is so rough, especially compared to the wondrous musicality of yours."

"I am glad you hear my language that way. I feel the same about it. I would not say your Gaelic language is ugly or that rough. I find it pleasant, very, oh – what is the word? Let me think a moment." The two men took several steps before Richard found the word he was looking for. "Evocative. Yes, that is it. I find your Gaelic very evocative."

"I never thought about it that way. Interesting. How are you with the language those Anglo-Saxons speak south of here?"

"Now THAT language is truly ugly," Richard exclaimed.

Peter laughed. "I totally agree with you!"

The knight and the monk walked the remainder of the distance in silence, each absorbed in his own inner ponderings.

———◆•◆•◆———

Peter's raven guide had watched unseen in a corner of the stables as he had observed the two humans leaving after visiting the horse.

"Open up, my beloved human," the raven thought. *"Surrender to this great opportunity for you. Open up to this other human who has been sent to help you, just as you are here to help the knight. Take the risk. Dare to love and be loved. Keep going, opening up more and more."*

After Richard and Peter had re-entered the infirmary, the raven flew away – with new hope swelling in his breast.

—————•◆•—————

A few days later, Peter sat on the edge of the knight's bed feeding Richard his lunch. Occasionally, however, Peter would hand the bowl and spoon to Richard so he could feed himself. They made a game of passing the bowl and spoon back and forth so sometimes Peter fed Richard and sometimes Richard fed himself. Each time the bowl and spoon were passed from one man to the other, both of them would giggle or break out in hearty laughter.

"This stew is exceptionally good," Richard remarked with great satisfaction.

"I am glad you like it. I thought so as well. I will make sure Brother Mark, who is the one who made this meal, is told how much you liked it."

"Please do. A good meal should always be a great work of art, not only in its preparation but also in how it is served and how we eat it."

"I like your philosophy, Richard – but how can EATING food be a work of art?"

"By enjoying the experience with great focus, passion and appreciation. Loving HOW you eat a meal is a work of art equal to preparing and presenting it."

"What a phenomenal philosophy!" Peter exclaimed.

"It is all part of being born on the Italian peninsula," Richard explained, "especially, I feel, in Venezia. Our tradition is to experience every moment and all we do as a passionate embracing of beauty and art. All beauty is vital to us, and not just visual beauty. You can CHOOSE to experience beauty through what you feel, how you experience every single moment and in everything you think, plan, do and say. And when you bring passion to every experience, that makes every moment beautiful and a work of art that YOU helped to create."

"I can feel that from you right now, Richard."

"I love to prepare food passionately, to look upon it passionately and to savour every mouthful passionately. This stew you are feeding me and which sometimes you hand to me to feed myself fills me with abundant passion!"

Peter nodded and smiled, as he fed Richard another spoonful then passed the bowl and spoon to a smiling Richard.

"I am afraid in this country," Peter added as he watched Richard feed himself, "we eat just to get rid of the hunger. I do not recognise any of us monks loving to cook, setting out the food or eating it with any real appreciation at all. It is more like everything is a DUTY or a responsibility to finish as quickly as possible. We just push the hunger away until the next time. After hearing your philosophy, I feel that we here are all so pathetic."

"What you describe, Peter, is how I experienced it in most countries that I visited. But in Venezia, a meal is a shared experience of emotional passion and appreciation of beauty. Where I came from, we cannot help but live our lives this way in everything we do."

"I think it is wonderful. We Celts seem to show passion only when we sing our poetry or are fighting one another. Again, it is just so pathetic."

Richard laughed. "Believe me, Peter, we Venezians are just as passionate about arguing and fighting amongst ourselves as we are about eating or making love."

Peter smiled and nodded. With a wry grin and an arched eyebrow, Richard handed the bowl and spoon back to Peter. With a shake of his head and a grin, Peter fed the next spoonful to Richard.

"Let me describe Venezians this way, Peter," Richard said after swallowing the latest mouthful. "We are extremely sensitive to our five senses. Every aroma triggers deep emotional reactions in us. Every flavour fills us with passion – and the more flavours we taste, the more ecstasy we feel. Our sense of touch is dynamic and varied, with hundreds of different sensations from head to toe, all as intense as through our fingertips. And oh, how we passionately react to every colour we experience around us. We lovingly caress every shade of every colour with our eyes and in our hearts and souls. We are highly enthusiastic for both music, poetry and art. We Venezians are living souls of passion, and we feel that this love of passion is our gift to the world."

"I think that is truly magnificent!" Peter suddenly laughed uproariously.

"Share!" Richard said.

Peter shook his head. "Honestly, Richard, I am not making fun of you or minimising anything you have said. Honestly. It is all wonderful."

"But?"

Peter laughed again. "I just had this awful thought."

"Then you MUST share it with me," Richard said with a wide grin.

"Honestly, I mean no disrespect. I love everything you have said. But this vision came into my head, and I cannot get it out. It is hilarious."

"Then share it, please!" Richard begged.

"Oh dear." Peter took a few deep breaths to work up the nerve to share his thought.

Richard waited anxiously.

"You tell me how passionate the Venetians – I mean, the Venezians are in EVERYTHING they do. I think that is fantastic. But I just had to wonder."

"Yes?" Richard prompted eagerly.

"Do Venezians poop with passion?"

Richard blinked, then blinked again. In the next instant, he threw back his head and laughed uproariously. He grabbed Peter to him in a massive bear-hug. Luckily, the stew was finished. Otherwise, as Peter dropped the bowl, there would have been quite a mess everywhere.

"Do we poop with passion? I LOVE that question with great passion! And I can only hope we do. EVERYTHING with passionate passion!"

The two men laughed together for several minutes before Richard finally released Peter and the monk gathered up the dropped bowl and spoon.

"I wish I had been born in your Venezia. I hope I will be born in Venezia in every lifetime after this one!"

"And I want you to know, Peter, that I enjoy the way you feed and bathe me when you do. You are not just efficient anymore. You show me so much consideration and loving care. That fills ME with great PASSION, as I hope it does for you as well."

Peter blushed anew. He had never thought about having such deep emotional experiences from such a simple meal or compliment. Peter wanted to immediately throw himself into Richard's arms, but that bold impulse filled him with the old familiar waves of insecurity and inadequacy – mixed with his constant passion for Richard.

But Peter hesitated to express his full desire for Richard, for fear that the knight might reject him. A part of Peter knew Richard would never do that, but Peter's lack of ownership for his own lovability blocked him from fully expressing his true feelings for Richard. So Peter remained trapped in his prison of expected rejection and abandonment, even though he knew there was no truth to it at all. His lack of self-love remained dominant.

———◆•◆•◆———

"I want to wing-slap the life out of your monk!" the cynical raven screeched.

Then the other raven wing-slapped his companion across the beak. *"Shut the feathers up!"*

PART II

PART

Eleven

"THE KNIGHT AND the monk certainly talk a lot about Venice, or Venezia, in the knight's tongue."

"So? And by the way, the knight and the monk have names – Richard and Peter. What is wrong this time?"

"I never said anything was wrong. I was simply making an observation."

"Okay."

"Is this Venice – or Venezia – really so special?"

"Oh yes!"

"How do you know? Have you ever been there?"

"As a matter of fact, I have. In fact, I lived there in my most recent previous lifetime."

"As a raven?"

"No, last time I was a pigeon."

"A pigeon? How disgusting!"

"Hey! No need to be such a bigoted elitist."

"Oh come on! Really? The way they can't walk without bobbing their heads back and forth? That would make me not want to stop puking. And anyway, compared to ravens, pigeons have the brain capacity of a dead gnat's ass."

"I guess that explains you."

"What?"

"Apparently you have somehow been born this time around into a raven's body but with, according to your definition, a pigeon's brain."

"How rude!"

"Yes, you are."

"Never mind. But tell me honestly, what is so special about this Venice/ Venezia?"

"I thought Richard explained it very well. Venezia embraces a passion for passion."

"Why in Venezia and nowhere else?"

The raven shrugged in the best way possible for a raven to do so. "A combination of things, I suppose. Partly the fact that it is a city seemingly floating upon the sea as a myriad of tightly interconnected islands with four rivers flowing in from the north and west and the sea flowing in from the east and south. Partly the exquisite architecture and art. Partly the myriads of canals acting like blood veins for the city, the hundreds of bridges connecting the more than one hundred islands. A combination of everything and who knows what other elements from Mother Earth and the Totality of the Cosmos feeding into the city from so many different levels."

"What was it like to live there as a – ugh, pigeon?"

"It was wonderful! So adventurous and exciting. Thousands of statues, rooftops and splendid trees to perch on while I observed all the passion and the splendour pass beneath me. The souls of the people who live there are very special, I suppose because of the physical design of their city. It is just so many things, much of it, I guess, incomprehensible and therefore inexplicable."

"So why did you not reincarnate there again this time?"

"Because Peter needs me now, and he is here in Alba."

"So Peter was in Venezia when you were there last time as a pigeon?"

"No."

"Then I do not understand your point."

"I am not with Peter every single lifetime. I was not with him in his previous life because he did not need me then. But I am with him in this lifetime because he needs me now."

"I do not understand how or why anything works as it does. I feel like I am forever missing the consistencies. And right now, I do not care. I am feeling hungry again, so I will go and hunt food for myself." With that, the other raven flew away.

The remaining raven reminisced nostalgically for a moment before returning his attention to Peter – but not before declaring to the world, *"Lunga vita alla passiosne Veneziana!"* {"Long live Venetian passion!"}

———————◆———————

It was the last week of November, and winter was reclaiming its domain. Everyone woke daily to glimmering frost, and snow could already be seen on the taller Highland peaks.

Richard was sitting in a chair by himself in the infirmary waiting for Peter to return with his lunch when corpulent Brother Clair jiggled into the room.

"Greetings, gorgeous knight!"

"Greetings to you as well, Clair. And thank you for the 'gorgeous' compliment. That is very kind of you."

"How are things going with you and our beloved Brother Peter?"

"Very well. He is always most efficient and takes care of all my needs."

"How is he with bathing you? Improved any?"

"He is very thorough, Clair, as he always is."

"Yes, but is he thorough EVERYWHERE, Richard? Is he thorough with your ENTIRE body?" Clair persisted.

Richard laughed. "Yes, Clair. He is thorough with my ENTIRE body."

"Great news!" Clair exclaimed with a whoop of glee. "The lad is learning! And Richard, does he thoroughly ENJOY taking care of your entire body?"

Richard considered his answer. "He is very thorough and takes great care in what he does."

Clair nodded with deep understanding. "Brother Peter is still frightened. This is all so new to him. He still lacks both self-worth and confidence in his own lovability. It will take time, but I trust that you will teach him."

"I hope so, because, Clair, I love him so much."

"I know you do – and he loves you, too. Both of you are blessed in that. But Brother Peter needs to learn what a great growth opportunity he now has in his life through you – and then SEIZE it – I mean, seize YOU – I mean, seize ALL of you – I mean, ugh, never mind!"

Richard laughed. "I understand thoroughly what you mean. And I agree, but it is still very difficult for him to express how he feels directly to anyone."

Clair nodded sympathetically. "Brother Peter's belief that he does not deserve love feeds his huge fear of rejection, which blocks him from expressing his love-feelings to you directly. And Brother Peter also fears receiving the love he is so desperate for because he always assumes love will automatically result in rejection, pain and abandonment. This silent war rages back and forth within him – and actually within all of us, each in our own different ways."

"You speak with great wisdom, Clair. I assume you are one of the 'other' monks hiding behind the 'real' ones."

Clair smiled. "Ah, Brother Peter has shared about us with you. I am pleased to hear that. Yes, I am one of the 'others'."

"How difficult was it for you to conquer your fears and accept love?"

Clair shook his head. "Oh dear, have I somehow given you that false impression? I am still learning too, as we all are. It is a life-long commitment – or more accurately, a LIVES-long commitment – to be constantly and consistently accepting, healing and transforming our fears. But the more we can do that, the more love we will feel for ourselves and can then give to and receive from others. Yes, often I feel self-love and can trust and value myself – but not always. Far less than always. So I take it one day at a time."

"As we all must. If I may ask you, Clair, what is the best advice you can give me on how to love myself more so I can receive love more from others – especially from Peter?"

Clair thought a moment. "We cannot give to others what we cannot give to ourselves. We cannot accept from others what we cannot accept within ourselves. So feel and accept your fear when it is there, but do not BELIEVE it. Everything we feel is real, but not necessarily always true. The challenge is learning to recognise the difference."

"You just lost me, Clair."

"For example, Richard, if I criticise myself a lot and feel unworthy of love, my feeling unworthy of love is a real feeling, but that does not automatically mean that I truly AM unworthy of love. I must allow myself to feel the unworthiness to know that it is there and even discern WHY it is there but then choose in that moment to not blindly accept or believe it is true.

"Emotions reveal our perceptions of ourselves," Clair continued, "especially where we constantly judge ourselves. Slowly we learn to no longer need to judge everything so incessantly. This takes time, commitment and patience. But with practice, we keep working through this process until we eventually see faster and faster what emotions are true and which no longer need to be blindly accepted as truth. Most emotions and fears are trying to reveal how we do not love, trust, value or honour ourselves. Once we see this and learn from them without judging, we can then accept their lessons but no longer need to believe the fears or negative feelings. This will bring us great joy, healing and great wisdom."

"Wait a minute!" one raven said to his bird companion.

"What?"

"That fat monk is saying the EXACT same thing you told me a few days ago."

"So?"

"So he STOLE it from you!"

"By the Cosmos!" the second raven cawed. *"How can Universal Truth be stolen? It is shared amongst everyone and everything."*

"But how did that chubby little monk steal it from you?"

"You are not listening! I just said it was not stolen. And anyway, if you really MUST know, I deliberately planted those words into the fat monk's recent dream so he would remember the words from the dream when he awoke and repeat them when needed to the knight. Clever, am I not?"

"You can do that?" the first raven asked.

"You did not know we can do that?"

The first raven shook his head.

"We animal spirit-guides, plus all other spirit guides and even all souls

who have died and returned to the spirit plane, can enter any incarnated soul's dreams to give guidance or leave messages for them to remember later in their awake state. We birds do this all the time. How can you have incarnated as a raven and not know this?"

"You know something?" the first raven replied with a grim sense of doubt. *"I am beginning to wonder that myself."*

"Ah, now I understand you. Thank you, Clair. What you said is powerfully wise and insightful. Please continue."

"The deepest purpose of fear," Clair continued, "is not to scare or hurt us but rather to remind us to recognise how and when we are not honouring, trusting and valuing ourselves. We need to create these challenging fear experiences to help us learn to love ourselves – so we are then able to receive love from others. So when we feel fear, we must remind ourselves that it is there to help and teach us – not to harm or punish us."

Clair paused a moment to catch his breath, then continued. "Only then can we start to work WITH our fears instead of fighting against them and trying to get rid of them, which will only result in our fears sticking to us ruthlessly. In my experience, Richard, self-destructive attitudes only cause us more pain and problems. Fear's REAL purpose is to help us reveal and heal our self-imposed limitations so that in working with and through these fears, we can finally transform them. It may sound odd," Clair concluded, "but LOVING your fears for the truth and transformation they are genuinely there to give you is quite liberating."

"Miraculous!" said the stunned knight. "I never thought about it like that before. Thank you for being so clear."

"That is why my name is Clair – to gain and share clarity. Now if only I can more consistently follow it myself!"

Clair was about to leave when he hesitated and thought for a moment before looking at Richard with a mischievous glint in his eyes. "To change the subject entirely, Richard, have you discovered yet whether or not Brother Peter has nipples as pretty as yours?"

Richard laughed to the tips of his tawny teats. "Thanks for your compliment. Well, I feel I am getting closer to both Peter and the answer to your question. And to be honest, I would also love to know the answer! But I must move slowly in order to not spook this shy and beautiful man."

"I have no doubt in my heart that Brother Peter's nipples are just as pretty and luscious as yours. Give yourself the time, my friend. It will be well worth the wait and the effort to find the answer to that question."

"I agree."

Then Clair wobbled merrily out of the infirmary.

———•◆•———

"What is all this talk about nipples?"

"Speaking as a member of a species that does not have any nipples, I do not have the vaguest idea, so I cannot help you."

"I thought you had all the answers."

"Whatever made you think that?"

"You."

The other raven would have frowned had he been able to do so.

———•◆•———

"I am always saying the wrong thing," young Brother Andrew lamented to the eternally cheerful Brother Clair an hour after the portly monk had left Richard in the infirmary.

"Nonsense, Brother. You are a deeply sensitive and compassionate soul, well-loved by us all."

The two monks sat on a rough-hewn wooden bench in the monastery's front courtyard absorbing the sparse autumn sunlight. They both shivered from the cold blasts of wind that shot through the courtyard. The wind blew icily, but it was also invigorating.

"I do not think Brother Peter or Prior Thomas would agree with you." Andrew's mouth drooped in a sad pout. "Both of them despise me."

"Despise you? Oh, no," Clair insisted. "I think you misunderstand them."

"Oh?"

"Here is a new thought for you to consider. Brother Peter and Prior Thomas are in actuality very SHY about their feelings."

"SHY?" Andrew asked incredulously. "Are you kidding? Both of them often deluge me with their disgust and extreme disappointment in me. Not shy at all!"

"Listen to me, Brother Andrew," Clair counselled with deep compassion. "You have so much to learn about people. Shyness does not always show itself as shyness."

"What does THAT mean?" Andrew asked.

"Sometimes," Clair explained, "shyness and insecurity masquerade as coldness, aloofness, abruptness, arrogance, anger – or as over-meticulous efficiency. People can use one emotion to cover up other emotions they do not feel safe with. So your challenge is to intuitively tune in and determine whether what people are saying is what they really mean. Because sometimes it is a cover-up to run away from something else inside themselves that they are too afraid to feel and express. Do you understand what I am saying?"

Andrew considered the other monk's words. "Well, those examples you used, the coldness and abruptness, the arrogance and over-efficiency, are all things both Prior Thomas and Brother Peter do."

Clair laughed uproariously. "Well, there you go! In all probability, both Prior Thomas and Brother Peter are among the shyest souls on the planet. Most people are afraid of certain emotions and hide them behind impenetrable masks or self-absorbed behaviour."

"Okay," Andrew said without true clarity.

"Let me explain it to you this way. I once had a priest instructor who was very insecure about his ability to teach and speak in front of people. So he would often act with anger and cruelty towards his students, not because he genuinely wanted to be cruel but because it helped him hide his painful insecurities. He just did not dare to see what he was doing and why – and also how it affected others. He was trying to escape his own harsh self-judgements and self-doubts by blaming and attacking us, his students. Can you follow what I am saying?"

Andrew nodded slowly. "Yes, I think so. Are you saying that Brother Peter really likes me but is afraid to show it?"

Clair immediately noted that Andrew asked only about Brother Peter and not Prior Thomas because Clair knew that Andrew both feared and disliked the prior. But Clair also had to be careful not to falsely lead Andrew on regarding Peter since Clair knew Peter was in love with Richard.

"Brother Andrew, I know our prior is hard on you, but please do not assume that Brother Peter feels the same way. Our Brother Peter is a man of many self-protecting masks, so how he treats you is not necessarily what he really feels about you."

"I understand. And I am glad to hear it."

"I am sure you also have noticed how much Prior Thomas and Brother Peter cannot tolerate being in each other's presence."

"That is SO true," Andrew agreed.

"Why do you think that is?"

"I do not know."

"Give it a try," Clair coaxed.

Andrew considered for a few moments. "Because they are so much alike?"

"Very good, Brother Andrew! That is it exactly. They both share similar fears about their repressed emotions. So they constantly try to protect themselves, they think, from their constant expectations of pain and rejection. The more you try to avoid something, the more you draw it to you."

Andrew nodded again. "Yes, I see what you are saying."

"Good."

"But on the other hand," Andrew said sadly, "it could still be true that Brother Peter does not like me."

"My dear young monk," Clair said affectionately, "you worry too much about whether or not others like you. You forget to love yourself."

"But that is a sin!"

"Excuse me?" Clair asked, blinking.

"To love yourself is vanity, and vanity is a great sin."

"The heartlessness of rigid religion strikes again," Clair thought to himself.

Aloud Clair said, "Hardly. It is not a sin to love yourself. But in a way, it is almost a sin to NOT love yourself."

Andrew gaped in shock, but Clair continued his explanation.

"Vanity is seeing yourself as BETTER than others, but its roots are actually buried in deep feelings of insecurity, envy, inferiority and a severe lack of self-love. The colder and more arrogant someone acts, usually the more a person dislikes himself but cannot face feeling the pain of that self-judgement and self-rejection. So TRULY loving yourself does not mean you think you are better than anyone else. Just the opposite, in fact. True self-love will ultimately show you that everyone is equally divine."

"Is this true?" Andrew gasped, his face shining with astonishment and revelation. "All my life I have been taught that loving yourself lets the devil into your soul and damns you to eternal Hell. The priests said so when I went to Sunday mass as a child. But now I hear you say something completely different. So, Brother Clair, how did you learn this?"

"From many, many, MANY years of experience and growth."

"How can this be so, Brother Clair? You are not THAT old, are you?"

"Oops!" Clair realised. *"I must be careful not to mention anything about reincarnation or else I will shock this one into rejecting everything I have said up to this point."*

Clair gave a little shake of his round head and said aloud, "Never mind, Brother Andrew. It just FEELS like so many years of experience. But please trust me that I have learned enough to profoundly feel the truth of what I share with you now."

The two monks sat in silence for several minutes. Andrew stared bleakly ahead while Clair secretly watched the younger monk out of the corner of his eye.

"We must be careful not to judge a person solely by what they say or how they act," Clair resumed. "You will soon discover that people rarely show what they truly feel inside."

"I see."

"Just remember this – to truly love yourself is to celebrate God's perfect creation and to thereby return the love to Him that He bestowed upon you by creating you in the first place. It is all about love and growth and NOT about rules, sin, judgement and punishment."

Clair knew he had to express this higher truth in words that would fit within Andrew's current limited belief system where religion had made inner divinity into something always outside of people.

"You mean that loving myself is also loving God?"

"You have stated it perfectly, my clever boy! And to love God is to love yourself. One is the other."

Andrew frowned in deep concentration. "I am not so sure about that. What I mean is, I never heard my father or any of the other priests explain it that way. I certainly never thought of it that way."

"Think about it, my friend," Clair suggested, trying to be as patient as he could. "You and God's Love are one and the same. Do not waste time seeking love or approval from another when you fail to give it to yourself first. That is another way of interpreting our Lord's words: 'Do unto others as you would have others do unto you.'

"Most people," Clair continued, "think that means you always have to love others first. But I say it means that you can only love or treat others well when you are first able to love and treat yourself well. AND, you can only love another to the extent that you are willing to love yourself."

"So you are saying that if I limit the love I show myself, I am limiting the love I can show to my neighbour as well as to God?" Andrew wondered.

Clair clapped his hands with ecstatic approval. "You have gotten it exactly!"

That conversation gave Andrew a banquet of food for thought.

———◆———

"That chubby little monk is good — real good! He bears more watching and listening to."

"Good at what?" the usually cynical raven asked in confusion.

"Cosmos give me strength!"

———◆———

"I think it is so cute when you do that."

"When I do what?" Peter asked. The monk sat on the edge of Richard's bed as he finished serving him his breakfast.

Richard smiled up at the monk, his eyes sparkling with affection. "I love how you puff out your cheeks and stick out your tongue whenever you are doing something with deep concentration – such as making sure the hot food goes in my mouth and not down my chest. But when that happens, it is fun and DOES feel rather nice in a drippy sort of way."

Peter gave a little bow. "I am glad you find anything I do cute or adorable." After a moment's self-doubt, Peter added, "And I THINK you are paying me a compliment."

"Of the highest order," Richard said with his dazzling smile.

"There. Now we are done. Another meal successfully delivered and devoured."

Peter handed the knight a cloth to wipe his mouth. "Richard, you are well enough now to sit at a table and feed yourself."

"I know, but I love it when you pamper – uh, I meant – FEED me."

Peter grinned. "You were right the first time, with pamper. But I understand what you say. And I DO enjoy feeding you. But you ARE improving, and you do need to do more things on your own."

Richard nodded. "I know."

But to himself Richard thought dismally, *"Actually, it is NOT good to see how much I am healing, because the sooner I am well, the sooner I must leave. That truth fills me with agonising fear."*

Peter busied himself tidying things up around the infirmary. When he was finished, Peter turned back to face the knight.

"I have a surprise for you," Peter announced with one of his rare smiles.

"Do tell."

"Brother Bartholomew has agreed that today you and I can take a walk towards the hills with your horse, Orion."

Richard whooped with joy as he slowly got out of bed, took the few steps to the monk and hugged Peter tightly.

"That is the best news you could have given me, Peter. I am so happy that I could KISS you!"

To himself, Richard thought, ***"Puzzi come il Paradiso tra le mie braccia."*** {"You smell like Heaven in my arms."}

"Well, yes, I – um, yes, I mean –" Peter stammered with self-doubt.

Richard's hands rose up to cradle Peter's head as he looked lovingly into the monk's astonished blushing face.

"I want to smother this man in kisses, make love to him in a thousand ways and hug him forever," Richard thought. *"But instead I know I must be patient and take things slowly and not scare him."*

Peter recovered from the sudden surprise of Richard's exuberant hug but remained sweaty-hot as if with a fever. "But remember, Richard, we must not over-tire you or cause any complications that could result in a setback. Not too far, rest often and be careful."

"As you say," Richard replied as he glided the back of his right hand down the left side of Peter's face. "You lead the way at your pace, and Orion and I will follow. I am so happy! Thank you, Peter – and my thanks also to Brother Bartholomew. ***Fai cantare il mio cuore di gioia!"***

"I did not understand a word of that," Peter said with a grin, "but hearing you speak in your native tongue like that makes me feel giddy."

"So please be giddy. It is a lovely feeling. And what I said was, you make my heart sing with joy!"

Peter continued to feel giddy. "Then later this afternoon we will collect your Orion and be on our way."

———◆•◆•◆———

"Are you ready for your first walk today with Peter and your horse Orion?" Bartholomew asked.

"Yes, I am eagerly looking forward to this walk. Thank you very much for giving me the approval to do so."

"My pleasure," Bartholomew said. "You are improving steadily each day. I have given you a thorough inspection, and I see no reason why you cannot go out today and enjoy the beautiful scenery beyond our monastery. But be sure you do not overdo the walk and dangerously exhaust yourself," the healer monk said, wagging his finger in warning. "Be careful!"

Richard nodded his agreement. After a moment's hesitation, Richard asked Bartholomew, "May I ask you something?"

"Of course," Bartholomew replied. "You may ask me anything anytime. How can I help you?"

"Peter recently shared with me that in your Celtic tradition the months are named after trees, as part of your close connection with nature."

"Yes, that is true."

"And he told me he was born under the tree-sign of the yew and I was born under the tree-sign of the willow."

"Okay."

"That makes me wonder, what tree are you?"

Bartholomew threw back his head and laughed heartily. "I like that, Richard. Not what tree-sign was I born under but what TREE am I. That is wonderful, and there may be a great deal of truth to stating it that way. I am a hazel."

The knight shook his head in frustration. "This is so annoying. I do not understand these tree names at all."

"The hazel is a tree that bears a small round nut that is a rich reddish-brown."

"Ah," Richard said with a nod. "I think I know the tree you talk about. What astrological sign are you, Bartholomew?"

"I was born mid-August, according to the month names used by the Anglo-Saxons far south of here. So I am a Leo."

"Excuse me from saying so," Richard said, "but somehow you don't strike me as a Leo."

"Not dramatic and dynamic enough?" Bartholomew asked with a grin. "I am often told by Brother Clair that I hold myself back too much, not willing to share my truth. There is much truth to that."

"But when you do speak," Richard said, "it is with warmth, compassion and great wisdom. That is far more important than being dramatic."

"Thank you, Richard. That is very kind of you. Unfortunately, we monks here do not share very much about ourselves between one another – and I think that is a great shame. Perhaps I feel protected because of that, but it is not such a good thing. Your words move me very deeply, and I am very grateful."

"My pleasure. Do you know the tree-signs of some of the other monks here, such as Abbot Paul and our wonderful Clair?"

"Oh, now, let me think." Bartholomew pondered for a few minutes. "Father Abbot is a Virgo – very attuned to clarity, efficiency and all the minutest details. So he is an apple tree."

"And hopefully all he endeavours will come to fruition," Richard added with a pun.

"Rightly so," Bartholomew agreed. "And in Celtic tradition, the apple is a symbol of the Goddess energy, having to do with intuition, psychic abilities, compassion, nurturing – all the qualities that go well with Father Abbot's role. And our sweet and dear Clair is a Pisces, the embodiment of all the signs as one. And he is an alder tree."

"Alder? No, I do not know this tree by that name."

"Oh dear, how do I describe an alder tree? I am not sure. Um, I only know it is a member of the birch family."

"Yes, I think I know what a birch tree is. Oh well, it does not matter if I cannot place a tree exactly. It is just very interesting to know more about all of you. Could you also please teach me the names of the seasons in your Gaelic language?"

"Of course, Richard. I can also write this down so you can read the names later and better learn them."

"Thank you. That would be very helpful, Bartholomew."

"Some of our words are rather a big mouthful – and winter is a typical example. Our word for winter is **Geimhreadh**. Then spring is **Earrach**, summer is **Samhradh**, and for autumn we say **Fómhar**. But again, I will write the words down for you."

"Thank you. I appreciate that. It makes me feel closer to you knowing these things that you are teaching me."

"I wish all of us monks were like you and shared more openly with one another – and also had the curiosity to get to know each other better. But we do not. We seem to feel some bizarre fake safety and security in being so closed off from one another. It is a great pity. If we were more like you, we might better enjoy our lives here together better – but unfortunately we do not. However, I greatly appreciate your curiosity. It is refreshing."

Richard nodded his thanks.

"Anyway," Bartholomew concluded, "you are well enough to walk towards the Highland hills with Brother Peter and your horse, and I hope you enjoy yourself immensely while you are out. But remember," Bartholomew repeated as he once again playfully wagged his forefinger. "Do not overdo it!"

———————•◦•———————

"Are you ready to begin our walk?" Peter asked.

"More than ready, I assure you," Richard replied eagerly.

Richard was now clad in a monk's robe like all the others. Standing next to Peter, the two men looked like identical twins. They both petted Orion's flanks, and the horse wasn't sure which human to pay attention to first, his owner or to this special monk who so closely resembled Richard – not only in physical appearance but also in his 'soul-scent'. So Orion decided to nuzzle both men with equal affection.

"Oh, I almost forgot!" Peter exclaimed.

Richard watched curiously as Peter searched inside his robe. "Aha!" he announced triumphantly as he pulled out several slices of apple. "I thought Orion might like to nibble on these before we take our walk."

Richard looked at Peter gratefully. "That is so considerate of you to think of Orion in that way. Thank you."

Peter handed the apple slices to Richard, who then put one at a time on his open palm and lovingly fed them to his beloved horse.

As Orion joyously devoured one apple slice after another, Richard gently petted the horse's long nose, a gesture that always thrilled Orion. Seeing the horse's enjoyment, Peter did the same.

"I was not aware monk robes had any pockets at all, much less on the inside," Richard said. "I do not seem to have any in my robe."

"They do not," Peter replied. "I secretly made this inner pocket for my robe so that whenever I went on walks into the Highland hills, I could have something to eat if I wanted it."

Richard laughed. "How deviously clever of you. I like you more and more with everything I discover about you."

Peter beamed happily. "Now we are ready to go."

———•◆•———

As Peter and Richard left the monastery with Orion, a tall thin monk stood watching them nearby just inside the archway. Prior Thomas observed the departing trio with venom-filled eyes.

Richard momentarily glanced back when he sensed the prior staring at them.

"My God!"

"What is wrong?" Peter asked.

"The glare from that man could stab my left side far deeper and deadlier than that highwayman's sword did."

Peter turned and recognised Prior Thomas standing under the monastery's archway entrance.

"That is Prior Thomas. Ignore him. We all do."

"Is he angry because we are together?" Richard asked.

"He is angry at everything – at Life itself. A foul mood is his natural state of being. Do not take it personally. He would look like that no matter who we were."

"Poor man," Richard said.

"What?"

"He must be very sad or in a great deal of pain to be so perpetually foul, as you say."

Peter stopped walking and stood silently for a moment. "I never thought of him like that before. I guess you are right."

With Richard leading his white steed, this band of two men and a horse resumed walking due west from the monastery toward the Highland foothills. The autumn wind blew cold and brisk. Freedom from his infirmary bed and also walking and stretching his body brought a new satisfaction and happiness to the knight – not to mention finally being alone with Peter away from the monastery for the first time.

Peter himself had always preferred to be alone and private during his long walks to the Highland hills. But suddenly he discovered great peace and joy while sharing his personal sanctuary with Richard and Orion. It gave Peter a sense of completion and family that he had never experienced before when walking alone.

"I love coming here in the spring," Peter explained to Richard, "when these hills come alive with the vibrant purple from the newly blossomed heather. Later in the autumn, these great swaths of purple heather are transformed into a vast sloping sea of rich reddish-gold. Absolutely breath-taking."

"I have never seen these foothills covered in springtime purple," Richard said. "I have only witnessed these foothills in the spectacular reddish-gold you describe. It was just beginning when I rode through here for the first time a few months ago. You are right – it is glorious."

"If you are still here in the coming spring, then you will finally be able to see the radiant purple as the heather blooms once more."

"That may very well be the case, and I will look forward to that." *"Please, dear God,"* Richard prayed silently, *"let that be so."*

"Richard," the monk said after a few more steps, "I think we should stop here and allow your body to rest."

"That is fine with me. I see a stream nearby where Orion can get his fill of water."

Telepathically understanding the men's conversation, Orion wandered off to drink from the stream while the men settled themselves upon the ground.

Peter supported Richard as the knight carefully lowered himself to the ground. Then suddenly and playfully, Richard grabbed Peter's hands and pulled the monk on top of him. "This is more like it," Richard said in a low husky voice.

Peter felt giddiness again, but also trembled with fear, arousal, panic and uncertainty. He was very clear he was in love with Richard, but he remained too terrified to say so out loud because his self-rejecting fear insisted it might cause ridicule or rejection from Richard.

Richard sensed exactly what was going on in Peter's mind. He knew that Peter's fear of rejection was not because the monk genuinely believed Richard himself would reject him but because Peter was still rejecting **his own** lovability and self-worth. So Richard knew he had to be patient and not push things so that Peter could get accustomed to the emotions storming inside him.

Peter rolled off Richard and sat himself into an upright position. However, Richard's hands continued to hold his, and the monk had to admit that he actually liked it.

"You know, Richard," Peter said after a few minutes of holding hands with the knight, "none of us at the monastery has ever asked why you came to this area – and how you arrived at the monastery exactly in my hour of need."

Peter hated bringing up his horrible experience with the three highwaymen. Remembering his near gang-rape and possible death still triggered nightmares and shame in the monk. But like all the other monks, Peter WAS curious – so he decided that now was the time to find out how Richard had arrived when he did.

As they sat face-to-face now, Richard released one of Peter's hands and once again brushed the back of his fingers down the left side of the monk's face, a repeated gesture that Peter loved more and more each time.

"La tua pelle sembra un paradiso." {"Your skin feels like heaven."}

"Excuse me?" Peter asked.

Richard shook his head with a wry smile. "Just thinking to myself. I will tell you another time. What did you ask me?"

"How you ended up here at the monastery when you did."

"Oh, yes. I was hired by King Oswiu of Northumbria to explore and research this area for him."

"To spy on our non-Celtic neighbours, the Picts, you mean?"

Richard laughed and once again brushed Peter's temple and cheek with the back of his fingers. "Straight to the point. I see I can hide nothing from you! Yes, to spy on the Picts for King Oswiu. By the way, am I pronouncing his name correctly?"

Peter gave a short laugh. "I do not have the vaguest idea. In fact, I do not think anyone here knows for sure. Your guess is as good as mine!"

"Well, that is why I came here. And that is why I was able to see the heather for the first time in its lustrous reddish-gold brilliance."

"But how did you end up at our monastery at the MOMENT you did?"

"Ah, yes – that. I had been observing you for several hours, following you at a distance, as it turned out."

"What? I do not recall anyone near me when I was out walking that day."

"I know how to camouflage myself and Orion. You, on the other hand, were very easy to observe and simple to follow once you headed back towards the monastery. You did nothing to conceal your presence."

"Why would I?"

"Good point," Richard conceded.

"But where were you?"

"When you approached the hills, I was sitting atop Orion among some trees about fifty metres north of you," said Richard, pointing behind Peter. "Being that far away, I could not see your facial features clearly, so I had not yet realised our extreme physical resemblance. I only saw that you were a monk walking by yourself, completely consumed by breathing in and loving your quiet environment. I could sense your absolute peacefulness and oneness with the nature. I also remember that at one point you looked up and waved to a passing raven."

"Ah, yes," Peter said. "There is one particular raven who often flies above me during my private walks. I have watched this raven for over three years. He – or she – often dips a wing to salute me, and I return the salute with a wave."

"That is charming," Richard said, meaning it.

"Sometimes I see this raven perched in several areas of the monastery with another raven, but for some reason I do not feel the same unity with this second raven as I do with the other one. I like to think that my raven friend is an animal spirit guide watching over me."

"That could very well be."

"Look – there it is now!" Peter exclaimed as he pointed up to the right.

Richard turned to look where Peter pointed, and then the magnificent raven circling above them dipped a wing in salutation to the two humans sitting on the ground below. Both Peter and Richard waved enthusiastically to the circling raven, and Orion lifted his head as well, aware of the soaring raven's greeting. The horse neighed a return greeting to the bird before it turned and flew off into the distance.

"Charming," Richard repeated.

After a minute, Peter had another important question to ask Richard.

"I now know why you came to this general area. But how did you end up in the monastery at the exact moment when I needed you?"

Richard nodded. "I followed you at a distance as you headed back towards the monastery. I was hoping there was a place nearby where I could spend the night on my way back south. Then I saw you quickened your pace because you ended up running the last short distance into the monastery. But I did not know why."

"Yes, I could hear commotion among the monks from quite a distance."

"I did not hear their voices until after you sped up your pace because I was so much further behind you. I wondered if you were simply late or if you heard or sensed there was a problem."

"From where I was, the noise was deafening."

"Yes, I finally heard it as well. Then I knew something was wrong. But I kept my distance until I saw you enter the monastery. After that Orion and I hurried to enter the monastery, but I felt at first to remain under the archway. By then you were giving the highwaymen your worst fury. And I have to say, beloved brother, I thought you were wonderful and very brave."

Peter blushed, but he was also trembling from the memory of the obscene act one of the highwaymen wanted to perform on him.

Richard continued. "I approached carefully and as quietly as I could, asking Orion to move forward ever so silently in case I needed to intervene."

"You certainly were needed!" Peter exclaimed.

"When I heard what they wanted to do to you, I jumped into action."

"For which I shall be eternally grateful."

Richard smiled with warm loving eyes as he once more slid his fingers down Peter's face. The monk thought he would ejaculate in that moment.

"I never saw you clearly until after I had knocked the first man down and killed the other two. THEN I saw your face, and I froze."

Peter nodded. "I vaguely remember that."

"In that instant, just before the first man rose and stabbed me in my left side, I instantly KNEW you were my soulmate. I was certainly more than surprised to discover my soulmate was a man and not a woman – but I did not care. It was meant to be. I knew you and I were of the same One."

"And then you were stabbed," Peter sighed in a half-whisper.

Richard nodded. "I thought I would die the moment I had finally reunited with my soulmate. But I did not – and that is because you have taken such wonderful and meticulous care of me. For that I am eternally grateful."

Peter smiled self-consciously. "And I am eternally grateful to Father Abbot for assigning me to you."

The two men embraced for a long time.

Peter's spirit-guide raven had returned for another visit with the three travellers. This time he circled above with his bird companion and indicated with a dipped wing the two men embracing one another below with Orion nearby.

"You see," Peter's raven said to the other raven as they flew in spirals high above the two humans and the grazing horse, *"the humans are aware of me and understand I am a guide. And they have also recognised their spiritual link with each other. There is a major CONVERGENCE of energy and consciousness going on here. It is exciting! And by the way, I found it very interesting when my monk said he never feels the connection to YOU that he feels with ME. Hah! I wonder why THAT is, hmm?"*

"Big deal," the other raven replied. *"Personally, I am far more interested in the horse. He is obviously very intelligent. Although why horses waste so much time helping humans is beyond me. Is it because they are as needy as dogs?"*

"Big deal you say? You are just envious because you do not have any human who connects so directly with you."

"Why would I want that?"

"That is your envy speaking again."

"Hardly. They are humans. No matter how wonderful you may think they

are right now, all human endeavours end up in total disaster. It will happen here as well, mark my words."

"Will you please fly off somewhere and stop pounding me with your negative judgements? Honestly, you are worse than the humans you judge as so negative and destructive."

"How rude!" the other raven screeched and flew away in a huff.

"You mean, how TRUE!"

———————◆———————

"Now I have a question for you," Richard said to Peter.

"Of course."

"What is the name of this country, this northernmost part of Britannia? I am never sure what to call it."

"That is complicated," Peter replied with a chuckle. "The Romans called our land Caledonia. But now it just depends on who you ask."

"Why is that?"

"Why indeed. To those of Celtic blood like myself, we call the land Alba. The Picts call it Scoti. And there are other tribes who call this land Goidi. It is like asking 'What does the name Venezia mean?'"

"I see that. People always complicate everything."

"Get three people of this country discussing anything, and you will end up with at least five theories."

Richard laughed. "I think I have mentioned before that Venezians are EXACTLY the same way."

The two men sat silently side by side for a moment.

"What?" Richard suddenly asked.

"What do you mean?"

"I can feel when you want to ask me something else."

"I am so sorry!"

"Please, no need to be. I enjoy our sharing, so ask away with whatever you want. It actually makes me feel better to answer your questions."

"Okay then, I have often wondered what King Oswiu is like."

"Who?"

"King Oswiu. You remember – the man you are spying for."

"Is THAT how you pronounce his name?"

"It is the way I pronounce his name."

"I have been pronouncing it Oswiu."

"Is that not what I said?"

"No, you said Oswiu."

"Did I? I had not realised," Peter said. "My father used to say, to pronounce the king's name correctly, say it as if you are sneezing with onions in your mouth."

"Ah, then I was right. It is Os-WIU!"

Peter laughed. "Just like that!"

"I still have not answered your question."

"Did I ask a question?"

Richard laughed. "You wanted to know what King Os-WIU is like."

"Oh yes."

"I can best describe him this way. He is an overweight peacock with the brain of a turnip, the manners of an earthworm and the wit of – well – no wit at all."

"Oh dear," Peter said. "That cannot be any fun for you."

"Believe me, he is just like most of the kings or overlords that I have dealt with over the years. If I had to describe Oswiu – OsWIU" Richard repeated as if with a great sneeze, "– in one word, it would be *cafone*."

"Okay. And that would mean what?"

Oh, sorry. There I go again. He is rather rough and ill-mannered."

"A lout?" Peter asked.

"A lout? I do not know. What is a lout?"

"Oh, someone who is rough and, well, *cafone*."

Yes, yes," Richard laughed. That is it exactly. **Cafone**!"

The two men quickly realised that Orion had re-joined them when the horse began nuzzling both their heads and then suddenly exploded with an enormous sneeze.

"You see," Richard exclaimed, "even Orion can pronounce the king's name correctly!"

Peter laughed again. "He can indeed, and without the onions in his mouth! But I think Orion is also hinting that our rest is over, and we need to return to the monastery," Peter said.

"I have always admired my Orion's clear and steadfast mind."

Richard pushed himself to an upright position as Peter quickly rose to give assistance to the knight.

"Are you feeling well, Richard? Any pain or aches anywhere?"

"No pain anywhere. In fact, I even feel a bit better than before our walk. Thank you. Come, Orion," Richard said as he stroked the steed's head and turned him around to head back.

"Can I ask you something again?" Peter asked.

Richard smiled warmly. "Please stop asking me if you can ask me something and just ask!"

"Oops, sorry about that. How did you choose 'Orion' for your horse's name?"

Richard gave a mirthful chuckle. "Actually, it is not the original name I gave him."

"Really? What was it, and why did you change it?"

"My horse's original name was **Il Cacciatore.**"

"**Il Cacciatore?** That sounds lovely. But what does it mean?"

"It means 'the hunter'. But when I first came to this island, the other knights around me had difficulty pronouncing Orion's name and chided me to rename the horse to something they could pronounce and understand. In other words, they wanted me to give Orion a name in their Anglo-Saxon tongue."

"So typical of the people of this island. But you renamed him Orion rather than The Hunter."

"Yes, I did not like the sound of the word 'hunter' in Anglo-Saxon. It had neither the impact nor the grace for me as **Il Cacciatore.** But I decided in the end on a name I felt comfortable with and which the other men finally accepted. That was Orion."

"But why Orion?"

"You tell me, Peter. What does 'Orion' mean to you?"

Peter thought a moment. "Well, Orion is the constellation of the —" With sudden understanding, Peter smacked his forehead and chuckled. "Orion is the constellation of the hunter!"

"Exactly."

"That was very clever of you, Richard."

The knight bowed his thanks.

Richard was gently leading Orion to head back to the monastery as the two men walked in silence for several minutes before the knight suddenly stopped dead in his tracks.

"Is something wrong?" Peter asked with concern.

Richard shook his head and laughed. "Now I just realised something."

"What is that?"

"With all these questions we have been asking one another, I just now realised I have NEVER asked you or any of the other monks what the name of this monastery is. I have no idea where I have been staying all this time!"

"Oh, Good Lord!" Peter said with a shock. "And apparently NONE of us ever bothered to consider telling you. How unbelievably inconsiderate of us! Well, the monastery is called Saint James."

"James?" Richard laughed. "That is San Giacomo in my language, and that is the name of the first, the biggest and most important church in Venezia. Once again, another sign of our soul connection."

Peter smacked his forehead again and laughed uproariously. "Holy shit!"

"I love a monk who talks dirty," Richard said, growling like a tiger.

"What I mean is, you had mentioned before that the large church in Venezia was called Saint James in your language. Yet I never made the connection nor informed you AT THAT TIME that our monastery shared the same name. What an idiot I have been!"

Richard gave the monk a powerful embrace, then moved back a step as he once more glided the back of his fingers down the monk's face. Peter wondered if he blushed a bright crimson as he felt feverishly giddy again and wanted to hurl himself into Richard's arms – but did not dare.

Richard noted it all and smiled warmly. He could sense the time for coming together with Peter on a more physically intimate level was coming soon – very soon. The thought pleased him with joyful anticipation.

The two men and Orion made their way back to the monastery as the sun began to set and an icier coldness descended across the land.

As they approached the monastery, Richard quickly glanced sideways towards Peter and thought to himself, *"Sei la risposta alle mie preghiera – ciò che ho cercato per tutta la vita. E ora finalmente ti ho trovato. Sei la mia anima soddisfatta."* {"You are the answer to my prayers – that which I have been seeking my entire life. And now I have finally found you. You are my soul fulfilled."}

Richard's heart swelled with loving gratitude as he, Peter and Orion passed under the entry arch of the monastery as the sun sank beneath the distant horizon.

Twelve

IT WAS THE first of December – Peter's twenty-sixth birthday. It had snowed the night before, and several inches of glistening white blanketed the monastery and all around it.

Richard sat upright in his infirmary bed with Peter sitting beside him on the bed's edge. When the monk finished feeding Richard his breakfast, he carefully set everything on the bedside table. The two men then looked deeply into each other's eyes for an extended moment. But it was Peter who broke the silence first.

"Honestly, Richard, you are quite capable of bathing and feeding yourself now," Peter insisted. "We have had this discussion before, you know."

"I know, but it is so much nicer when YOU do it. *N'est pas?*"

"What?"

"Excuse me. *Non è cosi?*"

"Sorry, still not getting it."

"What am I doing?" Richard asked with a laugh. "First I spoke to you in French, or what used to be called Gallic before Gaul recently changed its name to France, and then I spoke in my native tongue."

"French? You speak French as well?"

"Some. I learned French while living there."

"What other languages do you speak?"

"I also speak Spanish. *Buenos dias. Me llamo Riccardo.*"

"And I love you," Peter blurted out without thinking.

"That was not what I said." Richard said with a wide grin, but then he thought to himself, *"Did I correctly hear what I thought Peter just said?"*

"I know, but I was simply informing you that I love you."

Peter's eyes opened wide. He hadn't meant to speak his feelings directly out loud either time. He had known for some time that he loved Richard but had not dared to say so, fearing rejection or ridicule. But suddenly, in the heat of the moment, he couldn't help but speak directly how he truly felt. The monk was stunned by what he thought was his own audacity.

"I have just admitted to Richard – out loud! – that I love him!"

It was so sudden and spontaneous. But it was completely true – Peter DID love Richard. And somehow, it now felt wonderful to say so out loud as well as to feel it inside!

Richard's face lit up with joy. Peter had finally spoken those three magic words directly to the knight, and Richard was overwhelmed with gratitude.

Peter held his breath. *"What is going to happen next?"* the monk wondered. Instantly his inner question was answered.

Richard drew the monk down to him and said most clearly and directly, "I love you." Then the knight kissed Peter fervently for a very, VERY long time.

"Oh my God!" Peter thought ecstatically as the intoxicating kiss continued. *"I am being kissed by Richard! It is AMAZING! Holy shit!"*

When their lips finally parted, Peter laughed and said, "My God, but that was incredible! So this is what I have been missing all my life! All I can say is, I like it when we have translation problems. But what were we talking about?"

Richard laughed. "You said I am healthy enough to bathe and feed myself, and I told you that it is so much more fun when you do it. Then I added *'n'est pas'*, which is French for *'non è cosi'*, which is my language for 'is this not so'."

Richard's grin made Peter laugh. "Well," Peter said with a nod, "that is true – it is more fun for BOTH of us when I bathe or feed you. Alright then, let us get on with the bathing next!"

Both men continued laughing as Richard quickly stripped off his robe, pushed away several pillows and then lay back with his arms outstretched in total surrender.

This caused Peter to laugh yet again when he saw Richard's arms stretched out. "I am going to bathe you, Richard, not crucify you!"

"Do with me whatever you choose!"

However, Peter was still recovering from the fact that first he had verbally declared his love to Richard, and then he had been kissed by the knight – BOTH things happening for the first time in his life as well as occurring on his birthday! It was the most sensational kiss he ever could have imagined. Richard's lips had pressed against his with such immense passion that Peter feared he would pass out from the absolute strength and enrapturement of it.

"I am ready. Do to me what you must!" Richard declared, his arms remaining outstretched.

"God, I just want to jump into those magnificent arms!" Peter thought but didn't dare do. Instead, he began to sweat profusely from the thought of it. Aloud he said, "That was a lovely birthday gift you gave me."

"Gift? What gift?"

"The kiss. That was – wonderful!"

Richard grinned mischievously. "Oh no, beloved brother. Your birthday gift is much, much more than that and comes later."

"Like I hope YOU will 'come' later!" Richard thought gleefully.

"Holy shit!" Peter gasped, trying to guess what his later birthday gift could possibly be as he began bathing Richard.

"Keep talking dirty like that, and I cannot be held responsible for what may happen next! By the way, beloved brother, do you still like my nipples?" Richard asked teasingly.

"To quote Brother Clair, they are 'pert and gorgeous', as you well know." Peter replied.

"Wonderful. Brother Clair will be so pleased!"

Peter continued to slowly and gently massage ALL of the knight's body with a soapy cloth, then carefully wiped away the soap with another warm wet cloth. The monk took special care when washing Richard's extensive penis. Richard was both very grateful and very pleased with Peter's slow gentle thoroughness, and the knight's penis grew long and rigid to communicate ITS appreciative delight.

"You are so much improved in your technique, my beloved brother," Richard announced happily.

"I can see," Peter grinned, watching Richard's penis stand to attention, "and I am glad."

Richard observed his fully erect member. "I only do that to help you wash me as thoroughly as possible."

"That is very thoughtful of you, Richard. Thank you. However, I must point out that your penis is now directing itself more towards you than to me, so I do not see how that helps me be more efficient."

"Oh well, I try my best," Richard teased with a shrug. "I love seeing you enjoy doing this – much more than in the beginning when you were so nervous and embarrassed. Still the epitome of efficiency, of course, but it is lovely to see the genuine ENJOYMENT on your beautiful face."

"Thank you, sir," Peter bowed with mock seriousness. "I never before realised that joy could be experienced simultaneously with efficiency."

"I am pleased you have learned that invaluable lesson," Richard said happily. "It makes me happier, too."

When Peter finished drying off the knight, he helped Richard get back into his robe.

"There you are, sir, ready for the new day."

"Not just any day. Your BIRTHDAY!"

"Yes, my birthday. And somehow I know it will be better than any of my previous birthdays."

"I promise you it will be NOTHING like any of your other birthdays."

"Oh my," Peter said feeling giddy again. "I look forward to it."

At that moment, Brother Bartholomew entered the infirmary and greeted both men.

"How are you feeling today, Richard?"

"I am well, thanks to the both of you."

Bartholomew did a quick examination of Richard, checked the bandage on the knight's left side, listened to his heart and felt the pulse at the wrist.

Meanwhile, Peter continued to re-experience his very first kiss – a kiss of extraordinary length and passion – over and over in his mind. He could still feel the pressure of Richard's warm firm lips on his own as well as the strength of the knight's embrace. Peter sat down as his heart hammered fiercely. He felt dizzy from the somersaults of emotions bouncing wildly inside him.

"I am pleased with your progress, Richard," Bartholomew announced happily. "We will change your bandage again tomorrow. I think we can also let you walk around even more so you can exercise your legs and get used to increased movement."

"Thank you."

Bartholomew turned to Peter seated in his chair. "You look a little pale, Brother Peter, but you are taking very good care of our guest. Whatever you have been doing is working miracles on our patient."

Peter was simultaneously touched by Bartholomew's compliment while also stifling inner laughter.

"If you only knew," Peter thought. *"Apparently, me being kissed by Richard is working miracles on our patient's health as well! I would love to go further and see what miracles THAT would generate – on ME as well as on him!"*

Richard nimbly changed the subject by asking a question. "May I ask you something, Bartholomew?"

"Of course, anything."

"What led you to become a healer monk in the first place? I mean, did you always know you had these healing gifts?"

Bartholomew was deeply moved. "You know, Richard, you are the very first person to ever ask me that."

Peter immediately felt ashamed for his total lack of interest towards any of Bartholomew's previous life experiences before ending up at the monastery. Now he could add guilt to the erupting mixture of emotions regarding Richard that were already ricocheting in all directions inside him.

"Both of my parents had healing gifts," Bartholomew explained. "My mother was extremely knowledgeable in herbs, and all I know about herbs I learned from her. And my father was a healer Druid."

"Druid?" Richard interrupted. "I do not recognise this word."

"Well," Bartholomew said, scratching his head, "this is an ancient spiritual tradition among many of us descended from the various Celtic tribes that came to these islands several centuries ago. The Druids were their spiritual counsellors, healers, poets and teachers. They focussed on unity with Mother Earth, cooperation with all aspects of Nature, and deriving wisdom, strength and power from the natural forces of our world. It would take me a long time to explain the intricate complexities of Druidism. But in short, I come from generations of a family dedicated to healing and transformational growth through Oneness with Nature."

"Fascinating," Richard said. "I would love to learn more about this Druid tradition of yours."

Bartholomew smiled. "That would be very nice indeed. Thank you, Richard. I look forward to that. But for now, I leave the two of you to your healing work."

"Healing," Peter thought as he fought to suppress a grin. *"That is what Richard's kiss to me was — part of our healing work!"*

With a nod to both men, the healer monk left the infirmary.

Later around midday, an unusually agitated Richard sat in the chair next to his bed. Moments before, Peter had left to collect the knight's lunch.

"I cannot arrange this on my own," Richard said aloud. "I need help."

Immediately, as if on divine cue, Brother Clair entered the infirmary.

"Praise be to Heaven!" Richard squealed delightedly.

"Well, hello to you, too!" Brother Clair said with an enormous grin. "Thank you for that very nice greeting."

"You are just the man I wanted to see."

"That is also good to hear."

"I need your help."

"Whatever you need, I will gladly do it for you. And that would be what exactly?"

"Today is Brother Peter's birthday."

"So it is. I do not know if he told you, but birthdays are not so much —"

"He already told me," Richard interrupted, "but I do not care."

"Okay," Clair replied quizzically.

"I want to give Brother Peter a special gift for his birthday."

"Splendid. What did you have in mind?"

"Me."

"Excuse me?"

"I said, me — I want to give myself to Brother Peter. I mean, I want us to be together. No, let me try this again and express myself more clearly." Richard took a deep breath, exhaled slowly, and then let it out. "I want to make love to Peter."

"That," Brother Clair exclaimed excitedly, "is the most exceptional birthday gift I have ever heard of! He will LOVE it — I mean you — I mean, he does — love you!"

"So you think it will be alright?"

"Are you kidding? Rapturous does not even begin to explain how much he will appreciate it!"

"Thank you. I am relieved to hear that you approve."

"But, um, I am unclear on something. What can I do to help you — uh — give yourself to Brother Peter?"

"Two things. First, I want to surprise him in his own cell tonight."

"Richard, I can certainly tell you where Peter's personal cell is and how to get there. And the other thing?"

"Now, this one might be a bit more complicated. You see, I need to sneak into Peter's cell without him knowing I am there so I can properly surprise him when he arrives. But he will come to the infirmary to check on me before retiring for the night. Only I will not be here. I need you to handle him when he gets here and persuade him to quickly go to his cell, but without letting him know that I will already be in his personal cell waiting to surprise him. This could be very tricky, but can you do it?"

Brother Clair clapped his hands as his face lit up. "You are SO inspirational! Consider it done. I will make sure he hurries to his cell without worrying or wondering about you so you can — surprise him with his EXCEPTIONAL birthday treat. I will take care of everything. Oh, the lucky man."

"Clair, I cannot thank you enough."

"Actually, Richard, yes you can."

"Oh? What would that be?"

"Afterwards, you will have to report to me whether or not our beloved Brother Peter has nipples as pretty and pert as yours."

"Consider it done," the happy knight chuckled as he and Brother Clair shook hands.

———————

Brother Clair sat alone in the infirmary that evening, waiting for Brother Peter to come and check on the knight before retiring to bed. But this night, Richard was absent because he was already waiting for Peter in the monk's cell. There Richard had lit several candles to create a romantic glow, and now the knight eagerly awaited Peter's arrival.

Brother Clair went over again in his mind what he would say to Peter when his fellow monk came to the infirmary to check on Richard but found only himself. The happy, fat monk was sure he had figured it all out. But the moment Peter entered the infirmary, Clair's carefully conceived plan instantly vanished into a vast mental vacuum.

"Brother Clair, what are you doing here?" Peter asked with a perplexed stare.

"Oh, good evening, Brother Peter. How are you?"

"What? Fine. But why are you here?"

"Oh, um, just visiting."

"Visiting? This late at night?"

"Oh, well, I was in the neighbourhood and thought, why not?"

"But –" then Peter glanced around the room. "Where is Richard?"

"Who?"

"Who? What do you mean by who? Richard! The convalescing knight. Remember him?"

"Oh, yes, um, him. Right."

Peter scanned more thoroughly around the room. "Where is he?

Has something happened to Richard? Is anything wrong?" Peter asked with mounting panic.

"Oh, no, no, no, no, no. Nothing is wrong. Everything is fine, thank you."

Peter stared angrily at Clair and demanded, "I repeat, what – is – going – on?"

"Going on?" Clair asked, perspiration beginning to drip down his forehead. "Whatever do you mean?"

"You are here when you should not be. Richard is not here when he should be. I want answers, Brother Clair, and I want them NOW!"

"Calm yourself, Brother Peter. Really, there is nothing wrong – nothing going on. Just make your way down to your own cell so you can go to sleep."

"Go to sleep?" Peter shrieked. "Are you nuts? How can I do that when Richard is not here? What has happened?"

"Really, Brother Peter, nothing has happened – yet. Everything is fine. Go on back to your own cell and call it a night. Trust me!"

"Call it a knight? What am I supposed to call the knight, other than Richard? And anyway, I will not go to my cell!" Peter was yelling again as rising panic threatened to choke his breathing. "Not until I know what is going on. And SOMETHING IS going on since Richard is not here! Now out with it, Brother Clair. Where is Richard?"

"Um, uh, let me see, uh, he is out? Yes, that is it. He went out."

"Well, no kidding!" Peter barked at Clair. "Richard is not here, so he is out!"

"Well then, there you are!"

"What do you mean, there I am?"

"Richard is out. Good night."

"GOOD NIGHT! Brother Clair, out with it, and I mean RIGHT THIS INSTANT!" Peter roared. "Where the HELL is Richard?"

"Brother Peter, your language!"

"Shove my language up your ass!"

If looks could kill, Peter's enraged glare would have melted Clair into a puddle of drool.

Clair was so totally confused now he could not think straight about anything. "Yes, well, he is out – with, um, oh Lord! Yes – that is it! He is with Father Abbot."

"With Father Abbot? At THIS time of the night? Whatever for?"

"Um, just to visit."

"Watch my lips, Brother Clair! NO ONE goes to Father Abbot at this time of night, and NEVER just to visit!"

"Well, um, Richard did. So there you go. Good night."

"Will you stop saying 'good night'!" Peter yelled again. "You are being exceptionally infuriating! Now, once and for all, what is going on?"

"They, uh, just wanted to visit – and talk."

"This is crazy. I am going right now to ask Father Abbot what is happening."

"No, no, no!" Brother Clair shrieked as he quickly grabbed Peter's hands and prevented him from leaving the infirmary.

Peter stared down at his Clair's trembling pudgy hands. Their grip, shaky as it was, squeezed Peter's hands with enormous strength. "Why are you squeezing my hands so tightly?" Peter demanded. "And why are you trembling so badly?"

"Am I trembling? I had not noticed."

"Are you kidding? Your hands, and the rest of you for that matter, are shaking like you are having your own private earthquake! I am going immediately to Father Abbot to get to the bottom of this. However, you will need to let go of my hands first, please."

Clair's grip on Peter's hands tightened. "No, I cannot do that."

"Excuse me?"

"Okay. You are excused."

"What? Unhand me this instant!"

"Uh, no, I cannot do that."

"Cannot or will not?" Peter demanded with mounting anger.

"Yes."

"Yes to what? Cannot or will not?"

"Yes." Clair repeated.

"Let me go this instant!" Peter tugged hard, but with no success.

"No."

"Why not?"

"I am not supposed to." Brother Clair blurted.

"What does that mean?"

"What does what mean?"

"Are you having a complete nervous breakdown, Brother Clair?"

"Um, no, I do not believe so."

"Then let go of me!"

"No."

"What do you mean, 'no'?"

"I mean no. As in, I cannot."

"Because?"

"Because, because, um, you need to go to sleep now?"

"Honestly, Brother Clair, your brain is melting inside your skull. Now let me go!"

"No."

"LET ME GO!" Peter roared, trying to break free of Clair's trembling grasp. But the fat little monk held on for dear life.

"Brother Clair, you will release me this instant!" Peter shrieked. "I am going to Father Abbot to find out what the hell is going on with Richard. And after that, I will get Brother Bartholomew to come here and take care of you because you are obviously having a nervous breakdown!"

Clair shook his head "no" as he continued to steadfastly hold on.

"Let me go this instant!" Peter ordered furiously.

"No, you need to go to sleep now."

"What the hell is this all about? Who do you think you are telling me when to go to sleep?"

"Please, please listen to me," Clair begged as he continued to hold on to Peter's fighting hands with all the strength he didn't know existed in him. "Go to bed in your own cell right now. You will be very glad you did, I promise you."

"You are totally nuts! Why should I listen to ANYTHING you have to say?"

"Because it is important."

"To whom?"

"To you."

"Why?"

"Because."

"Because? What is THAT supposed to mean?"

"Go to bed now!" Clair screamed helplessly.

Peter stared in utter shock. "What has gotten into you?"

"Please, please, PLEASE Brother Peter. Just this ONCE in your life please listen and do what I request without needing to understand down to the tiniest detail. I beg you to TRUST me on this and do as I say."

"Trust you? When you speak and act like a madman — a raving lunatic?"

"Yes, even so. Please trust me and go to bed. Now!" Clair pointed his chin towards the infirmary door. "In your cell – please!"

"Why should –"

"JUST DO IT!" the rotund monk screamed. "Believe me when I say that you will not regret it," Clair added in a suddenly normal tone.

Peter stared with a whole new level of shock.

"Please, Brother Peter," Clair tried again with the greatest expression of false calm that he had ever managed. "There is a genuinely good reason for this. Trust me and just go to bed right now. Everything will be crystal clear if you do. Honestly."

Peter took two steps back in utter shock, dragging the corpulent monk with him since Peter's hands remained imprisoned in Clair's unrelenting grip. "You are weird, Brother Clair. There is no doubt about it."

"Yes, yes, I am weird. You are right, and there it is. But please trust me anyway and all will soon be very clear. Go to bed now."

"But I still think I should see Father Abbot first."

"No, no, no! Completely unnecessary. Open your heart to trust. Go to your bed. Right now. PLEASE!"

"You need medical care – and A LOT of it!"

"Probably. But please go to bed right now anyway."

"You certainly are eager to get me into bed."

"You would be too if –" *"Crap — shut up!"* Clair warned himself. "If?"

"Never mind. Bed, bed, bed!"

Peter was exhausted from both the bizarre conversation and trying to break free from Clair's iron-clad grip, which was surprisingly strong for such a normally sweet monk.

"Okay," Peter wearily acquiesced. "I am going to sleep now. Apparently everything will be fine if I do. I will listen to you, Brother Clair. God help me to see why I have agreed to this, but I will go now to my cell. But if anything is wrong with Richard –"

"There is nothing wrong with Richard, on the contrary. I swear. Go to sleep. Good night."

"Good night, Brother Clair. I hope someday you regain your sanity."

"Yes, that would help me a great deal. Thank you. Good night."

"Good night," Peter repeated. He continued to stare quizzically as Clair finally released his grip on Peter's hands.

Backing up a few steps, Peter rubbed his aching hands and then headed out of the infirmary to his own private cell as fast as he could, imagining that Clair might decide to come after him. Peter had had more than enough of Clair for one evening – or for the whole winter.

Brother Clair collapsed into a chair, sweating profusely and trembling from head to toe. "Well," he said out loud to himself, "that went well in the end – I think. Brother Peter is finally going to his birthday surprise. Oh, the night those two will share together! The heavens will sing in glorious rupture!"

"He meant rapture rather than rupture, right?" one raven asked the other.
"He just had a rough time with his fellow monk," the other raven explained.

"What the hell was THAT all about?" Peter asked himself aloud as he quickly made his way towards his cell. "I always knew that Brother Clair would eventually disintegrate, and tonight it finally happened. I have known all along it is dangerous to grin twenty-four hours a day every day, and now I have seen the proof. He is utterly mad!"

Then suddenly Peter stopped walking and wondered if he should go to Father Abbot's cell after all and make sure nothing had happened to Richard.

"*However*," he thought, "*if Richard is not there and nothing is wrong, then I will get a stern lecture from Father Abbot.*" Peter was not particularly in the mood for any stern lectures, especially after his harrowing conversation with Brother Clair.

But Peter still felt uneasy that Richard was missing and Brother Clair might be hiding something. On the other hand, Brother Clair kept insisting nothing was wrong – but who could trust a monk who had totally fallen apart?

In the end, a bewildered Peter resumed hurrying forward until he finally reached his cell. Opening the door, he entered, his mind totally exhausted and overloaded. Still holding his cell door open, Peter quickly noticed that there were several lit candles had been placed around his cell.

"*What the hell?*" his tired mind thought. "Hello? Who is here?" Peter called out.

"It is me. Or should I have said, it is I?"

"Who is this 'me' or 'I'?"

"Are you kidding?" came the laughing reply. "Who else do you know who speaks with this accent?"

"Richard?"

"Of course."

"What are you doing here?"

"Please shut the door."

"Why?"

"Can you just do something that is asked of you without always needing to have a full analytical explanation?"

"Brother Clair said the same thing just a few minutes ago."

"He is a wise man. Now close the door!" Richard ordered with another laugh.

Peter closed the door and then asked, "What is going on?"

"***Buon compleanno, mio amato fratello.*** And before you ask me," Richard added with a warm smile, "I just said happy birthday, my beloved brother."

"Oh!"

"Surprise!"

"This really IS a surprise!" Peter said happily. "Thank you for all these lovely birthday candles."

"Uh, no. The candles are not your gift. They are here just to set the mood."

"The mood? A mood for what?"

"Dio mio — I mean, my God, Peter! Richard sighed. "You really are naïve!"

"So many of the monks keep telling me," Peter admitted.

"I am here to give you your REAL birthday gift."

"Oh, my! What is it?"

"Me."

"What?"

"Me. My gift to you is me."

Peter blinked several times, not grasping Richard's meaning. "You mean, I am going to bathe you again?"

"DIO, DAMMI LA PAZIENZA!"

"What?" Peter repeated.

"I just asked God for patience."

"I see."

Then the monk finally noticed that Richard was not wearing his robe, but instead was wrapped in Peter's own wool blanket. Richard suddenly held out his arms to Peter, causing the blanket to drop and reveal the knight's tall, muscular and naked body – as well as Richard's massively erect penis and his two pretty and perky nipples. The knight's erect penis and his two nipples all pointed directly and proudly at the monk.

"Richard, has anyone ever told you, sir, that it is not polite to point?"

Richard roared with laughter. "I want to make love to you SO MUCH, Peter! I apologise for my *pene* – oops, I mean my penis. It is just SO HAPPY to see you, as is all the rest of me as well. *Il mio pene ti saluta!"*

"One more time, please, in my language."

"Oops again. I said, my penis salutes you!"

Now it was Peter's turn to laugh. "I can certainly see that."

*"Ti amo, ti amo, **TI AMO!** I love you, Peter, with all my heart and from the depths of my soul. I want to make love to you in every way our bodies can touch, and because I want to love you fully, thoroughly, eternally!"*

Peter blinked a few times, tears welling in his eyes. "Oh, my," he spluttered. In the next instant, he ran towards the knight and leapt into Richard's waiting arms, holding on to Richard with all his strength.

"I love you. I am so completely in love with you. ***Ti amo, ti amo, TI AMO!***" Peter repeated the words of love Richard had just spoken to him.

Peter felt ecstatic by the feel of Richard's hard, muscular body against his through the material of the monk's robe. Peter also sensed the hard erection of Richard's member against his left thigh, which filled the monk with an even greater euphoria.

Richard embraced the monk tightly, kissing him along the forehead, down the temples, across both cheeks. And then Richard kissed Peter's lips with a locking firmness that expressed total desire, devotion and passionately eternal love.

Their lips merged together for so long that Peter thought he had stopped breathing. *"Who cares?"* the monk thought breathlessly. *"He is kissing me, so just keep kissing him back!"* It was Richard who released his lips first and stared lovingly into Peter's tearful eyes.

"What is it, my love? You are crying."

Peter wiped away his tears and gazed in wonderment at Richard, as if seeing the knight for the very first time.

"Peter, what is it?" Richard repeated.

Peter needed a minute to formulate his thoughts. He looked at Richard and took a deep breath. "I have just realised something."

Richard nodded in encouragement.

"I just realised that the first time you kissed me earlier today was also the very first time in my life that I felt like I genuinely exist."

"Oh Peter," Richard whispered, then kissed the monk again. ***"Sei la passione del mio cuore.*** Oh, I have done it again! Let me repeat it now in your language – you are my heart's passion."

"What does he mean?" one raven asked the other.

"Which 'he'? Richard or Peter?" the other raven replied.

"Your pet monk of course. The knight translated what HE said. But what did your pet monk mean that this was the first time he felt like he genuinely existed? Where does he think he has been all this time – in some alternate Universe?"

"My monk, who is NOT my or anyone's pet, is beginning to learn something new about himself that is essential to his spiritual growth."

"Which is?" the first raven prompted impatiently.

"He just revealed that being kissed by the knight triggered his first real awareness of existing as a physical being."

"No, I am still not getting it."

The second raven sighed like only ravens can sigh. *"Peter is starting to understand that his defensive behaviours – such as impatience and his obsessive need for everything to be neat and organised to HIS fanatic standards – are not SOLELY a defence against his fear of emotions or his fear that love automatically will lead to rejection and pain."*

"I take it there is more, because I am still not following."

"Cosmos give me strength! Pay attention this time! Peter is now realising that his obsessive behaviours were ALSO created because he never relates to himself as a physical being. He additionally created these obsessive behaviours in order to make an IMPACT upon others as a way of proving to himself that he is physically real. You see? If people react in any way to anything he says or does, then he therefore must actually exist."

"No, sorry. I do not understand the human mind at all," the first raven confessed.

The second raven swiped his wing fiercely across the first raven's beak, causing the second raven to dance back and forth as he attempted to re-balance himself on the tree branch.

"Why did you do that?"

"Because you deserve it."

"I do not! But continue – I am still not getting it."

"Peter has never related to himself with any sense of love or value as an individual physical being. For example, remember that he noticed how handsome the knight is, but my monk could not make the connection that looking like Richard means he too is handsome. Being practically identical to Richard did

not allow Peter to see himself as he sees Richard. This is how severe Peter's lack of self-acceptance as a physical individual has made him."

"But I thought your monk does that to avoid owning and feeling his *emotions,*" the first raven pointed out.

"Yes, that is true, but it is not the full story. This new revelation means that he can go much deeper into his self-awakening."

"I THINK I understand?"

"You see," the second raven continued, *"when Peter told Richard that being kissed by him allowed the monk for the first time to identify himself as a physical being, this greatly elevated his growing self-awareness – not ONLY as a spiritual being but also as a spirit incarnated into a physical body. Peter is finally seeing his physical body as an integral part of who he is as a unique individual. This is an enormous breakthrough for Peter. I want him to go even deeper into this new understanding of who he is. This will be a major transformation for him."*

"Okay, I just MIGHT be following you now – somewhat."

The second raven rolled his eyes (which is almost impossible for a raven to do). *"Yeah, sure. We will see."*

———— ◆•◆•◆ ————

Richard gasped from the impact of Peter's admission and realised that tears had come into his own eyes as well. He ran his right forefinger down the left side of Peter's face, the knight's a repeated gesture that filled Peter with desire and joy.

"I want to make love to you, Peter, if that is what you want."

"GOD YES! I mean, yes, that is what I want as well."

Peter was shivering in Richard's arms.

"Are you cold?" Richard asked.

"No, I am not cold." The monk looked down. "I am –"

"What, my love?" Richard asked.

"Nervous."

"About what?"

It took a moment for Peter to raise his head and look into Richard's eyes. To Richard, the monk appeared shy and uncertain.

"Speak to me, my love. Is there a problem?"

Peter nodded and took a deep breath. "This will be – my very first time."

Richard sharply sucked in his breath. "So you are – a virgin?"

Peter nodded again.

"Oh, my love," Richard whispered as he held the monk tightly against him, with the knight's rigid penis pressing hard against the monk's thigh. Then Richard laughed. "In a way, Peter, I can say the same for myself. Because this will be the first time I ever make love to a MAN." He laughed again. "Well, we will just have to be very patient and tender with each other as we – uh – grope in the dark and find our way."

Peter glowed with love and safety in Richard's arms.

Richard released Peter, took a step back and lifted the robe completely off the monk in one graceful movement. Richard gazed for the first time at Peter's totally naked body – so slender and muscular. That first view of Peter – plus the romantic glow of candlelight softly illuminating the monk's cell – filled Richard with love and desire.

But then Richard suddenly giggled.

"What?" Peter asked, immediately feeling self-conscious.

"Brother Clair will be so pleased."

"Brother Clair? About what?" Peter asked.

"That you really DO have pretty nipples. VERY pretty nipples indeed!"

Peter blushed a deep crimson but smiled gratefully.

Richard then noticed Peter's very long and erect penis. "NOW who is rudely pointing?" Richard asked playfully.

Peter glanced down and then looked back at Richard, with the monk's face turning even redder.

"But I love it!" Richard murmured.

Peter smiled appreciatively.

Richard stepped forward and tenderly kissed each of Peter's nipples before gently lifting Peter and lowering the monk onto the bed. Richard slowly and sensuously laid down on top of Peter.

First hesitantly and then with mounting passion, the two men physically expressed all the immense love they felt for one another in all the ways their bodies could possibly do so.

At one point Richard murmured to Peter, *"Fai cantare il mio cuore di gioia."*

"Now wait a minute," Peter whispered to the knight between gasps of ecstatic pleasure. "You have said that to me before. I recognise it. But I cannot remember what it means."

"You make my heart sing with joy."

"Oh my!" Peter gasped. "Just hearing you say that makes me want to come all over you, and in BOTH languages!"

"You know how to come in more than one language? That is a very nice gift." Richard added with a grin.

"I did not mean to say it in that way. I meant – oh, to hell with it! Kiss me again, Richard. I love you, and you speaking to me in ANY language makes me want to come again and again and again!"

Richard's smooth and muscular body covered Peter completely. In the next moment, the monk broke out giggling.

"What is so funny?" Richard asked with a grin.

"I am so sorry, but sometimes I get the strangest thoughts at the oddest moments."

"Please share with me," Richard encouraged.

"When you covered me with your body the way you just did now, it felt like a total eclipse of the sun – I mean, I was the sun and you were the moon – I think?"

Richard smiled. "I like that very much. Let me see if I can cause a total eclipse of your lips." With that, Richard's mouth pressed passionately against Peter's mouth.

———————•◆•———————

"What is it with their sexual organs?" one raven asked.

"What do you mean?"

"Well, they are – so long and floppy. They just hang down in front of those two men flip-flopping everywhere. And then suddenly they become like hard rods pointing one direction and then the other."

"Is there a point to all of this?"

"Well, that is just it – what IS the point?"

"I really need to explain this to you?"

"It must be so uncomfortable for them, not to mention so inconvenient. It is so — so —"

"Handy?"

———————•◦•———————

In the middle of the night, Peter woke up on his right side with Richard lying behind and against him, the knight's left arm draped over the monk. Peter's eyes teared up again with immense happiness about Richard's extended lovemaking. Peter sighed joyfully and wondered if he glowed like the nearly melted down candles still flickering on his table and windowsill.

When Peter slightly shifted, Richard awoke and caressed Peter's left shoulder and arm.

"Ti amo. I love you so much," Richard whispered contentedly into Peter's ear, sending thrills that caused the monk's entire body to tremble anew.

"Are you cold, Peter?"

"No, just in love with you."

Richard smiled and kissed Peter's shoulder.

"Toccarti è toccare Dio. Baciare le tue labra sta baciando l'estasi."

"That was a mouthful!" Peter murmured.

"Just like you," Richard teased. "I said, to touch you is to touch God, and kissing your lips is kissing ecstasy."

Peter started to cry again. "You just described what I feel being loved by you."

"What you and I just shared," Richard said dreamily, "was the most incredible lovemaking I have ever experienced in my life. I had no idea it could be this intense. Nor did I fully understand until now with you that sex could be so emotionally loving."

"It was — unbelievable!" Peter said. "I had no idea love could be expressed and shared like this. I love you so much."

"Peter, I have never felt sexually attracted to another man. But the moment I met you, I felt something so deep — far more than a physical attraction. It was a binding of my heart to yours, of my soul to yours. It had nothing to do with you being a man. Instead, I fell in love with your

SOUL! Or maybe," Richard paused a moment to be sure he expressed clearly what he meant, "I remembered that I have ALWAYS loved your soul – since before time existed."

"I understand," Peter replied wistfully. "For me, too, it had nothing to do with you being a man. In fact, I have never before felt attraction to ANYONE. But as I got to know you, you captured my heart. And now I know that my soul is bound to your soul forever."

Richard kissed Peter's left shoulder again and stroked the monk's back and arm. Then the knight turned Peter around to face him and stroked a forefinger down Peter's left temple and cheek and shoulder and arm.

The touch of Richard's forefinger once again sent shivers through the monk, and Peter wondered if he was going to ejaculate again right on the spot.

"Holy shit!" Peter moaned.

"Oh God, you are talking dirty again, and it arouses me! Do it some more."

"Really?" Peter sighed. "Well, then – shit-crap-poop and damn it all to Hell."

"I am all yours, my love!" Richard exclaimed as he once again glided the back of his fingers along one side of Peter's face.

"I love it when you do that. Your gentle touch gives me so much joy."

"I will always remember that," Richard said as he re-traced the back of his hand down Peter's left arm. "Your body is beautiful. It is amazing to see how our entire bodies are so similar, not just our faces."

"But you are far more beautiful," Peter said.

"No, beloved brother. Do not deny yourself. You are beautiful as well. Own it and celebrate it."

Peter looked down and shrugged, still in denial about his own physicality. After a moment Peter put his arms around Richard's neck, and the knight responded by embracing the monk tightly.

"Thank you," Peter murmured.

"For what, my most beloved brother?"

"For teaching me how to love," Peter whispered.

Richard smiled. "I will always love you." Then the knight passionately kissed the monk on his lips. "I want us to make love again."

"Oh yes!"

"By the time we finish ejaculating again, your bed will be a total mess!"

"Maybe I will never clean my bed again."

"You ARE changing!" Richard laughed. "But that is a bit too extreme, do you not think?"

"I see your point. Okay, I will compromise and clean my bed again – eventually."

"But not tonight! I love seeing you so playful and happy. **Grazie Dio!**"

"What?"

"Thank God," Richard murmured.

"Oh, yes. Him too."

Richard began playfully rubbing his body against Peter, showering the monk with kisses and sending his "beloved brother" into endless waves of ecstatic joy.

"Fissare nei tuoi occhi è incontrare la Divinità. La tua è la felicità del cielo tra le mie braccia."

"Richard, when you talk to me like that, I want to ejaculate forever."

"I have no problem with that. And I just said before that staring into your eyes is like meeting the Godhead. You are heaven's bliss in my arms."

"Oh Richard," was all Peter could manage before new tears welled up in him. The monk clung to Richard with all the love he could feel and communicate through his entire body.

At one point, Richard lowered himself so his face was directly in front of Peter's erect penis. The knight sensuously licked the long shaft up and down several times and then took it completely into his mouth. Peter wanted to scream aloud. After several minutes of licking and sucking, Richard released Peter's penis and raised himself to stare passionately into the monk's eyes.

"Beloved brother, your **pene è molto gustoso!**"

Peter was still gasping from the intense pleasure. "I THINK that is a good thing?"

"A very good thing. I just told you that your penis is very tasty."

Peter didn't have a clue how to respond to that. After a moment, though, he managed, "Um…thank you?"

"Actually, beloved brother, thank YOU! I will also go so far as to say *hai un sapore come Dio* – which means that you taste like God!

"Oh my!" Peter was dumbstruck. He had no way to react to Richard's words except by crying. Richard smiled as his fingers wiped away the monk's tears.

Finally, Peter managed to say, "You described how I experience you. You taste like God. You taste like all the love that exists in eternity."

"What would THAT taste like" Richard asked.

"Like you."

Richard smiled gratefully. "Oh – and by the way, Peter, happy birthday!"

Peter laughed and kissed Richard fervently. "To be loved by you makes every day my birthday!"

"Then we will have to celebrate your birthday every day."

The two men continued their celebration of Peter's birthday as they loved each other through the night.

———————◆•◆•◆———————

In the early morning, the two ravens were perched just outside of Peter's window.

"Humans have the strangest ways of copulating," commented the first raven.

"What is wrong this time?" asked the second raven.

"Whatever was the knight doing with the monk's, um, extremely long sexual organ?"

"Never mind. Just move on."

"And not only that – what was going on when the knight stuck his long and hard sexual organ into your monk's posterior? That HAD to hurt!"

"Trust me – you do not want to go there."

"I still say they display very weird sexual behaviour."

"Oh, do shut up, will you?" the second raven said. *"All you ever do is complain about the humans. You never see anything good in them. It is annoying as Hell."*

"That is because there is seldom anything good to see," the first raven

insisted. *"After all, what good can you say about a species that sticks a hard, long sexual organ up another person's butt?"*

The second raven chose to ignore the other raven's last question. *"You refuse to see ANY good in them. Look at what just happened – pure love emanating from both their souls across the expanse of Mother Earth. How can you criticise that, even if you apparently understand nothing whatsoever about human sex?"*

"You just wait," the first raven replied. *"Humans always find a way to destroy any of the good they create. It is their nature."*

The second raven jabbed his beak into the other bird's neck.

"Hey! Be careful. That hurt!"

"It was meant to!"

"Do not blame me when humans destroy everything good in their lives."

"That is not always true," the second raven replied as he repeatedly jabbed the other bird everywhere his beak could attack.

"Ouch! Stop that, you shit! You are hurting me! Stop that at once!"

"I certainly hope so. You are painful to listen to. I want you to feel how destructive and vicious your words are!" the second raven cawed as he continued to peck angrily at the other bird. *"In fact, just fly off and stop blaming the humans when you are a hundred times worse!"*

"Well, I never!" the first raven retorted.

"If only. Now, fly off and be gone!"

The first raven flapped his wings angrily to ward off the other bird, and then he flew away in a huff.

"Finally, some peace," the remaining raven sighed. *"Congratulations, my human,"* he telepathically thought towards Peter. *"Well done. You finally opened up to another human, to give and accept love. Your barriers are coming down. I am proud and happy for you."*

———◆◆◆———

In early morning just before the sun rose, Peter again awoke to feel Richard behind him. As Peter settled more firmly against Richard, the knight woke up and hugged Peter gently to himself.

"Good morning, my beloved brother," Richard mumbled sleepily. "How are you feeling?"

"In love with you," Peter murmured back.

Richard nuzzled his face into Peter's neck and shoulder. "And I love you."

Peter sighed and then laughed curiously.

"What do you find amusing?" Richard asked.

"I do not know why, but just this moment a memory popped into my head, and it made me want to laugh."

"Then please share it with me." But sensing it might be something important, Richard stopped nuzzling Peter in order to listen more closely.

"I do not know why, but suddenly, while being held so closely by you, I remembered that some of the older priests, all from before I ever arrived at this monastery, used to go on and on about how evil, dirty and satanic the human body is and that sex is also dirty and evil and should be performed solely for procreation – and other bullshit drivel like that. I often asked these idiots if sex is so evil and dirty, then why did God make sex so necessary for procreation? But they never had an answer for that."

"Of course they could not," Richard agreed. "That is a good insight, Peter."

"I cannot believe how these old priests blathered so much about evil sex and the dirty body when sex and the physical body are so beautiful and wondrous. They can give us so much joy, ecstasy and – PASSION!"

"Men fear what they cannot understand or control – or possess," Richard replied, hugging Peter more tightly. "Personally, I believe a lot of this negative judgement comes from a fear of women."

Peter turned around onto his back to face Richard as the knight shifted himself to rest alongside Peter's body. "In what way?"

"First, let me kiss your pretty nipples good morning."

"Oh my," was all Peter could manage as he felt a new wave of passion and pleasure while Richard gave thorough attention to each of the monk's nipples.

"How was THAT greeting?" Richard asked with a grin.

"Perfect, like you."

"Where were we?" Richard asked. "Oh yes. Women have been feared by men for centuries because they are so much more in touch with their emotions, intuition and other spiritual gifts that most men never dare to recognise or celebrate within themselves."

"Yes, I totally agree," Peter said. "But why so much fear about women? I mean, there must be more to it than that."

"Well," Richard replied, "I feel that most people confuse male and female with masculine and feminine."

"Ah! Yes, that is very interesting. Go on."

"Most people think male and female mean exactly the same thing as masculine and feminine. But they do not."

"No," Peter agreed. "Masculine and feminine relate to energies of consciousness – while male and female relate to physical bodies."

"Exactly. Energy in its purest form has no sexuality. But all energy DOES have two complementary aspects, each with its own qualities and purposes. However, all this has nothing to do with different anatomies of male and female bodies."

"Yes, I agree," Peter said with increasing interest and animation.

By now both men were sitting cross-legged in bed and facing each other.

"Feminine energies," Richard explained, "have to do more with emotions, inspiration, intuition, creativity, caring, compassion, sensitivity, openness, flexibility and so on. Masculine energies physically carry out and complete all the creative inspiration of feminine energies, as well as provide determination, strength, endurance and stamina.

"Somehow, sometime," Richard continued, "the feminine qualities became identified with women and the masculine qualities with men, and that was a big mistake. Because whether we are born into male or female bodies, we must develop an equal and integrated balance between our masculine and feminine energies. Otherwise we become narrow, incomplete and very limited human beings."

"I absolutely agree with you, Richard. When women show any kind of strength or intelligence, they suddenly threaten men who think women should be submissive and nurturing with no brains in their heads at all. And men who show sensitivity and emotional depth are just as threatening."

"Exactly," Richard agreed. "Men should act one way and women the other, and the two should never cross over. This thinking is hilarious but also pathetic, dangerous and destructive."

"Maybe," Peter wondered, "this is why the Church is so fanatically opposed to homosexuality. Church leaders tend to believe that homosexual men have too many feminine qualities they think belong only to women, and that scares the shit out of them. Conversely, these same Church leaders see any kind of strength, power or intelligence in women as threatening their control over everybody and everything – but especially over women!"

"That is how I see it," Richard said. "Any crossing over in behaviour or talents threatens the control of Church and kings. And all because they fear accepting that male and female have nothing to do with masculine and feminine. For our so-called religious and government rulers, it all comes down to power and control. This is exactly what I have observed in all my travels from country to country."

"Yes, I think you are right."

Richard smiled as he gazed lovingly into Peter's eyes. "Now that you and I have thoroughly analysed the negative state of the world and come up with a solution, what do we do now?"

Peter smiled. "I have an idea."

"That being?"

"Holy shit damnation crap and poop and more shit and damnation."

"Oh yes!" Richard growled. "You arouse me to the height of passion when you do that – so do it again. ***Dimmi porcherie!***"

"What?"

"Talk dirty to me!"

Peter did just that – and more.

Thirteen

RICHARD LIMPED WHILE leaning heavily on his walking staff as he slowly made his way to the monastery stables to visit Orion. Just before arriving, Richard paused because he heard Peter speaking intimately to the white steed.

"I love to visit you, Orion," Peter murmured. "You soothe and comfort me, which I greatly appreciate."

Listening to his lover, Richard smiled as a few tears welled up in his eyes. The knight too experienced Orion as always soothing and comforting. Then he carefully peeked into the horse's stall to see Peter brushing down the horse's flanks with broad strokes.

"Do you know what I love most about your owner?" Peter asked the horse, half-expecting a reply.

This made Richard totally alert, with his heart pounding.

"What I love most about Richard is his SOUL. And I can describe Richard's soul in one word, Orion – PASSION!"

Richard's heart was beating so strongly he thought it would burst – and tears started dripping from his eyes.

"I love Richard's passion for passion – his passion for compassion too. Every movement of his body, every look from his eyes, every word he utters, whether in my language or in his. It is all so intense and – PASSIONATE!"

Quietly sobbing now, Richard had to step back so Peter would not see or hear him. His love and gratitude for Peter was endless.

"Orion, the touch of Richard's hand thrills me beyond description.

With just the back of his forefinger, just the merest touch of a knuckle, he will trace a line down my cheek. And that, Orion, sends me into an ecstasy that I never knew was possible to feel. Richard IS passion, Orion. Sometimes I do not think I have enough room in my heart for all the love I feel for him."

Orion nodded in agreement with one big dip of his head and neck.

"Just hearing the sound of your master's voice is like being made love to. You and I are the two luckiest beings in this world, Orion – lucky to know him, to love him and to be loved by him."

Richard shakily wiped the tears from his bearded cheeks. Then he quietly turned around and walked unsteadily back to the infirmary to fully absorb what he had just heard Peter sharing with Orion.

Soon every monk in the monastery knew about the fiery love affair between Peter and Richard. Reactions ranged from happy approval to severe condemnation.

There was also another shock to absorb as more monks met and saw first-hand Richard's physical similarity to Peter. Some saw it as beautiful. But other monks said that love between two men is Satanic and therefore their physical similarity was deliberately designed so that the Devil could more easily recognise His own kind.

"So typical of them," Brother Clair complained one day to Brother Bartholomew. "Once again fanatic religion breeds narrow-minded hate."

"Remember," Bartholomew responded, "that some of us are hiding among these religious ones in order to protect our own personal spiritual beliefs."

"What has that got to do with their condemning attitudes?" Clair asked. "Religions are often anti-spiritual."

"Sometimes, but not always," Bartholomew reminded Clair. "Some people gain deep spiritual growth, tolerance and love through their religious beliefs and structures."

"Rare exceptions to the rule, as you well know."

Bartholomew sighed patiently. "Be careful, Brother Clair, that you do not become what you judge THEM to be. What good would that accomplish?"

"You are right, of course. But I still believe that the heartless ignorance and intolerance of fanatical religion is the greatest destructive force in our world."

"What is REALLY wrong with you, Brother Clair? You are usually radiant and happy all the time. Why are you suddenly so judgemental and negative?"

"I do not know. Some days the idiocy of humanity just gets on my nipples!"

Both of Bartholomew's eyebrows shot up in surprise. "I see."

"And another thing —"

"Now what?" Bartholomew asked.

"On and on our fellow monks talk about how similar our two lovers look."

"What is wrong with that? After all, it IS very odd that two unrelated men from different countries can look so much alike. They are reacting normally."

"But," Clair complained, "everyone here pretends they cannot tell Richard and Brother Peter apart."

"I too have difficulty telling them apart, now that Richard wears a monk's robe like the rest of us."

"For Heaven's sake, Brother Bartholomew, it is obvious which is which."

"Really? Please enlighten me."

"Richard's hair is longer than Peter's — and thicker — and even slightly darker."

"It is?"

"You cannot see it?"

"No. Forgive me."

Clair shrugged irritably but had no more to say. Bartholomew never understood what was genuinely causing so much judgemental anger in the usually jubilant Clair. What Bartholomew did not see was that Clair was equally stumped by his own emotions. Something was niggling deep in Clair's subconscious that boded trouble ahead, possibly even disaster. But Clair could not make any sense of it and continued to brood in mysterious discomfort.

Father Abbot and Brothers Bartholomew and Clair, of course, were ecstatic for the relationship between the Peter and the knight – and also grateful to Richard for the love and emotional liberation that he was bestowing upon their Brother Peter.

Young Brother Andrew was also happy for his beloved Brother Peter but sad for himself. "I always knew there was no hope for me. I am not good enough for Brother Peter."

Meanwhile, the eternally dour Prior Thomas talked to no one and kept almost exclusively to himself. If looks could kill, the other monks said, they would all be dead – slaughtered by Prior Thomas' continuous expressions of disgust and condemnation.

The weeks passed by, Christmas and New Year's came and went. Throughout January and almost all of February, the monastery was draped overhead by constant darkness while below it was snowed in for weeks at a time. It became a common daily sight to see Peter and Richard walking together when visiting the knight's horse, Orion, or they would on occasion brave the severe wintry weather to venture beyond the monastery walls towards the Highland hills – a few times knee-deep in accumulated snow. Richard now always wore a monk's robe, so the two men looked like identical twins.

The days were colder with bitter icy winds, and the landscape remained buried in snow and icicles. Even when the wind howled like a wounded beast, the two men would trek, sometimes with Orion, into hills blanketed by snow and passing forests where the trees looked like paralysed armies of ice giants.

Occasionally Peter led Richard to the library's scriptorium to view the manuscripts being copied, repaired or translated. There the two lovers enjoyed reading aloud to one another and also debating translations and the deeper meanings of various Biblical passages.

On one occasion in mid-January, Peter was sitting on a stool in the monastery's small library doing intricate repair on an old manuscript, completely absorbed in his detailed work. Then he jumped up in shock, knocking the stool over, when he suddenly felt a sharp poke in his lower back. Whirling around, he sighed with relief to see Richard standing behind him, a playful smile on the knight's face.

"You scared the life out of me!"

"That was not my intention," Richard said, running his right forefinger down Peter's left bearded cheek.

"What did you poke me with?" Peter asked, noticing nothing in Richard's hands.

Richard's smile increased as he pointed downwards.

Peter looked down to see a pointed protrusion beneath Richard's robe in the area of the knight's groin.

"My *pene* has been looking for you. It was very lonely."

"I have a feeling more than your *pene* was looking for me."

Richard nodded. "All of me was very lonely for the man I love."

"Well, here I am. What can I do to help you?"

Peter giggled as Richard embraced the monk tightly, with the knight's still erect penis now jabbing into Peter's lower abdomen, just above Peter's own quickly hardening member.

"I need to taste you," Richard whispered sensuously.

Peter giggled again. "Taste away. I love it when you taste me – or when I taste you."

Richard licked ravenously along both sides of Peter's neck and inside both ears, which made Peter howl with laughter. Then the knight kissed the monk with sumptuous mastery all over Peter's face.

"Yes!" Richard sighed contentedly. "THAT is the taste I hungered for." Richard kissed Peter deeply on the lips again.

Peter went limp (except for his penis) and completely surrendered to Richard's embrace.

"When was the last time I told you that I love you?" Richard asked with a baritone purr.

"Well, if you count loving my taste, about twenty seconds ago."

"That is far too long."

"I love you, Richard." Peter returned Richard's strong embrace with his own.

Richard released Peter and smiled lovingly at the monk. "That will hold me a little while."

"Whenever you need to taste me, I am right here."

Richard grabbed Peter's buttocks and pulled the monk tightly against him again.

They held one another for a long while.

———◆•◆•◆———

Beginning with the bitterly cold and snow-packed days of January, many monks quickly noticed that since the knight had arrived, there had been a vast transformation in Peter. Before Richard's arrival, the other monks had always experienced Peter as aloof, unapproachable and defiantly rigid in his exactness and ultra-orderliness. But now Peter greeted all the monks warmly and showed a genuine willingness to listen to his fellow brothers as they offered their personal opinions and suggestions.

Even the more fanatically religious monks, who looked upon sex between two men as sinful and satanic, were impressed and felt gratitude towards the knight for the overwhelming change in Peter's personality that had been triggered by Richard's love.

Brother Clair, of course, was ecstatic when Richard confirmed the superb prettiness of Peter's nipples. "I never doubted it for a moment," Clair replied.

———◆•◆•◆———

One freezing afternoon in late February, Richard and Peter were out walking with Orion in the Highland hills and enjoying their snow-covered wonderland. Both men wore heavy full-length cloaks over their robes. On this day, Richard had been allowed by Brother Bartholomew to ride his steed for the first time since his sword-piercing injury the previous autumn.

Peter had never before ridden a horse, and the knight had Peter sitting astride Orion with Richard behind the monk. Peter was thrilled to be riding a horse for the very first time in his life, while also feeling

Richard's powerful body seated behind him. Richard's left arm wrapped snuggly around the monk's waist, and every so often Richard would nuzzle against the back of Peter's neck or lick along the monk's nape until Peter found himself almost screaming with pleasure.

After riding Orion for some distance, Richard tightened his grip around Peter and suddenly brought Orion to a standstill.

"Is something wrong?" Peter asked with concern.

"No."

"Why have we stopped?"

Richard whispered sensuously into Peter's ear, *"Voglio fare l'amore con te."*

"What?"

Richard again whispered sensuously into Peter's ear, "I want to make love to you."

Peter took a deep breath and willed himself to not ejaculate right then and there.

"Actually, Peter, I want to make love to you *per sempre.*"

"Right now?"

"I said forever. But on the other hand, right now is also true."

In one graceful movement, the knight dismounted from Orion, and then he smoothly guided Peter off the horse as well.

Richard kissed Peter passionately, their lips pressing together with an intense longing. Orion immediately sensed what was going on and gently sauntered away to occupy himself with investigating the icicled shrubbery. Then Richard began lowering Peter down upon the snow-packed earth.

"What?" Peter gasped. "Here, now, in the SNOW?"

"Why not?"

"Because we will freeze to death!"

"I can assure you, my beloved brother," Richard said in a sultry voice, "I will keep you warm for the entire time we are – occupied with one another."

Peter was about to object with some insane list of logical reasons why this wouldn't work, when from deep inside he felt, "*Shut up, you moron! He loves you, you love him, and he wants to make love to you RIGHT*

NOW! If he says he will keep you warm, believe him, accept it, and for God's sake ENJOY it!"

Aloud, he said to Richard, "Yes, I would love to make love with you right here on the snow."

"Good man!" Richard said with a laugh. ***"Tu sei la mia vita e il mio piu grande amore."*** {"You are my life and my greatest love."}

Richard removed his heavy outer cloak and spread it upon the snowy ground behind Peter. Then he began to disrobe the monk. Peter's expression turned to utter panic, causing Richard to throw back his head and laugh. "I promise to keep you more than warm enough throughout."

Peter nodded, kissed the knight and then let himself be laid down fully naked upon Richard's cloak. Immediately Richard flung off his robe and sprawled naked on top of Peter.

"Sei piu sexy sulla schiena!"

"I understood the word sexy. That is promising!"

"I said you are sexiest on your back."

"Nice to know," Peter said.

"Warm enough, beloved brother?"

Peter gave the knight his most teasing smile. "Well, I am not sure –"

So then Richard kneaded himself deeper into Peter's body, sending the monk into fits of joyful screaming. The knight kept sliding his body back and forth against the monk while saying, "Warm enough there? How about if I do this? And this? Or if I move against you like this, and then rub this way against you like that?"

In between howls of laughter, Peter continued to tease the knight. "No, not yet. No, that is not working either. Harder like that. Oh, I did not mean harder as in – oh, just shut me up for God's sake! Harder is fine too. Ooh, that was rather nice, do that again!" And so on until Richard was laughing with high-pitched exuberance.

In addition to body pressure, Richard was kissing, licking and sucking every part of Peter he could get to with ecstatic abandonment and kept the monk VERY warm for an extensive passage of time. Finally, the two men climaxed simultaneously within a cocoon of oblivious joy.

"La tua anima mi riempie di passione!"

"Um, I –"

Richard placed a playful forefinger across Peter's lips as he told the monk, "I said your soul fills me with passion."

"Well, I am certainly filled up with SOMETHING," Peter said as he removed Richard's finger and sucked it.

"I am ready. Give it all to me. *Ho fame del tuo tocco. Bramo i tuoi gusti – la tue pelle – le tue labra.*"

"Oh my!" Peter gasped.

Richard smiled. "I keep forgetting which language I am speaking in. I said I hunger for your touch. I crave your taste – your skin – your lips."

"If I had known you would be so hungry, I would have brought some food to eat," Peter joked.

Richard laughed with a shake of his head. Then when he stared at Peter's chest, both of his eyebrows arched.

"What?" Peter asked.

"The cold has made your pretty nipples extra perky."

Peter looked at Richard's chest, passing tentative fingers across Richard's two dark and firm nipples. "The cold is doing the same to YOUR pretty nipples as well."

"How convenient for us. The more to enjoy each other's nipples," Richard said as he playfully licked and sucked both of Peter's extra perky teats.

"Warm enough now, beloved brother?"

"Oh, yes," Peter sighed with pure contentment.

"Good, I am glad to hear that. **Sei mio per sempre.**" {"You are my forever."}

Richard bent forward and kissed each of Peter's eyes.

"Occhi stupendi," Richard whispered.

"What?"

"I was commenting on your beautiful eyes."

"Oh."

Richard kissed the tip of Peter's nose.

"Bel naso."

"What?"

"I was admiring your beautiful nose.

"Oh."

Richard nuzzled against one side of Peter's throat, then kissed the other side.

"Bella gola."

"What?"

"I was appreciating your beautiful throat."

Finally, Peter understood Richard kissed whatever body part the knight would mention next in his native tongue.

Richard carefully and delicately, kissed each of Peter's lips.

"Belle labbra."

"You are appreciating my mouth."

Richard momentarily shook a forefinger back and forth and emitted a funny sort of growl. "Not exactly."

Peter thought a moment. "Oh, I get it! You did not say mouth. *'Labbra'* must mean lips."

Richard rewarded Peter with a deeply sensual kiss. "You are correct."

Richard next lowered himself slightly to Peter's chest and curled his tongue enticingly around each of Peter's nipples.

"Bellisimi capezzoli!" Richard exclaimed triumphantly and kissed each nipple.

"You like my nipples."

"That I do, my love. That I do."

"I like your nipples, too. A lot."

"That is always good to know."

"I have an idea!" Peter exclaimed.

"Please share it."

"Perhaps from now on, we should refer to our nipples as our 'Clairs'."

Richard laughed uproariously. "And we each have two nipples, so our nipples are brothers. Therefore, our 'Brothers Clair'!"

Peter joined him in the laughter. "That is hysterical. I think Brother Clair would be most appreciative of our newly baptised 'Brothers Clair'."

Richard next kissed each of Peter's shoulders.

"Bella spalla."

"I like your shoulders, too."

"Thank you."

Richard lowered himself some more and kissed Peter's navel. ***"Bellisimo ombelico."***

"I love your stomach as well."

Richard looked up at Peter and shook his head.

"No?"

"No."

"But you kissed my stomach."

Again, Richard shook his head.

"Funny, I could have SWORN that was my stomach."

Richard stuck the tip of his tongue into Peter's navel and tickled with his tongue back and forth inside Peter's navel.

"Oh, oh, oh!" Peter laughed. "Not my stomach! My navel!"

"Bellisimo!" Richard crowed.

"This is fun! Where to next?"

The two men's lips locked with an intense force of ecstatic love.

Releasing their lips to better breathe, Richard stared deeply into Peter's eyes and murmured, ***"Mi fai cantare il cuore."***

"And the same to you," Peter said.

Richard smiled and ran his forefinger down Peter's nose, lips and bearded chin. "I said you make my heart sing."

"Then I was right."

Richard lowered himself back down upon Peter and rubbed his penis alongside Peter's hard shaft. But in the next moment, Orion nuzzled the back of Richard's head and neighed impatiently, causing both men to break out in hysterical laughter.

"Our lovemaking seems to have reached its climax," Richard said.

"That is very funny," Peter said, wondering if the pun had been intentional or accidental.

"Our time is up. Orion wants the three of us to go home."

"Orion always knows best," Peter replied. "We should do as he suggests."

Richard helped Peter to an upright position, and then the two men quickly put their robes and capes back on.

Before mounting Orion, Richard paused with a sudden thought.

"What?" Peter asked.

"I could teach you my language."

Peter seriously considered that for a moment, then shook his head with a chuckle.

"What?" Richard asked.

"I am afraid that if I could speak your language, I would end up ejaculating all over myself all the time."

"We have a word for someone like that in my language."

"I am sure you do!" Peter said with a laugh.

"Ti amo," Richard murmured.

"I love you, too."

Orion neighed impatiently, shaking his head.

"Immediamente, Orion!" Richard called out to his horse.

"That word sounded a lot like immediately."

Richard nodded. "You see, you are already learning my language."

Orion stomped a front hoof and neighed.

"Orion has spoken again," Richard said with a laugh.

"Okay, I suppose we SHOULD be getting back to the monastery," Peter said. "Anyway, thank you very much for an afternoon of keeping me sufficiently warm."

Richard embraced the monk and held him tightly again with all his enormous strength.

"Believe me, my beloved brother, it has been MY greatest pleasure."

Peter was about to remount Orion when the knight held the monk back a moment and then turned Peter to face him. Richard stared adoringly into Peter's eyes.

"What is it?" Peter asked.

"There is something I wish to say to you from the depth of my soul."

"Yes?"

Richard took a deep breath before he began. "From the first time I held your hands, my soul and my body knew that our hands were meant to hold one another passionately and forever. This is why, for me, it has never felt like I was just meeting you for the first time or gradually getting to know you. Instead, from the very beginning it has been me REMEMBERING you from somewhere before.

"It has been to me as if we have lived together lifetime after lifetime, choosing to come back again and again to re-meet and fall in love, over and over again for eternity.

"I am grateful to have found you again my great love," Richard continued, "because all I ever want to do is to live every lifetime loving you forever."

Peter cried with a depth of joy he never knew possible to experience. To look into Richard's eyes was to see into the infinite depth of the Divine. Peter threw his arms around Richard's neck and kissed the knight with all the passion he could generate.

Orion neighed with extra vigour.

"Hey, have a little patience, please," Peter implored the horse in between kisses to Richard. "This is a very deep and loving moment we are sharing here!"

Orion shook his head and neighed again.

"Okay, okay, we are leaving. Forgive us for daring to want to express our love to one another!"

Richard laughed as he helped Peter mount the steed. Then Richard mounted Orion behind the monk and held Peter in a tight left-arm embrace.

"Home to the monastery," Richard said as he guided his horse towards the east.

———◆◆◆———

Richard and Peter entered the monk's private cell. Richard no longer needed to sleep in the infirmary, so he now slept each night with his beloved. As Peter shut the door, Richard threw off his cloak and robe, lay down on Peter's bed and held out his arms to the monk.

"Amato fratello. Ti adore," Richard said in a husky whisper.

Peter remembered what those words meant – "Beloved brother, I adore you." Between hearing the Italian words spoken by Richard's sensual baritone voice and looking at the knight's muscular naked body with the fully erect penis pointing directly at him, Peter felt that he would either explode in ecstasy or melt into the Earth.

"Richard, you know that every time you speak in your language, it makes me want to ejaculate!"

Richard grinned mischievously. "In that case," he announced, **"La luna è blu. Scoreggia come una scimmia paradisiaca. Patate e cuccioli di orso. Sedersi sudi me e spin. Baciami, stupido. Mi benedica quando scoreggia come un angelo!"** {"The moon is blue. You fart like a heavenly monkey. Potatoes and baby bears. Sit on me and spin. Kiss me, you fool. You bless me when you fart like an angel."}

"Now you have done it!" Peter shrieked. "I am ready to ejaculate!"

"So come and grab me! No, no, that is not right," Richard corrected himself with a grin. "I mean, grab me and come!"

Peter threw off his cape and robe and plunged on top of Richard, who smothered the monk in endless kisses.

Afterwards the two men cleaned each other up most thoroughly and playfully. Finally Peter had mastered the art of enjoying his work.

———————◆◆◆———————

"I can see from that look in your eyes," Richard said with a smile, "that you want to ask me about something."

"I am sorry."

"Oh, no. Please, never be sorry. I enjoy your curiosity. So please ask me."

"Okay. You have travelled so far and have seen so much, while I have hardly gone anywhere. So I was just wondering, who were the most interesting people that you met on your travels?"

"That is a very good question, Peter. Let me think a moment."

Richard's thinking process, of course, required him to kiss Peter now and then. After several kisses, this apparently enabled Richard to find the answer to Peter's question.

"When I was in España, or Spain, I met some fascinating people in the town of Toledo in the centre of the country. They were an amazing group of Hebrew, Muhammadan and Mithran philosophers, doctors and teachers."

"Mithran? You mean followers of the fire god Mithras?" Peter asked with surprise. "Apparently, during the Roman occupation of this island, there were many Roman soldiers who worshipped Mithras. I have also heard that some of their small temples still exist along the great wall you crossed over from Northumbria to enter Alba."

"Yes," Richard said. "These Mithrans I met in Toledo were descendants of those who had come to ancient Egypt from Sumeria further east – all in search of deeper spiritual knowledge."

"That must have been quite a fascinating group of people," Peter remarked with heightened interest. "But in this group of scholars you met, you did not mention any Christians."

"There were none in that group."

"No Christians at all among them?"

Richard shook his head.

"Interesting. But please, continue."

"Somehow these men from vastly different religious and cultural backgrounds lived and worked together quite harmoniously in Toledo. And all of them were dedicated to understanding the workings of life and the Universe to the greatest depth that they could achieve. It was magnificent to behold their group commitment to the Highest Truth."

"How did they end up in Spain together?"

"That was the most interesting thing about them. They all claimed to be descended from ancestors who had left ancient Egypt a few years after Moses led the Hebrews to freedom after their many years in slavery."

"What? You mean that not all the Hebrews left Egypt with Moses?"

"According to these men, no. Some Hebrews stayed behind because they felt their destiny was to go elsewhere than to the Promised Land with Moses."

"Why?" Peter was completely intrigued.

"Apparently, some Hebrews felt they had a separate destiny that required different studies and investigations into the Cosmos. They also believed that this would lead them into different lands and cultures."

"I have never heard of this before," Peter said with wonder.

"Nor had I. But it intrigued me. And it also felt so true in the depths of my soul."

"So then what happened?" Peter asked.

"According to these Toledo scholars, their ancestors felt guided to leave Egypt a few years after Moses had departed with the majority of the Hebrews. Those Hebrews who had remained, along with some Egyptian mystics and many Mithrans living in Egypt but originally from Sumeria, left together, headed north to the port that is today called Alexandria and then sailed to the southern coast of Gaul, or what is today France."

"Of course," Peter pointed out, "there would have been no Muhammadans with them at that time. Muhammadans have only been around for – what? – less than a hundred years? So the Muhammadans you met must have joined that group very recently."

"I would think so. Maybe some came to Spain crossing over from North Africa."

"But why the exodus from Gaul – I mean, France?" Peter asked. "Why didn't they remain there?"

"Their ancestors felt – knew within – that France was not the right place for them. They continued journeying until they arrived in what is today Toledo, south of Madrid, in central Spain."

"I wonder why that was their rightful place?"

Richard shook his head. "Who knows the deeper reasons for anything that happens in our lives?"

Peter nodded. "True enough. Then what happened?"

"According to them, many generations of their ancestors remained in central Spain, pursuing their spiritual studies. But several centuries later, some of the descendants in Toledo began to feel an inner call to continue migrating further north."

"What is Cosmos up to?" Peter wondered.

Richard chuckled. "Many of us would like to know the answer to that."

"Do you know what Richard is talking about?"

"No," Peter's spirit-guide raven replied. *"I have never heard about any of this before."*

"But I thought you knew –"

Peter's raven swiped a wing towards the other bird to quiet him. *"Shhh, I want to hear all of this!"*

———————◆◦◉◦◆———————

"So," Peter asked, "some chose to remain in Spain after several centuries of living there, while others felt to move on?"

"Yes," Richard nodded.

"And where did the ones who left Spain end up?"

"On the island of Eire." {Ireland}

"Eire?" Peter asked with great surprise. Why?"

Richard shrugged. "Who can answer that? The Toledo scholars told me that many centuries ago their ancestors split into two factions – those who remained in Spain and those who migrated to Eire. The ones who left Spain felt they were being guided to begin a new culture on a special island enhanced with mystical energies and Nature Spirits whom they would learn to work with."

Peter frowned, lost in deep thought.

"What is it?" Richard asked.

"Good God!" Peter gasped.

"What?"

"When the ancient Celts first arrived on Eire over eight hundred years ago, they too arrived from Spain, after many centuries of migrating across Europe. We have always been told by our Druid bards that our Celtic ancestors encountered a race of beings on Eire known as the *Tuatha dé Danann.*"

"I have never heard of them," Richard said.

"They were supposedly the inhabitants of Eire when these original Celts arrived. Some Celts said the *Tuatha dé Danann* were a sacred race of beings – not human but from other dimensions of existence. Beings such as faeries, leprechauns and elves. But I just wonder –"

"What?"

"Maybe the *Tuatha dé Danann* were not otherworldly beings at all but humans like us – descendants of those ancient Hebrews, Egyptians and Mithrans who had settled on Eire long before the arrival of my Celtic ancestors but who had actually worked with the genuine otherworldly beings."

Richard shrugged. "Who knows. Anything is possible. But tell me, what does *Tuatha dé* whatever you said mean?"

"*Tuatha dé Danann*. It means the tribe of the Goddess Dannan – also known as Danu. She was the river goddess and also Mother Goddess of all Celtic deities. She generated fertility and abundance."

"I see. She sounds most impressive."

Peter nodded. "If the *Tuatha dé Danann* were in fact descendants of Hebrews, Egyptians and Mithrans who left ancient Egypt so long before, they would most probably have APPEARED as alien and godlike to most people, including my own Celtic ancestors. And if the *Tuatha dé Danann* did indeed manage to communicate and cooperate with genuine otherworldly beings, then all the more reason to see *Tuatha dé Danann* as otherworldly as well."

"Anything is possible," Richard agreed.

"I am curious about something."

"Good. Ask me," Richard said.

"Why did you not stay with them? Not that I wish you did – because then I would never have met you!"

"At the time I was there, they were enduring mounting problems with envious intolerance and fear from the Christians settling across Spain and who were seizing more control over the country. As fascinating as I found the group, I did not want to remain in that escalating conflict that can only eventually end up in bloodshed as it almost always does with fearfully intolerant Christian nations. And while they felt it was right for them to be there, it somehow did NOT feel right for ME to remain there. I felt the urge to move north, but not to Eire."

"To here," Peter said.

"Yes, to Alba. And now I know why."

"Why?" Peter asked with genuine innocence.

Richard gave Peter his happiest grin. "In order to find and love YOU."

Later that night Richard and Peter lay naked together on the monk's bed. Peter's right cheek rested on Richard's right nipple, while Peter's left hand rested on the knight's other famous nipple. But Richard was in deep troubled thought as he lightly stroked the monk's hair.

"What am I going to do? Spring is coming soon, and the roads will be free of snow and ice. I am sufficiently healed and have no real excuse for staying much longer at this monastery."

Slow tears leaked from Richard's eyes as he continued to stroke Peter's dark hair. The knight's practical thoughts were now tinged with growing stress and fear.

"Soon I must go back south to Northumbria. But how can I possibly leave this man I love with all my heart and soul? I cannot live without Peter.

"Do I dare suggest that Peter leave his community and come with me? Would he want to? Would he be allowed to? And what happens if he does come with me? How could I explain his presence with me? How could we possibly share a life together that would be accepted by others?

"And worse still — how do I explain to Peter all that I have not yet shared with him? The secrets I have withheld from him. Will he leave me once he knows the whole story?

"MY GOD, what have I done?" Richard cried inside himself, with new tears streaming down his bearded face. *"I have created a situation that will erupt in our faces and destroy us both. But I cannot bear that thought. I need Peter in my life — but I have secrets that might destroy our love. I HAVE TRAPPED MYSELF WITH NO WAY OUT!"*

While Richard lay tormenting, Peter pretended to be asleep on the knight's firm breast. But Peter's mind too was racing with fears.

"The time is coming soon when Richard must return to the king of Northumbria. Richard is almost healed now and able to leave — but it will be the end of me. I will return to my life of utter loneliness and duty — without the man I love. Soon I will lose him forever."

Peter considered some alternatives to that disaster. *"Or could I somehow go with Richard? Would he want me? Do I dare ask him? Or would that pressure Richard in some way? Would I look needy asking him that? And even if I dared to ask Richard, would he possibly say no?*

"I am so pathetic! Like that young weakling Brother Andrew with his neediness and — OH MY GOD!"

Peter was having a shocking epiphany.

"That is the REAL reason why I have scorned Brother Andrew all this time. Not because he is weak and needy, but because HE WAS MIRRORING ALL THOSE SAME PROBLEMS INSIDE ME! I am afraid that I cannot live without Richard and his strength. And yet I am too scared to ask Richard if I can go with him. I would be shattered by a no answer because I do not love and trust myself and my own strength. I FEEL SO TRAPPED!"

The two men continued pretending to be asleep as they lay suffering quietly in each other's arms but not daring to speak openly to each other about their similar fears.

<hr />

"CRAP!" thought Peter's raven as he sat just outside the window to Peter's cell. The raven was telepathically attuned to the misery that these two men were inflicting upon themselves.

"Why do humans constantly imprison themselves with both the fear of communicating and the fear of anticipated negative results? These unacknowledged blockages create great pain for humans over and over, lifetime after lifetime – but without them ever seemingly learning from it. I am helpless to assist. They must make their own choices and live out the consequences. CRAP!"

The pain inside the two lovers – and within the disappointed raven as well – was all too much for him to bear any longer. With a shake of his head, the raven flew away into the dark of night, sending the two humans the only thing he could give them – his loving compassion.

Fourteen

PETER LAY IN bed on his stomach with Richard on top of him.

Richard thrust his erect penis rhythmically into Peter's anus, sometimes slow and gentle and at other times with speed and passion. This created an ongoing slapping sound between their naked bodies. With each thrust from Richard, Peter pushed his bottom back against the knight's body.

"Mi – dai così – tanto amore – e piacere," Richard spoke between his forceful drives into Peter.

"What – did – you – say?" Peter asked between the plunges of Richard's erect penis.

"You – give – me – so – much – love – and – pleasure."

"As – you – do – to – me."

As Richard continued to rhythmically penetrate inside Peter, the knight thought to himself, *"Entrarvi è entrare nell'Anima di Dio."* {"To enter you is to enter the Soul of God."}

After his prolonged orgasm, Richard gently pulled his penis out of Peter and turned the ravished monk over onto his back. Richard smiled lovingly into Peter's eyes.

"As much as I savour entering you," Richard said softly, "nothing compares with looking into your beautiful eyes and lying with you nipples to nipples."

"Or," Peter suggested, "would that be Brothers Clair to Brothers Clair – or Brother Clairs to Brother Clairs?" referring to the nickname the two men had given their nipples.

Richard pondered the question a moment. "That is the same as asking how you correctly pronounce the name of the Northumbrian king."

"You have a point."

Richard resumed lavishing kisses on Peter's face, shoulders and most importantly the monk's Brother Clair nipples. "I want to fill you with all the love and passion I can every day and every night."

"You certainly are filling me up with a lot of something!" Peter said with a straight face.

"*I got it – I got it!*" the usually cynical raven cried out triumphantly.

"*What ARE you cawing on about this time?*" asked Peter's raven.

"*Listen to this – **Lunga vita alla passione Veneta!***"

"*Did you just say 'long live Venetian passion'?*"

"*Yes I did! You were right – we ravens CAN speak any language on Earth because of our telepathy. I tried it, and it worked!*"

"*Good for you.*"

"*It is wonderful to be a raven!*"

"*Actually, all birds and the whole animal kingdom can do this.*"

"*Not as good as we can.*"

"*Sure – whatever.*"

The next morning a strange mounting energy smothered the monastery and all its surroundings. Without anyone understanding what was taking place, all the monks moved slowly and spoke in hushed tones and as little as possible. Something was coming, building up slowly but incessantly – and no one knew what it was or why it was coming.

Throughout the day all the monks struggled with every movement as if weighed down by invisible hefty stones upon their shoulders. Even the surrounding nature was unusually silent and still. Most mornings one could hear at least a few birds chirping or the occasional scampering of deer through the neighbouring woods. Today, however, there was no sense of movement or sound anywhere. It was as if Life Itself had come to a deathly standstill.

"This heavy silence is driving me nuts!" the usually chirpy Brother Clair said to Father Abbot Paul. "You can hear a worm fart!"

But the shocked Father Abbot could only nod in silent agreement.

The sky was a vast and unbroken grey slate -- no sense of cloud shapes, no sense of movement, not even the slightest wind or breeze. Just this utter silence and the burdensome stillness

The whole day dragged heavily with a sense of impending doom.

Almost all of the monks were unusually nervous, wondering if it was the preamble to the end of the world or the initiation of some horrific plague or release of a monstrous annihilation.

Even Richard and Peter were quiet, each caught up in his own thoughts and fears – but both still choosing to keep their inner torments to themselves and not open up to one another. Since noon Clair, known to all as the eternal jovial monk, was suddenly nowhere to be seen. As for the constantly grim Prior Thomas, none of the monks had seen or heard from him in several days, although most of them were actually grateful for that.

However, one individual HAD seen the prior two days before this mysteriously brewing morning. Richard had been in the stables brushing down Orion's flanks and murmuring lovingly to his beloved steed.

"I gain so much peace from taking care of you," Richard murmured to Orion. "Brushing your back and legs is like a meditation for me, calming my nerves and helping me feel safe and secure."

Orion snorted to let Richard know he understood what the knight was telling him.

"But all this sweet talk is not feeding you, my friend. So I need to find you some fresh hay. After all, *le belle parole non danno da mangiare a un cavallo*!" {"After all, pretty words do not feed a horse."}

Passing by, Prior Thomas heard Richard's warm baritone voice, although the prior was still too far away to make out any specific words or ascertain Richard's foreign accent. The prior entered the stables and saw Richard dressed in a monk's robe and brushing down the horse.

"Well, this is a sweet picture!" Thomas commented with bitter irony.

Richard stopped and stared at the prior.

"So lovey-dovey with the horse, but always cold and arrogant, belligerent, and insufferably obsessive with the rest of us."

Richard raised both eyebrows in puzzled innocence.

"Do not try that innocent look with me, you horrendous fake! You are hard as stone, except with that knight who has become your latest obsession."

Now Richard understood. The prior was confusing him with Peter. Then the knight's stare softened to a look of compassion.

"Do not dare use that condescending look with me, you vile monster!" Thomas spat, completely misunderstanding the look in Richard's eyes.

"You poor, poor man," Richard said quietly. "I feel deeply for you."

Thomas stepped awkwardly backwards as he suddenly realised he had made an incorrect assumption. 'Brother Peter' was speaking with that foreign accent!

Richard nodded. "Yes, Prior, I am not Brother Peter. I am Richard, sir, the knight and your very grateful guest."

Thomas felt stupid at his error but immediately attacked again. "How dare you call me a poor, poor man! You can go to Hell!"

"Prior, I feel very sorry for you, truly," Richard said with quiet patience. "You are obviously trapped within your own self-created Hell. And by the look of it, probably for a very long time. Your pain must be unbearable."

Thomas began to cry, something no one at the monastery had ever witnessed before.

The knight tried again. "If you ever feel the need to —"

Before Richard could finish his sentence, the prior turned and fled the stables.

Orion waited patiently for Richard to resume brushing the horse's flanks, as the knight stared after the departed prior.

"Pur troppo un po pazzo. Povero uomo," Richard commented with great compassion. {"Sadly a little bit crazy. Poor man."}

That was the last time anyone saw the prior alive – but only Richard knew that.

———◆◆◆———

"That Prior Thomas is certainly parsimonious with his compliments and compassion," one raven said to the other. *"How he ever became the prior is beyond my understanding."*

"I do not know about all that," the usually cynical raven replied, *"but he seemed rather stingy to me."*

"That is what I said."

"No, you did not. You said he was par-par-sim-something or other."

"Parsimonious. That means stingy."

"Then why not just say so?"

"I did."

"No, you did not. You said par – oh, never mind. You just use fancier words to try to impress me."

"It is not my fault you are lacking in a more expansive vocabulary."

"Do shut up! Why is Prior Thomas so par – uh, stingy?"

"He has desires that are unfulfilled. He feels deeply rejected, but he does not understand that he is rejected because of his cruelty towards others."

"Then why be so cruel all the time?"

"He is in constant emotional pain which results in physical pain as well. But his need to deny and escape all his self-created pains, emotional AND physical, is what results in his cruel behaviour that then turns people away from him. It is a never-ending circle, and he does not yet grasp this."

"I am so relieved I am not a human. These karmic lessons they must learn are too hard and complex for me to even think about."

"I would not be surprised at all if your insistent judgemental ignorance results in YOU needing to become a human."

The other raven cawed fearfully. *"Is that even possible? Can we ACTUALLY end up incarnating as humans?"*

His companion raven's lack of a response sent shivers down his feathery back. *"Shit!"* the cynical raven cawed as he flew away.

"And now I know how to get rid of that pest whenever he starts to incessantly bitch about humans."

———•◆•———

Peter was walking quickly down the corridor to collect Richard's lunch when he passed three monks in animated conversation. The increasing build-up of atmospheric energy was turning him, like everyone else in the monastery, into a nervous shambles. He was now super-sensitive to everything, which was bad news to the already nervous trio of monks Peter approached in the corridor.

"It is a pity," Peter overheard one of the monks say to the other two, "but the truth is, if you do not accept Jesus as your Lord and Saviour, then you are certainly condemned to eternal hellfire. That is just the way it is."

Infuriated, Peter marched right up to the group of gossiping monks and slapped the one who had spoken last across his forehead. The slapped monk's eyes teared up with fury while the other two monks gawked in shock.

"So," Peter spat angrily, "according to you, you brainless nitwit, anyone living in a far distant land is condemned to eternal tormenting damnation just because he never heard of Jesus and therefore was not able to accept Jesus as his Lord and Saviour? Are you out of your idiotic mind? God is a God of infinite love and forgiveness, but if you do not believe in Him the 'right way' you are condemned to Hell? Really?"

Peter was about to leave when he instead slapped the monk across the forehead a second time."

"Why did you do that again?" the monk cried.

"Stupidity should be PAINFUL!" Peter next put his face right up to the monk he had slapped again and yelled in his loudest voice, "Oh, and another thing – Christ's name was not Jesus. Jesus is a Greek name, and they were not speaking Greek in Israel when he lived there. They were speaking Aramaic. So NO ONE there called him Jesus! They would have called him Yeshua. Why can Christians not worship someone with his correct name? Grow a brain, you sententious little shit!" Finished with his fury, Peter stormed off.

The three monks stared after the departing Peter in fuming shock. "What idiot said Brother Peter has become a nicer person since meeting the knight?" asked the twice-slapped monk.

———◆◆◆———

"Do humans honestly believe that load of crap?" one of the ravens asked.

"Oh, you are back. That is a shame. Oh well. Unfortunately, many of them do," the other raven conceded.

"This invention of religions has to be the dumbest and most profoundly destructive thing humans ever came up with. Why have they not annihilated one another a long time ago?"

"Now, now. Try to calm down and look at this in another way," the second raven counselled. *"Their creation of religions provides an extremely important tool to help humans learn deeper truths about themselves as spiritual beings. This belief in religions is a stage most humans must go through and learn from – each in their own way and in their own time."*

"And when do you think these idiotic humans will learn these deeper lessons – a million years from now?"

"Linear time is irrelevant," the second raven insisted.

"Tell that to the human souls reincarnating again and again to suffer as victims of this religious crap over the next million of your LINEAR years!"

"Never mind," the second raven sighed hopelessly.

"And another thing – what in damnation is going on with your monk? I agree those other monks are brainless idiots, but your monk is completely out of control."

"Have you not noticed there is a tremendously powerful energy surge in the atmosphere around here? Something is coming that will change everything, including us. This energy surge is affecting everyone on a deep emotional level – including YOU, I might add."

"As if humans need the excuse of an energy surge to get themselves all riled up."

"Anything else you want to complain about?"

"Well, not exactly complain, but –"

"What?"

"Your monk called the other monk sententious. What the hell does that mean?"

"It means someone who makes very pompous judgements on moral issues, as the slapped monk did about those who do not accept Jesus – or Yeshua – as their Lord. But why did you not understand the word 'sententious'? Being telepathic, you should automatically understand everything."

"I forgot."

"You forgot? What – to be telepathic? How do you think you and I are communicating?"

"I do not understand anything. I am thoroughly confused."

The second raven sighed and shrugged as only ravens can do. *"By the way, have you thought any more about my theory that YOU could eventually end up reincarnated as a human?"*

The other raven cawed fearfully and once again flew away.

"Yes!" The remaining raven exclaimed. *"I have him now!"*

———◆◆———

Richard stood up with a gleaming smile when Peter walked into his private cell with the knight's lunch. Peter set the lunch on his small table, walked over to Richard and then pleasantly shocked the knight by grabbing Richard's bearded face and passionately kissing him. Richard blinked several times in wonderment.

"I love you, God damn it!" Peter announced dramatically. When Richard was about to say something, Peter immediately held up a halting hand and said, "I know. My cursing just now has aroused you. It arouses me too. But I just wanted you to know that I love you more than I can ever express with words. And any monks who disapprove of our love can sit on it and spin for all eternity!"

Raising both eyebrows, Richard was about to ask what monks Peter was referring to. But Peter grabbed the knight's face and kissed him again.

"I want you inside of me and all over me, and I want to do the same to you," Peter announced. "But I really must get back to my work immediately. However, I will return. And then I want to love you some more." Peter turned to leave but stopped to once more face a grinning but stunned Richard. "Oh, and one more thing – you can manage your lunch on your own, you beautiful man I love more than Life Itself."

Richard stared in awe as Peter left his cell, and then the knight laughed uproariously.

"God, how I love you, Peter!"

Later that day Peter was in the library's scriptorium working on transcribing a biblical text onto parchment, when the door to the library burst open. Richard entered quickly and then slammed the door shut behind him.

"Can this door be locked?"

Peter was double-jolted, first by the door slamming and then by Richard's question. Seeing it was indeed Richard, Peter relaxed immediately.

"Locked? Are you kidding, Richard? This is a monastery in the middle of nowhere in Alba. There is no such thing as a locked door here."

"Damn!" Richard hissed.

Peter smiled. "Oooh, now YOU are talking dirty. That excites my *pene*."

"Your excitement has me excited."

"And that is why you want the door locked?"

"Ho fame per tuoi gusti!" Richard stated with lust in his eyes.

"Um, I need to understand you in order to give you what you want."

"I hunger for your taste."

"Ah!"

"I need to taste you, Peter – and smell you and feel you against me. Something is building up in this heavy atmosphere, and it is driving me insane. I must embrace you and explore you with all my senses. *Adesso!*"

"I am guessing *adesso* means RIGHT NOW?"

Richard nodded, licked his lips seductively and looked at Peter with tormented eyes.

Peter laid down his quill, stood up and stretched out both his arms to Richard. "If you cannot wait, then certainly you should not have to. I am all yours."

"But what if someone comes in?"

"They will look at what we are doing and then run for the hills as if the Devil Himself were after them."

So Richard rushed to Peter and embraced the monk, smothering him with exuberant kisses.

"Your robe is in the way," Richard complained.

"So is yours."

Richard whipped off his robe in a few seconds and then did the same with Peter's robe.

"This is so much better!" Richard announced, once they were both naked.

"I quite agree."

Richard held out his arms. "Now I am **pronto**."

"I guess that is good. Should I be as well?"

Richard laughed. "I only said that I am ready. But what if someone enters?"

"I thought YOU were going to do all the entering."

Richard grinned. "What a marvellous idea! But really, Peter, what if someone does come in here?"

Peter turned Richard around to look at the knight's taut naked butt and grinned. "Then they will see this magnificent full moon."

Richard turned back to face Peter and started kissing the monk all over his body. "You taste heavenly. Both sweet and spicy at the same time."

As Peter moaned, Richard's tongue swirled around both of the monk's nipples and then glided upwards along the right side of the monk's neck. When Richard reached Peter's lips, he kissed his beloved brother with frenzied rapture.

"Ah," Richard whispered. "Here comes a new sensation that is you. **Sonti l'odore della Terra nella fresca rugiada del mattino.**"

"That sounded wonderful, but what does it mean?"

"My passion for you makes me forget to speak in your language. I said you smell like the Earth in the fresh morning dew."

"Oh, Richard! Is that a good thing?"

"My love, you have no idea!"

Then Richard sniffed both sides of Peter's neck, his hair, the cleft between his breasts and of course both nipples too.

"You smell – of the Divinity."

"Oh my!"

"Now it is your turn, Peter. What do I taste and smell like to you?"

Peter grinned. "I will certainly enjoy exploring you!"

Peter licked Richard's shoulders, upper arms, breasts and abdomen. Then Peter pushed his tongue against Richard's lips until they parted. Peter's tongue caressed Richard's thoroughly.

When Peter finally removed his exploring tongue, Richard laughed and asked, "What was THAT?"

"I was curious to taste your taster."

"And?"

"Somehow you taste of apples and silky bread, of meaty sauces and earthy wonder. And now for your smell."

Peter sniffed all over Richard's hair, face, neck, shoulders and chest. "Oh, you smell like angelic glory, like divine passion, like love and lust, peace and eternity."

Richard and Peter stood naked and kissing each other with a strength that roared with passion and soul-love.

Then the library door creaked open and someone DID enter – Brother Clair. He took one look at Richard and Peter naked and embracing, murmured, "Glory be to Heaven!" and stepped back out, closing the door as silently as he could.

"Was somebody just here?" Richard asked without removing his lips from Peter's.

"Who cares?"

"You are right."

After more kissing, the men finally parted lips.

"Whatever is happening outside in the atmosphere, it feels too overwhelming. When will you be finished here, Peter?"

"I think in about another hour."

"I will wait in your cell. Come to me as soon as you can. I want you and need you – more today than ever before."

"I will be with you as soon as I can."

"Hurry," Richard said as he kissed Peter once more before heading for the door.

"Uh, Richard."

Richard turned. "Yes?"

"Full moon?" Peter said, pointing to Richard's naked body.

The knight glanced down to his still erect penis. "Good God!" Richard said with a grin as he quickly grabbed his robe and pulled it back on.

"I will be with you soon," Peter repeated as he also re-dressed into his robe.

Richard headed back to Peter's cell and thought contentedly to himself, *"Il tuo amore mi sostiene."* {"Your love sustains me."}

———◆•◆•◆———

But Richard was restless in his heart as well as in his body. He could not simply go back to Peter's personal cell and passively wait for his beloved brother to return to him. His nervousness towards what was building in the atmosphere made him need to keep moving, to talk to someone, to do anything except sit alone in a cell and wait.

So Richard wandered aimlessly around the monastery courtyard, oblivious to the patches of snow and ice and the blowing arctic wind. He re-entered the monastery and marched up and down the hall, desperately needing to hold Peter in his arms, needing the safety and security of company, desiring to calm his restlessness.

The knight continued his endless back-and-forth pacing in the hall when he heard a magnificent singing voice coming from inside the infirmary. It was a beautiful tenor voice, rich in emotional texture that stimulated Richard's heart and brought tears to his eyes. He could not understand the words because the voice sang in a language unknown to him. And yet not understanding the words made no difference. The singing vibrations moved him profoundly and filled him with feelings of longing, wistfulness, enrichment, familial love and exalting hope.

"Who is singing in this magnificent voice?" Richard asked out loud. He had to know immediately. Listening to this tenor music filled

204

him with joy and a calming peace to his previous frustration, restlessness and vague fear.

The knight reached the infirmary door, quietly opened it and then peeked in. Brother Bartholomew was moving quickly around the infirmary tidying up the large room and making sure everything was neatly in its proper place. With the infirmary door open, Bartholomew's voice was now louder, richer and deeply moving to Richard on all levels of this thinking and feeling. Then the knight realised he was actually trembling with wonderment at Bartholomew's voice, and he felt suddenly healed and transformed by this monk's magical singing.

"Magnifico!" Richard announced with awe.

The singing stopped abruptly, and Bartholomew turned towards Richard's voice at the door.

"Are you, Richard or Brother Peter? I swear I cannot tell you two apart when you are both clad in our robes."

"It is I, Richard. I am sorry to disturb you, but I heard you singing, and it was so beautiful, so powerful, so MOVING!"

Bartholomew blushed a bright crimson as he gave a little bow. "That is very kind of you, Richard. Thank you. No one has ever before praised my singing – and with such abundant praise!"

"I find that very hard to believe, Bartholomew. Your voice has healed and inspired me. I was feeling very distressed by whatever storm is building up outside, so I went in search of Peter for comfort. But he is still working in the scriptorium, and I could not interrupt him with my personal sorrows. I was headed back to his cell when I found myself wandering aimlessly around the monastery, not knowing how to calm my nerves. And then I heard you singing and was instantly transformed. Your voice is beautiful and powerfully healing."

A few tears glistened on the bearded cheeks of Bartholomew's still-blushing face. "Oh my! Did my signing do that for you? No one has ever said THAT to me before as well."

"Yes, your voice helped me so instantly and profoundly. And again, I find it very hard to believe no one has experienced for themselves what I just did with your voice, much less share it with you. Surely everyone not only notices the beauty and healing gift of your voice, but they have also have benefited greatly from it."

Bartholomew shook his head. "Unfortunately, as I believe I have mentioned to you before, all of us monks here at the abbey have a tendency to never compliment one another, ask questions about our lives or share much of anything between us. Not a good tendency for a so-called family of monks, but there it is."

"That is a shame. You deserve to be fully and constantly complimented. I am deeply moved and transformed by your voice, and I am most grateful."

Bartholomew nodded but was unable to say anything as he felt slightly uncomfortable with the abundant praises from Richard.

"Could I ask you, Bartholomew, what were you singing? What kind of song was it, and what do the words mean?"

"Again, no one has ever asked me that before. I am deeply moved, Richard. Thank you for your interest. I appreciate it."

"And I appreciate you too – for all you have done to nurse me back to health. And now also for your beautiful, comforting singing voice. What were you singing?"

"Well now, let me think for a minute. I need to translate this vey old Celtic dialect so you will understand the words." Bartholomew stood silently musing over the lyrics. "I can do it now for you, roughly in our present dialect. What I was singing was this:

Long ago the trees' last leaves
Dropped and decayed.
And now their limbs shiver in the cold
Beneath their old protective barks
New growth waits in patient dormancy,
Kept safe from winter's cruel breath.
Lovers embrace to stay warm,
Bestowing hot kisses on skin undressed."

Richard gasped in wonder. He was deeply moved by the lyrics, identifying with the words with the weather that was stewing outside. The knight also felt a kinship with the lovers in the last line, feeling the song sang about Peter and himself and what he wanted to experience with his beloved brother as soon as possible. Richard could see from Bartholomew's expression that the monk was also identifying the lovers in the song with Richard and Peter's relationship.

Richard smiled, and then Bartholomew did the same.

"You are a man of many talents and great depths," Richard said to the healer monk, "and I am most grateful to have met you. I appreciate you as a great gift from Cosmos for which I am eternally grateful."

"Thank you, that is very kind of you, Richard. But I am just an ordinary man living an ordinary life."

"Hardly," Richard responded. "There is so much more to that, for whatever reason, you are reluctant to accept in yourself. But I see it, I see YOU, and I am full of abundant gratitude. Thank you for sharing your magnificent voice with me. It has eased my soul. If the other monks do not see or appreciate these deeper aspects of you, it is their loss – and a very deep loss indeed. I hope they will grow to recognise and appreciate you far more in the years to come."

Tears welled up again in Bartholomew's eyes. Like the other monks, Bartholomew remained uncomfortable accepting praise. The two men gazed quietly at each other for a long moment, while the howling wind could be heard outside.

Then Bartholomew spoke. "This storm is accelerating itself and will soon explode in all its dramatic splendour. I am sure that you and Brother Peter will keep each other sufficiently occupied and comforted when the storm finally unleashes itself upon us."

"Perhaps you can help us all by singing to the storm and asking it to be merciful to us," Richard suggested.

Bartholomew blinked several times in shocked surprise. "You know, Richard, I had not thought about that. The Druids believed we could control the weather or at least somehow work cooperatively with it by singing, invocation or supplication. There may be some truth to it. Thank you, Richard, I might very well do that after all. It could prove to be a most fascinating experience!"

Richard grinned and nodded his agreement as he departed the

infirmary and make his way back to Peter's cell to await his beloved brother's return.

———•◆•———

"I am beginning to appreciate this healer monk Bartholomew more and more," Peter's totem raven commented.

"Is it true?" the other raven asked.

"Um, you will have to give me more than that. Is what true?"

"Humans can use singing to heal?"

"Absolutely. Singing is a powerful tool of theirs for healing and in all other manners of transformation as well."

"I will be damned. I never would have thought they had it in them."

"I am so not surprised."

"Do we ravens have the ability to heal — and transform — through our cawing?"

"Yes, but in a different way."

"You mean in a better way."

"No, I meant in a different way."

"Since we are ravens, it has to be in a better way."

"How did you escape being reincarnated as a cockroach?"

———•◆•———

As night approached, the atmospheric energies began to steadily intensify. The greyness of the sky became darker and more ominous, appearing as if it were haemorrhaging bilious cloud-tumours. "The storm is coming – a threatening and monstrous storm." That was what most of the monks expressed as night was soon to descend upon them.

After the monks had anxiously completed Vespers, they all ran to their private cells and either knelt in prayer at their bedsides or fell into their beds and pulled the blankets up over them in desperation.

The more religious zealots among the monks wondered if they were to be punished for standing by while Brother Peter and Richard enjoyed their "illicit and satanic" relationship.

"I am surprised that those fanatic monks below do not ejaculate all over themselves from their passion for judging and condemning others," the cynical raven remarked.

For once, Peter's guiding raven had no reply to his companion, so the cynical raven continued.

"Does it ever occur to these rabidly dogmatic humans that it is their own bigotry and unloving judgements that create the very storms that they fear so much?"

"Are you kidding?"

"Right. Never mind."

Father Abbot and Brothers Bartholomew and Clair, on the other hand, were among the few who saw the coming storm as a positive purification and transformation of energies – allowing something old to die and something new and promising to be born.

Bartholomew mentioned to Paul and Clair his conversation with Richard about the healing power of singing as well as the lack of openness between the monks.

"How very true," Paul said. We keep so much within ourselves, and I have allowed far too much of it to continue for far too long. I must look into this and alleviate that situation."

"Well," Clair added. "The monks do believe that prayers can bring hope, healing, answers and changes into our lives. But the tonality of the singing voice alone as a healing instrument is fabulous. It MUST be true."

"Perhaps we should all sing with this storm and work with it instead of experiencing it as some kind of destructive enemy," Bartholomew suggested.

"Good luck with that suggestion with the other monks," Clair replied.

"Who wants to can do it," Paul said. "Those who do not simply do not. It is that simple. But I think I will join you, Brother Bartholomew."

"Count me in!" Clair added enthusiastically.

Bartholomew grinned with pleasure.

But whatever the beliefs and thinking of each monk, they all waited breathlessly to see what would happen next, what it would mean and how it would personally affect each of them.

Richard anxiously paced back and forth in Peter's cell while waiting for the monk to return from the library's scriptorium. Richard had again lit candles on Peter's small table and windowsill, marvelling at how accurately the weather was mirroring his own inner turmoil. He wished Peter would hurry up and come so he could hug the monk tightly to offer safety and security as much to himself as to Peter. Between the approaching storm and his tumultuous emotions, Richard was desperate to smother Peter in comforting and loving kisses.

In the next moment, thunder could be heard rumbling towards the monastery from the north. Every soul in the monastery stiffened with heightened alertness. There it was – the storm had arrived.

Over the next several minutes, each new roll of thunder increased in volume as everyone sensed the storm moving in on them, drawing nearer and nearer.

"Peter, where are you?" Richard cried out, shivering from apprehension as much as from the cold. "Hurry up, please, and get back here. God, how I need to kiss you and hold you and feel your strong body against mine."

In fact, Peter was not that far away, having just left the library's scriptorium and making his way to his cell where he assumed Richard would already be waiting for him. The monk held aloft a lit candle in his right hand, and with each new sound of thunder rumbling louder and closer, Peter noticed the crazily flickering candle-flame caused by his shaking hand. His whole body, actually, shivered with fear.

"Finally!" Peter muttered as he reached his cell. The monk quickly entered and shut the door, turning to face the waiting knight.

"Oh Richard, I –"

The next explosion of thunder was deafening. Richard and Peter (along with all the other monks and most of the outside wildlife) shrieked in terror. Two ravens cawed shrilly as they frantically flew to the closest spot of protective cover, through a narrow gap in the trunk of a dead tree.

"Good God!" Peter screamed, "the thunder is right on top of us!"

As he uttered his words, the first lightning bolts flashed across the sky. He and Richard could see the flashing light through the cracks and spaces in the wooden window shutters.

Many of the monks inside their own private cells, whether kneeling or in bed, began to fervently utter desperate prayers asking forgiveness for whatever sin they might be guilty of that was causing them to be punished in this way.

Peter literally jumped into Richard's waiting arms as they clung to each other tightly. Richard devoured Peter's lips in a hungry frenzy. Peter thought Richard was going to kiss the life out of him, but he wasn't going to complain because it did, after all, feel sensational.

Finally, Peter managed to pull his lips away from Richard's (not that he really wanted to). But he DID want to express something important to Richard, and he needed his lips in order to do that.

"This approaching storm is scaring the life out of me!" Peter exclaimed. "Help me please to calm down."

"And how may I do that for you?" Richard asked.

"Make love to me in your language."

"You want me to speak to you in my language as we have sex?" Richard pretended to enquire.

"No – well, yes! That too. But I mean, right now speak to me in your language so listening to you will calm me down."

"Ah, now I see. Anything in particular you want me to say?"

Distant rumbles of thunder could be heard, causing Peter to shake even more in Richard's arms.

"I do not care what you say, so long as you say it in your mother tongue. Tell me to sweep the floor, or get you more food, to roll over in bed or lick your face – oh! That would be nice. But just say ANYTHING to me in your language, because everything in your language sounds romantic and sexy!"

"Very well. Hmm, let me think. What should I say to you in this moment?"

The thunder rumbled louder as it approached nearer to the monastery.

"Anything at all, Richard, but for God's sake, say it NOW!"

"Very well." Richard held Peter tightly and stared with pure desire into Peter's eyes. "*Scoreggia nella mia faccia e fischia il mio buco del culo. Soffocami con la merda di mucca, esotici babbuini bluastre.*" {"Fart in my face and whistle up my asshole. Smother me with cow shit, you exotic blue-assed baboon."}

The thunder roared ever nearer as Peter tightened his hold on Richard. As an afterthought, Richard added, but in Peter's language, "Oh, and by the way, Peter – I love you."

The next claps of thunder crashed and bellowed so deafeningly loud that it forced Richard and Peter to let go of one another and cover their ears with their hands. The deafening crashes of thunder lasted nearly thirty seconds. Finally, when a full minute passed without hearing any more thunderous booms, the two men carefully removed their hands from their ears. But both men experienced a heavy deafness that lasted several minutes before they felt their hearing return to normal.

Richard grabbed Peter tightly to him again and planted his lips VERY firmly upon Peter's with an anxious ferocity that promised their lips would never part again. Richard kept pressing his lips tighter and tighter against Peter's until the monk was certain that if Richard kissed with any stronger intensity, the knight would end up BEHIND him. However, Peter was again NOT complaining.

The whole monastery trembled from the constant booms of thunder, but at least it was no longer so deafening that they had to cover their ears. Still, the thunder remained extremely close overhead.

More and more flashes of lightning illuminated the sky with each thunderous roar, and Peter and Richard again observed the flashes through the spaces in the window shutters.

"How are you feeling?" Richard asked when his lips finally released themselves from the monk.

Peter stared deeply into the knight's dark eyes. "As long as you are holding me, I am fine."

Now, along with the ominous thunder, the wind began to pick up and screech as if a massive flock of murderous super-vultures was about to descend upon the monastery. The howling of the wind intensified in pitch, and then a torrential rain began pounding the monastery's roof and window shutters. The entire building shook under the intense pressure of gusting winds and pounding rain. Lightning flashes continued, followed immediately by the deeply rumbling thunder.

"Is Mother Nature upset about something?" Richard mumbled without releasing his lips from Peter's.

"If this kind of communication from Mother Nature results in you holding me and kissing me as you do," Peter managed to say, even though their lips still remained locked against one another, "then I am all for it, and She can screech and howl and thunder to Her heart's content."

When the two men finally needed to part lips in order to breathe properly, Richard murmured into Peter's ear, *"Ti voglio ora.* Oops! I mean, I want you right now!"

Peter nodded. "And you can have me RIGHT NOW!"

The rapidly intensifying rain sounded like the sky was pouring an entire ocean down upon the monastery's roof. The building vibrated as thunder crashed and drummed, lightning flashed again and again, and the wind howled a deranged mournful litany.

Peter shivered more from fear than from the cold. "My God," he gasped fretfully, "that howling outside sounds like the keening of the **baintsi**."

"The what?" Richard asked.

"Oh – the **baintsi**, or sometimes now referred to as the **banshee**, is a legendary female spirit who wails like what we are hearing right now from the wind to herald the approaching death of a family member."

"If such a being is wailing outside, she is not doing so for either of us."

"But how do you know –"

Peter was prevented from finishing his question by Richard's lips pressing firmly against his. Once again, Peter did not mind this at all.

Richard pulled Peter down upon the bed and covered the monk completely with his own body.

"Amo la tua anima. Sei il mio tutto. La mia anima è riempita da te." {"I love your soul, you are my everything and my spirit is replenished by you."}

"Oh, my!"

Richard kissed Peter fervently.

"I will always protect you," Richard announced.

"From what?"

The knight shrugged with a grin and smothered Peter with comforting kisses.

"I like this protection," Peter said between heavy gasps. "Keep it up."

"I intend to keep it UP as long as I can."

Peter laughed. "That is not what I meant, and –"

Richard's mouth again devoured Peter's. After several minutes, Richard released their lips, pulled back and stared adoringly at Peter.

"You give me great *uccello!*" Richard exclaimed.

"I give you what?" Peter asked.

"Uccello, ucello! Oh, I am sorry. I said that you make my penis very erect."

"Uccello means erect?"

"In actuality, *uccello* means bird. But we sometimes use that word to mean an erect penis. Of course, I could have simply said *eretto,* which means erect. But I like to use *ucello* instead."

"Why would you use the word for bird to mean an erect penis?" Peter asked curiously.

Richard had to wait to reply as more thunder rolled across the sky overhead, followed by lightning flashes and the screeching of the wind.

"Who can ever explain how or why we create the special phrases that we do?"

"You do have a point."

"All I know is, *attraverso te mi trovo. Amarti e amare Tutto Cioche È.* I know I just spoke in my tongue yet again. When I feel most passionate, I feel the need to speak in my mother tongue. And when I am with you, I feel the most passionate. What I said before in my own language is that through you I find myself, and to love you is to love the All That Is."

They loved and comforted one another as the mysterious storm raged on.

———◆◆◆———

As the storm continued to howl and rage, the two thoroughly drenched ravens perched tenuously on the window ledge outside Peter's cell, the wind whipping them in all directions.

"Trying to find protective cover inside that dead tree trunk was not such a good idea, was it?" the first raven asked.

"For a moment, I thought that last lightning bolt was going to fry us for someone's dinner as it obliterated the tree," the second raven replied

The two birds sensed telepathically what was taking place in Peter's personal cell.

"Again?" the first raven asked.

"What?"

"They are procreating AGAIN!"

"Well, they are not exactly procreating," the second raven explained. *"After all, they are not trying to produce young since they are both, you have noticed, males. But they ARE expressing their deep love for each other."*

"Why do they need to have sex so often?" the first raven asked.

"Why do you care? They can express their mutual love whenever they want to."

"Day after day, night after night, on and on and on!"

"Ah, now I understand," the second raven replied. *"I see what is going on in you."*

"In me? What do you mean?"

"You are jealous."

"Jealous? Of what?"

"Oy vey! *Never mind."*

———◆◆◆———

Richard hungrily kissed and licked every inch of Peter's body, including all ten toes. Returning to Peter's chest, Richard once again kissed, licked and sucked the monk's nipples.

"*I tuoi capezzoli hanno un sapore delizioso!* Your nipples taste like exquisite heaven."

"Oh my. You better keep tasting them just to be sure about that!"

Richard amiably followed Peter's advice for the remainder of the torrential storm.

"What was that?" Peter asked suddenly.

"My tongue on your delicious nipples?"

"No, no. That noise."

"The storm?"

"No, Richard! That other noise."

Richard lifted his head from Peter's chest to better listen.

"Am I now going crazy, or do I hear singing?" Peter asked.

Richard grinned. *"Bartholomew is singing with the storm,"* the knight thought with joy. *"And by the sound of it, he may have gotten a few monks to join in with him. How marvellous. Peter and I should join them. But on the other hand, we ARE rather preoccupied with our own expression of celebration. Well, each of us to our own. But bravo, Bartholomew!"*

Aloud Richard said, "Yes, you hear singing. The storm is celebrating with us."

"What do you mean?"

For an answer, Richard smothered Peter in kisses, and that was a good enough response for Peter.

Bartholomew, Paul and Clair sang old Celtic songs throughout the night in their attempt to work in unison with the storming energies.

———◆◦◆◦◆———

Ceaseless howling winds, torrential rain, booming thunder, flashing lightning (and three monks singing) continued throughout the night until just before dawn.

In the early hours of the morning, as the rain continued in its final moments to pummel the monastery, Richard suddenly awoke, sensing he was being watched. He was right. Peter lay beside him, the monk's eyes gazing into Richard's face.

"Good morning, my beloved brother. What is happening?"

"Nothing."

"You stare at me with such intensity."

Peter nodded. "Would you do something for me?"

"Yes, anything. What would you like me to do?"

"Smile."

"Smile?"

Peter nodded again.

Richard laughed and gave Peter his widest grin.

Peter sighed with utter contentment. "Yes, that is it exactly. Thank you."

"For what?" Richard asked.

"When you smile, the light from your face is like the morning sun chasing away the storm."

Richard rolled on top of Peter and smothered him with passionate kisses.

"Ah, that is more like it," Peter sighed as he returned Richard's kisses with equal passion.

———————◆———————

When the sun was fully risen, the storm quickly vanished into nothingness. Peace and calm reigned anew. The landscape was drenched but serene. Even a few birds (but not the two ravens) sang their joy for the new day.

Richard and Peter slept contentedly in each other's arms, but they still avoided sharing with each other their fears for the future.

Richard awoke to find Peter sleeping peacefully in his arms. Feeling that his chest would burst with the abundant love the knight felt for Peter, he smelled the monk's silk-smooth skin and gently kissed along a shoulder and arm.

"Quando ti fengo, va tutto bene. Il tuo tocco mi fa sentire completamente in pace." {"When I hold you, everything is fine. Your touch makes me feel thoroughly at peace."}

Peter didn't hear Richard's words as he still slept. Richard hugged him tightly and prayed that his last statement was true, as he attempted to fall asleep as well.

Fifteen

THREE DAYS LATER on the first of March, the ground was pulled out from under Peter and Richard's feet forever.

Early that morning Peter was leaving his cell to work in the library's scriptorium. But before he could reach the cell door, Richard leapt naked out of bed, grabbed Peter, turned the monk around and then Richard hugged Peter as if they would never see each other again.

"I love your smell," Richard whispered. "It is like breathing in a new-born day. And the taste of you is rich with healing."

"Richard, I love you with all my being. But is something troubling you?"

"No," Richard lied, immediately regretting it. "I just – love you."

"And I love you."

<hr />

Bartholomew was busy in the infirmary, having taken inventory of all his supplies and now absently straightening things up around him. He felt nervous but couldn't understand why. Something was about to happen, and his instinct told him it was not going to end well.

As the healer monk continued to nervously move items back and forth, Richard suddenly burst into the infirmary.

"Richard," Bartholomew greeted the knight with a smile as he straightened up. "How are you doing?"

"I am fine," Richard lied, wondering why he kept lying instead of sharing a deep sense of dread that gnawed at his innards.

"Is there anything I can do for you?" Bartholomew asked.

"Not really. Peter is working in the scriptorium again, and I am just waiting for him to be finished so we can go out for another walk with Orion."

"I see," Bartholomew said, not genuinely seeing at all. He sensed a nervousness in the knight that mirrored his own. And yet neither of them was being honest about what they were both feeling. "You're welcome to stay here with me if you like."

"Thank you, Bartholomew. I think I would prefer that to being with myself."

"Certainly. Anything particular on your mind?"

"No," Richard answered too quickly, wincing imperceptibly, again wondering why he was not being honest.

Bartholomew sensed the knight's discomfort and wondered why he himself was not speaking up about his own edginess. *"What is going on?"* the healer monk asked himself.

"May I ask you something?"

Bartholomew smiled. "Certainly."

"Could you tell me more about your Druid tradition? I find it fascinating and would like to learn more."

"Of course. Anything in particular you want to know about?"

"No," Richard said. "Whatever you feel to share with me will be greatly appreciated."

"I see. Fine." Bartholomew could sense that Richard was desperate to have the healer monk speak to him in order to calm the knight's nerves. *"Well,"* Bartholomew thought to himself, *"It might help me to calm down as well!"*

Richard seemed relieved that Bartholomew was willing to share and took a deep breath and appeared to relax.

"We as a people were deeply influenced, guided and supported by our Druids," Bartholomew began.

"Yes, I am most interested in your Druid tradition, especially in how it was structured."

"Okay, I can talk about that. The Druids are our most highly developed and highly trained priests and priestesses. Most of them are tested in childhood or adolescence to determine if they exhibit any particular talents in healing, dream interpretation, judicial perception, telepathy with animals or nature spirits, past-life memory or singing. If so, they are then given to Druid masters to train them in whichever particular fields they are showing their greatest gifts."

"So, you are saying both men and women can become these higher Druid leaders?" Richard asked with fascination.

"Yes, there was never any discrimination whatsoever towards women in terms of Druid training. We see and accept male and female as equal spiritual beings."

"I am very glad to hear that," Richard said with evident satisfaction.

"Some Druids tended to specialise as singing poets called Bards who learned to sing the accumulative history of the clan and perpetuate the history of our people through poetic narration as well as composing new clan stories. Then there were those who were trained to be judges in clan disputes or in disputes between different clans or with people outside the clans. Then there were the healer Druids for both the clan people as well as for animals, using herbs and other elements of nature or healing through creative expression. Then there were teachers, dream interpreters or those who could read the karmic history of reincarnating souls."

"How is THAT achieved?" Richard asked.

"These Druids know how to meditatively attune to the auric energy of an individual and receive the past-life information that is most needed for that person to work through unresolved lessons, unhealthy relationships, traumatic or repressed emotional memories and especially work with how these various aspects manifest in the physical bodies as imbalances, illnesses or diseases."

"Fascinating," Richard breathed excitedly. "It is remarkable how your people have developed this."

"Well," Bartholomew said with raised eyebrows, "we have had many centuries to develop these skills and understandings within our culture. Every individual has the opportunity to explore these various areas of Druid expression and be tested to discover if the gifts have been developed to be experienced and expressed in this lifetime. If so, then they are offered every opportunity to develop to their highest potential. Those who are chosen to pursue a life as a Druid explore the particular areas of their expertise and to be the highest possible self they can be in whatever field of spiritual expression that manifests within them.

"And for you it was as a healer."

"Yes," Bartholomew replied. "For me it was as a healer, following in the tradition of my family for many centuries back into our ancestral history. I was very fortunate to come into this lifetime with the gifts to be a healer. That was always what I wished to do, following in the footsteps of both my parents, my grandparents, and for generations back. I have been very lucky indeed."

"Fascinating," Richard repeated. "I just wonder if –"

Before Richard could continue, a short thin monk entered the infirmary.

"Brother Luke," Bartholomew addressed the monk. "You know our visiting guest, Richard."

"Oh," Luke said, "I thought you were brother Peter."

Richard smiled. "Many people make that mistake with me since I have been dressing in a monk's robe."

"Can I help you?" Bartholomew asked the short monk.

"Actually, Brother Bartholomew, it was the knight Richard I was seeking."

"Oh? What can I do for you?" Richard asked.

"A messenger has arrived who has apparently been riding for months seeking you."

"What?" Richard and Bartholomew asked simultaneously.

Luke nodded. "Yes, the messenger arrived just a short while ago, asking specifically if we had seen you, and he was very happy and most relieved to hear that you are here, Sir Richard."

Bartholomew glanced at Richard, whose face suddenly paled as the knight's eyes took on a frightened expression.

"Are you alright?" Bartholomew asked the knight.

"Mio Dio. È la fine per me adesso!" {"My God. It is the end for me now!"}

"Richard?" Bartholomew asked with concern. "What is the matter?"

Richard shook his head and tried to maintain a semblance of calm. "What? Oh, nothing, nothing at all."

"So, can you come with me now to Father Abbot's meeting room where the messenger awaits you?" Luke asked.

Richard took several deep breaths to try to capture and retain a sense of calmness. "Yes, of course. I will follow you now."

As Luke turned to leave, he paused and turned back to face Bartholomew. "Oh, and Father Abbot asked that you join us in the meeting room," Luke informed the healer monk.

"What? Oh, certainly. Of course."

Luke took a few steps then turned and waited for Richard and Bartholomew to follow him. After a moment's hesitation, Richard followed the little monk as Bartholomew fell in step beside him.

"God help me," Richard muttered under his breath.

———•◆•———

Later that morning, Peter sat in the scriptorium examining a manuscript that required detailed repair. He tried to focus on the needs of the manuscript, but his mind kept wandering. Finally Peter gave up, put the manuscript away and sat at the table with his head in his hands.

All Peter could think about was the coming spring weather and the fact that Richard would soon leave to give his report to the Northumbrian king. But would Richard ever return? And for the rest of his life would Peter be left alone and miserable without the man he loved?

Over the past week Peter had repeatedly asked himself, *"Do I dare ask Richard if I can go with him to Northumberland? Would Father Abbot allow it? Can Richard's life include me? And if so, would we only end up being condemned, banished, punished or possibly killed? Does Richard even WANT me to go with him? I am so terrified he will say no to my joining him. But on the other hand, is that really what I fear, or is it in truth something else deeper in myself that I am afraid of?"*

Peter rubbed his eyes and forehead but felt no closer to any answers. Fearful questions dominated his mind, blocking out any clarity or truth.

"Stop it!" Peter shouted out loud. "This is achieving nothing. If I keep tormenting myself like this, I will only make myself sick!"

Peter then took several deep breaths. He repeatedly clenched and opened his hands, trying to force himself into a calm state – but of course that didn't work. Next Peter stood up and paced back and forth.

"What do I do? What do I WANT to do?"

That last question was the breakthrough. Peter had FINALLY asked himself what he WANTED instead of just wondering what he SHOULD do. And then Peter instantly knew what he wanted most deeply in his heart – and THAT was his answer. He must dare to tell Richard that he wanted to leave the monastery and follow the knight wherever he went – IF Richard wanted that as well. Peter knew now that he must be direct with his knight and pray that Richard's wish would be the same.

Peter ceased his pacing. He had made his decision. Now he must quickly find Richard and hope the knight would agree and embrace him with joy. Otherwise – "NO!" But then Peter stopped himself. "There is no otherwise," he decided aloud.

Peter raced back towards his cell, hoping to find Richard still there. On the way, he literally crashed into the short and thin Brother Luke who occasionally helped Brother Bartholomew in the infirmary.

"Greetings, Brother Peter," Luke said, tidying himself up after his collision with Peter.

"And to you, Brother Luke. I am looking for Richard."

"That is a coincidence. I happen to know your knight is in the meeting cell with Father Abbot and, I believe, Brothers Bartholomew and Clair."

Peter liked the way Brother Luke had said "your knight," but he didn't have time to dwell upon that.

"What? They are all there? Why?"

"Goodness me! You do not know?"

"Obviously!" Peter answered irritably. "Know what?"

"Interesting. Well, a messenger arrived here about half an hour ago. Apparently the messenger is from Oswiu, the king of Northumbria. By the way, Brother Peter, is that how you correctly pronounce the king's name?"

"What? Um, say it with a big sneeze, I think."

"*Crap!*" Peter screamed inside his head. *"It has happened already. I have to get to Richard as fast as possible and let him know how I feel!"*

Aloud to Brother Luke he said, "Excuse my rather abrupt behaviour. I feel jittery today for some reason. But thank you for letting me know where to find Richard. I will go to Father Abbot's meeting cell immediately."

"Oh, one more thing," Luke added as Peter tried to hurry away. "Have you by any chance seen Prior Thomas lately?"

"Prior Thomas? Heavens no! Not for several days, in fact."

"Yes, that is what every other brother answers as well. No one has seen him for a very long time, and many of us are quite concerned."

Peter wanted to escape Luke and find Richard as quickly as possible. "I am sure he is fine, just brooding alone somewhere. He will turn up eventually, when he feels like it."

"I hope you are right. But some of us are starting search parties and seeking him throughout the monastery, as well as in the surrounding woods."

"I am sure you will find him safe and sound."

"I hope so."

"Thank you again, Brother Luke."

Peter then dashed away as fast as he could before Luke could detain him with any more questions.

Just before Peter arrived at Father Abbot's meeting cell, Peter saw a diminutive, bald-headed monk also approaching the meeting cell carrying a large platter bearing a stone pitcher filled with wine, assorted fruits and six stoneware goblets.

Peter had a sudden flash of an idea. He raced to the burdened monk and blocked his way.

"Excuse me," the monk said irritably.

"I will take that from you."

"You most certainly will not!" the tiny monk objected harshly. "I have been assigned to bring the refreshments to Father Abbot, the messenger and the other brothers inside. So please get out of my way."

"And now I am taking over." Peter tried to grab the platter from the small monk, but the monk resisted with a strength Peter didn't think existed in someone barely taller than a dwarf.

"By what authority do you say you will take over my responsibility?" the little monk barked with hostility.

Peter thought quickly. "Father Abbot asked me to take this from you and bring it in myself."

"You lie!"

"I do not!" Peter lied. He tried to pull the platter away again, but he was met once more with strong resistance.

"Get out of my way!" the little monk repeated.

"I cannot do that," Peter said. "I must bring this in. It is extremely important."

"Why?"

"*Crap!*" Peter thought angrily. He hadn't gotten that far yet in his made-up story. He had to invent something immediately. "Because I am needed in there, and I was asked to take this from you."

"That is absurd. I do not believe you."

"I do not care whether you believe me or not. I must take this from you now and get in there."

The little monk maintained his resistance. "I still say you are lying. You can follow me into Father Abbot's meeting cell if you insist, staying BEHIND me the whole time, and then Father Abbot will say whether or not you should be in there and whether or not he truly asked you to take over for me."

"*Who IS this monk?*" Peter wondered with mounting fury. "*I cannot for the life of me remember his name. Is it Timothy? Joseph? Is he another Paul or Peter? Damn, I cannot remember this idiot brother's name, and right now, in actual truth, I do not give a damn!*"

"That," Peter barked, "will be completely unnecessary. Just let me have it so I can get in there."

"I will not!" Peter's opponent brother yelled.

The two monks engaged in a bizarre tug of war, each trying to gain control of the platter as the pitcher, goblets and fruit teetered back and forth, constantly threatening to spill or tumble everywhere.

"This is absurd! Let go immediately!" Peter demanded.

"No! YOU let go!"

Peter lost all patience. He had to get into Father Abbot's meeting cell before it was too late. He forcefully pushed the platter, causing the other monk to teeter just like all the objects upon the platter. Then Peter quickly stuck out a foot that caused the tiny monk to topple backwards with a shriek. As the tiny monk hit the ground, Peter had to sway to and fro in order to get everything on the platter to remain ON it and upright without anything spilling, falling or shattering. Finally, Peter managed to get everything quiet and still upon the platter.

Quickly Peter hurried the few steps to Father Abbot's meeting cell door and had to manipulate the platter and all its contents as he opened the door with the other hand and stepped inside.

When Peter entered the small over-crowded meeting cell, no one noticed his arrival at first. Father Abbot and Brothers Bartholomew and Clair stood in a semi-circle next to Richard, who was intensely reading a parchment letter.

In front of Richard stood the messenger, a young lad with long frazzled red hair. He was clean shaven with sharp angular features, a very long and thin nose and deep-set dark blue eyes. He was tall and very thin with narrow, sharp shoulders and very thin arms. The messenger's dark clothes were filthy from weeks of travel. A leather bag with a long strap hung from the messenger's left shoulder.

Peter still stood in the doorway bearing the platter with all that was heaped upon it. Still no one turned to notice or acknowledge his presence.

Richard finished reading the document and then folded it as he looked at the messenger.

"The king's message to you is clear?" the lad asked Richard in a shrill voice.

"Yes, completely."

"Do you have a reply for the king?"

"Please tell him I am on my way. I will be a day or possibly less behind you."

"Very good. I will tell him." After a moment's pause, the messenger turned to Father Abbot. "Excuse me, sir, but I dare not ever ask this anywhere near the king himself. When I say Oswiu, am I pronouncing the king's name correctly?"

Paul blinked several times before shaking his head and shrugging, with Bartholomew and Clair aping the same movements.

Richard, who stood preoccupied in his own thoughts, suddenly spoke up and said, "Say it as if you are sneezing."

"Excuse me?" the messenger asked, turning back to face the knight.

"OsWIU!" Richard stated as if sneezing.

Peter, still bearing the heavy platter, mouthed the sneezing pronunciation silently along with Richard and smiled as if sharing a secret joke.

"Really?" the messenger said with wonder. "Like that? Thank you, sir."

The messenger turned to leave then suddenly stopped. "Oh, I almost forgot," he said as he dug deep into his shoulder bag. "I have another letter for you, sir."

"Another letter?" Richard asked. "From the king?"

"No, this one is from someone else. I have been carrying this letter for you for the last six months as it has taken me that long to find you, not to mention to find this monastery. Ah, here it is!" the messenger said as he pulled another parchment from his leather bag.

"Alright, I will take the other letter. Do you know who it is from?"

"Actually, yes." The messenger held out the parchment for Richard to take. "It is from your wife."

C R A S H!

------◆◆◆------

"Cazzo!" hissed Peter's raven, perched along with his companion outside Father Abbot's meeting cell.

"What did you just say?" the other raven asked.

"Excuse me. For some reason I just lapsed into Richard's language. I said, SHIT!"

"I understand your sentiment. I am not surprised by this pathetic human scene. I am not one to say 'I told you so', but then again — yes I am. I told you this would not end well."

"Crap!" hissed the first raven. *"Crap, crap, crap, crap, crap, crap, crap, crapcrapcrapcrapcrapcrapcrapcrapcrapcrap!"*

"I told you so! I told you so!" gloated the other raven.

The first raven savagely pecked his companion on the head, causing a few drops of blood to dribble down the bird's face.

"How dare you!" the second raven cawed furiously. *"You are just angry because I am right – again! Humans always screw everything up. They lie, they cheat, they judge, they attack, they blame, they destroy everything in their paths!"*

"Stop describing yourself to me!" the first raven retaliated. *"That is all you ever do."*

"Go on, peck me again for being right. Human love is a travesty! Peter's precious knight has a WIFE! He deliberately deceived your monk! Welcome to the REAL human world, you idealistic fool!"

Peter's raven swiped his wing at his companion, who fluttered off the windowsill.

"Go to Hell!" the second raven screamed telepathically as he flew away.

"The same to you!"

Then the first raven looked back towards Father Abbot's cell.

*"Crap and **cazzo!**"*

———————◆———————

All heads in the meeting cell except Peter's turned towards the disastrous scene of scattered fruit, shattered pitcher and goblets, and spilled wine pooling around Peter's feet. In the midst of it all stood Peter, his ashen face frozen in pain-ridden shock.

"Crap!" Father Abbot, Bartholomew and Clair uttered in unison.

"Cazzo!" Richard hissed.

The red-haired young messenger stared aghast at Father Abbot and the other two monks for uttering such an obscene word. Richard's word he hadn't understood.

Brothers Bartholomew and Clair glanced at one another with pained expressions, and then they turned to observe a stunned and deeply hurt Peter.

Richard's eyes welled with tears of agony and guilt as he stared at Peter.

"Have I said something wrong?" the perplexed messenger asked while looking from face to face.

But the messenger was completely ignored. Peter stood in the doorway as if he had been turned into stone after staring at Medusa's face. His arms hung at his sides, with one hand barely clutching the platter.

No one moved or said a word. The messenger felt uncomfortable and confused. "Um, here is the letter from your wife," he said holding it out again to Richard.

Without taking his tearful eyes away from Peter's pain-ridden face, Richard absently held out a hand so the messenger could hand him his wife's letter.

Peter closed his eyes briefly. *"The messenger said that word again,"* he thought miserably. *"He said – WIFE."*

Everyone remained frozen.

"This is creepy," the messenger spoke up again. "Will someone please tell me what is going on?" But the messenger remained ignored.

Father Abbot shifted his gaze to stare pleadingly at Brothers Clair and Bartholomew. But the two monks slightly shook their heads, indicating to Father Abbot that they had no idea what to say or do next.

At that moment, the tiny monk who had originally been carrying the platter appeared in the doorway behind Peter.

"Brother Peter deliberately –"

Peter immediately smacked the little monk in the chest with the platter, sending him reeling backwards and out of sight.

Richard started to step towards Peter, but his lover shook his head, causing Richard to halt. Peter's eyes remained wide open with shock as he shakily attempted several deep breaths. The messenger stared from person to person and finally decided that everyone in the room was totally crazy.

Finally Peter stepped back, turned and fled the meeting cell, dropping the platter behind him. Richard's tall muscular body appeared to cave in as his shoulders drooped and he stared at the ground, his whole body shaking. The knight heaved with deep sobbing.

*"**Non potrò mai perdonarmi per quello che ho causato. Il mio cuore**"*

non si riparerà mai." {"I can never forgive myself for what I have caused. My heart will never heal."}

The Northumbrian king's messenger stared at Richard as if the knight were an alien two-headed monster.

"I am leaving!" the messenger muttered. "Everyone here is devil-possessed, and this quivering knight most of all!"

The original platter-bearing monk made a second attempt to enter the meeting cell. "That idiot man —"

"Shut up and get out!" Father Abbot and Brothers Bartholomew and Clair screamed simultaneously. The little monk backed away with furious confusion.

"This is a house of lunacy!" the messenger announced. "You now have both your letters, Sir Richard, and you can follow behind me when you can. But I am getting the hell out of here now!"

The messenger sped out of the meeting cell, leaving the knight and the three monks to their own madness. As he left, the messenger had to carefully step around the short bald monk who was ranting in the corridor like another madman.

Meanwhile, Peter ran as if he were being chased by a demon spectre. The hem of his brown robe flapped wildly as he ran faster and faster towards his own cell. Peter completely ignored any monks he passed who attempted to call out a greeting to him.

When he reached his personal cell, Peter quickly stuffed all of Richard's belongings into the knight's leather bag, then sat on his bed weeping bitterly while he awaited Richard's arrival.

Peter's whole body ached as he wept uncontrollably. His life was over. He had now descended into Hell, where he would spend the rest of his life. His heart felt shattered, just like the stoneware pitcher and goblets when they crashed upon the floor.

"I cannot survive this!" he wailed. "I wish I were dead!"

Sixteen

PETER DID NOT have to wait long. In less than five minutes, Richard entered the monk's cell and stared at Peter with guilt-laden grief.

Peter looked up at the knight. "How is your wife?" he asked miserably.

"Peter —"

"You lied to me. All these months — you deceived me." Peter sounded exhausted.

"Please let me speak."

"Let you speak? Why? To tell me MORE lies? You deliberately did not tell me you had a wife so you could get whatever it was you wanted from me." Peter choked back tears, his heart crumbling into fragments of anguish and desolation.

"That is not true," Richard whispered, barely holding back his swelling fear of losing Peter.

"What do you mean, that is not true?" Peter cried shrilly, the tears flowing freely down his bearded cheeks, his voice full of agony. "All these months and you never told me you had a wife. You deliberately kept her a secret from me. What other explanation is there?"

"Stop it!" Richard pleaded as he too wailed with tears. "Please, please stop it!"

Peter turned away, unable to control his crying, the pain in his chest burning unbearably. Richard stepped forward and grasped Peter's bearded chin, guiding the monk to look at him.

"I love you, Peter." Richard whispered. "Please believe that. I love you with all my being. I did not mean to hurt or betray you. I did not purposely lie. I honestly do not know why I never mentioned my wife. From the first moment I saw you, I fell instantly and madly in love. I sensed you were my completion, my soulmate, the one I have been searching for my entire life – probably for many lifetimes. I wanted and needed you so much – and I still do."

Peter remained silent, too overwhelmed for a reply.

Alright," Richard sighed with shameful defeat. "I admit it. I knew that mentioning my wife would have killed any possibility between you and me. But my love for you is so great, so intense, so all-encompassing. That is all I know."

Peter slapped away Richard's gentle hand and pulled himself into a standing position. When Richard grabbed the monk's shoulders, Peter tried to push the knight away – but Richard only tightened his firm grip.

"Why did you marry your wife?" Peter asked in suffocating pain. "Did you love her?"

"The truth is no, I did not."

Peter could only stare at the suffering knight. The torment was a tidal wave engulfing both of them.

"The marriage was arranged," Richard said. "It was supposed to better my circumstances and lead to future advancement."

"How convenient!" Peter sneered. "You did not love her, so therefore all your deceit was not a problem."

Once again Peter tried unsuccessfully to pull away from Richard's grip. The monk wanted to curl up like an unborn foetus and die.

"Peter, please do not do this. That is not what I meant at all."

"And do you love her now?"

"After a period of time, some semblance of love and respect did develop between Anne and myself."

"Oh, great!" Peter cried. "Now I know her name as well!"

"Peter, please stop torturing me – and yourself!" Richard begged as fresh tears poured down his face.

Peter's whole body ached with the next onslaught of pain. "When you return to your Anne, will you be honest and tell her about me?"

"Please stop this!" Richard begged. "I love you. Please believe me and accept that. You are my greatest love."

Peter sobbed and shook his head. It was just too much. He wanted to crawl into a deep hole and disappear forever.

"Whatever I tell my wife is my own responsibility, Peter. I must accept that burden and deal with it however I can. But I do not want this terrible drama to destroy the total love I feel for you."

"No matter what you claim to be your responsibility," Peter said in a dulled monotone without looking at Richard, "every choice or action you take affects other people."

"Yes, I know that," Richard agreed between sobs. "I accept my responsibility in this. But please be willing to still love me as I will always love you. Hold on to the love that we discovered and built together. It is eternal, I hope. It is ours. Do not use my marital responsibilities and failures as an excuse to reject what is forever between us. And for Heaven's sake, Peter, please do not reject ALL future love and happiness for yourself because of me and my mistakes."

Richard was weeping desperately, as was Peter. They stood facing each other, crying ceaselessly. Peter felt his heart was shattered beyond any hope.

"I cannot handle this," Peter blubbered between sobs. "I cannot take any more. My heart is destroyed. I will never love or trust again."

"No, no!" Richard screamed. "Please do not say that! What we feel for one another is real. Judge me however you must, but please do not deny any future love and happiness for yourself. I beg you!"

Peter then completely lost control and started screaming, terrifying the knight. Richard finally released his hold on the monk. Peter slumped to his knees and then rocked back and forth. With every wail emitted from the monk, Richard cried anew.

That Peter would now forever reject and hate him, Richard understood. This sudden realisation filled the knight with a new wave of merciless pain that he prayed would kill him quickly.

"I take full responsibility for the situation with my wife," Richard repeated. "That is mine. But above all, Peter, please do not reject love itself."

Peter could not respond from the shock of complete loss.

"Whatever rage and blame you feel towards me, Peter, you have the right to feel it and I accept that. But please do not use me as an excuse to reject love. I have stupidly fulfilled your life-long expectation that love always automatically leads to pain, suffering and loss. I am very sorry for doing that to you."

Richard had to pause a moment as his last statement caused him to erupt in a new wave of tears. After that, he faced Peter and started again.

"But it is not true, Peter. I promise you. Love does not always automatically cause pain and suffering. I have horribly fulfilled your expectations, and I can never apologise enough for doing that. Please listen to what I am saying. Love will always heal you."

Gasping and sobbing, Peter could no longer even look at Richard. The monk needed to escape to his hills and be free of this relentless torture – far beyond what his soul could tolerate. Peter needed to escape before the pain consumed him to the point of total annihilation.

So Peter turned away from his knight and finally managed to mutter, "Goodbye, Richard."

Richard shook his head with a sadness beyond his ability to bear. "In my heart, you will never be gone from me," Richard managed between crying fits. "**Perdonami.** I ask for your forgiveness, Peter, some day."

Peter had no reply to that.

"*Sono molto dispaiciuto. Come vivo con questa colpa?*"

"You are still speaking in your Venetian language!" Peter yelled.

"I apologise. I said I am so very sorry. How do I live with this guilt?"

Once more, Peter had no response.

Richard knew he was defeated. He had set into motion what must now be played out, and there was no escape. He picked up his bag.

"*Il mio cuore è distrutto irreparabilmente.*" {"*My heart is shattered beyond repair.*"}

Peter clutched his chest, feeling that HIS heart as well had been pulverised into thousands of tiny fragments.

"Farewell, my beloved brother. I am so very sorry. I hope someday you can forgive me. Please let yourself someday – somehow – love again. And please allow yourself to find happiness."

But still, Peter could not respond, his tears pouring down his face.

"Mi sono perso," Richard whispered with immense grief. {"I am lost."}

"Please stop speaking in your language!" Peter screamed. "I cannot take it anymore. It is too much for me to hear!"

"I am sorry. When I feel this deeply, it is hard for me to speak in any other language but my own."

"Then please leave now so you can speak to yourself in your own language to your heart's content!"

Richard stood motionless by the cell door, his leather bag in his hand. The silence between the two men was both deafening and heart-breaking.

Richard was about to leave Peter's cell but paused instead. He couldn't leave like this. It was too agonising to endure. He had to do something to say goodbye while showing his absolute love for Peter. He took a few steps back so he was standing in front of the still-kneeling monk.

Peter was breathing in deep gasps while fighting off the overwhelming grief that was strangling him. He had assumed that Richard had left, but suddenly he was aware that the knight was standing in front of him.

With confusion, dread and intense pain, Peter looked up and found himself staring into Richard's tormented face, tears pouring down the knight's face mirroring the tears streaming down his own cheeks.

Wordlessly and with great uncertainty, Richard leaned down and shakily glided his right forefinger down Peter's right bearded cheek. The gesture that had always filled Peter with so much love, desire and happiness now had the opposite effect.

"NOOOOOOO!" Peter screamed, crying hysterically and gagging so that he sounded as if he was choking.

"Peter, my love, I only wanted to –"

Peter shook his head and wailed with wild abandonment.

"I am so sorry. I am so very sorry," Richard repeated. He stared helplessly at the tortured kneeling figure of Peter. "I have only made things worse. I am sorry. I will go now."

Peter remained in his kneeling position, rocking back and forth as he cried and howled. Richard stared for a few seconds then painfully surrendered to his hopeless loss.

"Addio, amato fratello." {"Farewell, beloved brother."}

Peter heard the door open and close as Richard left the cell and departed from the monk's life forever.

"Addio, amato fratello," Peter repeated hoarsely but perfectly Richard's parting words in the knight's beautiful native tongue.

Immediately Peter erupted with a shrill wail that quickly escalated into a screaming fit that penetrated throughout the monastery and sent shivers down all the other monks' spines. He screamed and screamed, unleashing endless agony. This screaming fit lasted for nearly half an hour before he finally stopped from sheer exhaustion.

After several minutes of tormented silence, Peter hissed bitterly, "I hate love. It hurts! It destroys! I will never let myself be trapped by it again!"

He covered his face with pale, trembling hands and cried endlessly, reaching again a fevered pitch of animalistic howls until he was once more totally spent. He clutched at his aching heart and took several deep breaths.

"I will not feel this pain!" he ordered himself. "I will not feel this loss. I will feel NOTHING!"

Over one hundred times Peter repeated these three sentences until he was able to feel his emotions gradually shrink and disappear deep inside him, replaced by a heavy numbness. Slowly Peter consciously imprisoned all his emotions into a secret corner of his unconsciousness.

"I will feel NOTHING!" he shouted aloud again and again.

Gradually Peter rose unsteadily to his feet, willing the trembling in his body to calm and cease, ordering his legs to support him, refusing to acknowledge one shred of emotion.

"I feel NOTHING!" he repeated out loud as a continuous self-brainwashing mantra, convincing himself to believe the lie.

First with one hesitant foot and then with the other, Peter forced himself to move forward step by step, willing himself to leave his cell and make his way out of the monastery.

In the next instant, Peter lost control again as he felt an all-encompassing wave of grief and loss overwhelm him. He cried out in agony, breathing heavily and bracing himself against a corridor wall to remain upright. He cried and screamed his torment, lifting tightened fists before him and then screaming for the emotions to stop, to go back into their proper hiding place. He willed his mind to take over and totally suppress all emotions, ordered himself to not acknowledge any feelings, demanded that he feel absolutely NOTHING.

Throughout the monastery, all the other monks could hear Peter's harrowing ordeal. Some monks shivered in terror, some felt pity and compassion for Peter, and other monks thought Peter was being rightfully punished for daring to love another man.

It took a long time for Peter to succeed in re-imposing mental control over all of his emotions. But finally the old cold numbness once again took over Peter's consciousness, with all his emotions safely banished.

"No feelings of any kind are allowed!" he ordered himself defiantly. "I have no pain, no loss, no loneliness, no abandonment, nothing whatsoever. I feel nothing!"

"Sure, as if you actually believe that," some of the monks muttered to themselves as they continued to listen to Peter's screaming torment.

"You poor, poor man. God bless him," a handful of monks added.

Peter lurched forward, clutching his shattered heart as another wave of pain demanded to be acknowledged and felt. He breathed long and deep breaths, willing his emotions to vanish.

"I have to get away from here. I need to get back to my hills. They are my only hope."

One slow and tremulous step after another, Peter gradually made his way down the corridor, battling the pain and grief and willing them to be buried beyond reach.

<hr />

Meanwhile, in the monastery's meeting cell, Father Abbot sat glumly with Brothers Bartholomew and Clair. Whenever they heard Peter's screams or demands to feel nothing, the three monks cringed in sympathetic pain.

"What a fine mess we have made – again," Father Abbot said with the deepest despair.

Bartholomew emitted a deep sigh. "We have completely failed. Richard is gone, and Brother Peter is right back where he was before the knight arrived. How could we have prevented this?"

Clair shook his head. "Maybe nobody could have prevented this because it was SUPPOSED to happen."

"How can you possibly say that?" Bartholomew asked, raising his voice slightly.

"Look," Clair replied, "everything happens for a reason so that lessons can be learned. We all get so caught up in WHAT is happening that we often miss the actual PURPOSE of these experiences. There are lessons here that all of us are missing. They HAD to be acted out just this way in order for Richard and Peter – and for the rest of us as well – to learn whatever needs to be learned."

"Brother Clair is right," Abbot Paul said. "We become blind to the real lesson or purpose of any difficult situation because we focus on WHAT is happening, then JUDGE what is happening, and then REACT negatively to that judgement."

"What possible lesson," asked Bartholomew, "could Brother Peter and Richard need to learn by Richard not revealing he had a wife and then having to leave the very day the truth came out?"

Paul shrugged and shook his head. "I feel that Brother Peter always expects love to end with pain. Therefore, perhaps he only creates repeated experiences of love ending in pain in order to teach himself that life will always mirror that negative expectation back to him so he can see it and eventually change it and no longer need it. Or maybe our Brother Peter could only accept love coming from Richard but never from himself. So we have to trust that life always gives us what we most need in order to learn, heal, grow and transform – even if we are not ready to accept or learn the lesson in that moment."

Abbot Paul paused briefly to reflect more deeply, then continued.

"We have to trust that Brother Peter has received what he truly needs," Paul continued, "whether he is willing to accept it yet or not. It could be any of these things we have discussed or all of them or even something more. I only know that right now I am too exhausted and saddened by it all to understand ANYTHING for certain."

"So what do we do?" Bartholomew asked.

"For now," Paul replied, "we let Brother Peter return to his hills. We give him time to find whatever peace and comfort he can find with Mother Earth. Then later we will approach him slowly and delicately, with patience, compassion and love, to see if there is anything we can do to help him – or not."

"It is just so sad," Bartholomew said, "that these two men, obviously soulmates, have to end up this way."

"But," Paul reminded the other two monks, "just because two people are soulmates does not mean that they can automatically live together for a long time in happy love and harmony. Life always has its own agenda."

"That is so true," Clair agreed with a nod.

"Excuse me?" Bartholomew interrupted.

Father Abbot continued. "Many people who know about soulmates incorrectly believe that soulmates always automatically fall in love with one another and live happily ever after. They also tend to misperceive that soulmates are always automatically paired as male and female."

"Then what is the point of being with your soulmate if it is not to be together in happiness and love?" Bartholomew asked, visibly distressed by Father Abbot's words.

"Oh dear," Clair said as he glanced at Paul.

"Oh dear indeed," Paul agreed with a nod. "Brother Bartholomew, the greatest gift soulmates can give to each other is learning the most important lessons they need to achieve, as well as whatever healing or transformational evolution will most benefit each other."

"Exactly!" Bartholomew agreed, so far at least.

"But sometimes there is immense fear, denial and deep resistance in us to learning certain key lessons. In those situations, soulmates will often agree to come together on Earth as enemies or as sources of drama and even excruciating pain – if that is what it takes to get each other to release their blockages and learn their spiritual lessons."

"Crap!" Bartholomew muttered with a sense of helplessness.

"Yes indeed," Paul agreed with a sad nod. "Sometimes our most powerful act of love is to unconsciously – or even consciously – create conflict and pain in someone we deeply care about. That is what good parents have to do sometimes. Life will do what is necessary to guide us into our most urgent lessons so true happiness will eventually blossom and prevail. It is not always pretty, but it does work in the end – no matter how we feel about it at the time."

After several moments of deep thought, Bartholomew said, "I had not thought of it that way before."

"Well," Father Abbot continued, "sometimes a specific lesson is far more important than being all lovey-dovey, even if the lesson has to be experienced in a very painful and even shocking way. This is how it has apparently turned out for Richard and our Brother Peter.

Peter screamed again in the distance causing all three monks to cringe again. Then Paul continued.

"It may take several lifetimes for both of them to heal this. And I have a feeling that we three will be there to help them."

The three men sighed.

"Crap," Bartholomew muttered again, but this time with resignation.

There was a sudden knock on the meeting cell door.

"Oh, no," Paul hissed. "Not now."

The three monks remained silent and motionless.

The knock repeated, but the three monks remained silent and unmoving.

On the third knock, the door creaked open, and an older grey-haired monk hesitantly poked his head into the cell.

"Please, Brother Clarence," Paul begged, "could we have a moment? I will come to you later."

"I am very sorry, Father Abbot, but this is important."

"Please, Brother, can it wait?"

"No, Father Abbot, I am afraid not. This is an extreme emergency."

Paul took a moment to calm himself and gather his thoughts. "Yes then, Brother Clarence, what is it?"

"Prior Thomas has been found."

"Thank God. I will come to assist him as soon as we are finished here."

"No, I am afraid not." Clarence took a deep breath. "Prior Thomas is dead."

"What?" Paul, Bartholomew and Clair shouted together as they simultaneously stood up with deep shock.

"Prior Thomas was found in a small wood a few hundred metres north of the monastery."

"What happened? Is it known how he died?" Paul asked.

"It is quite evident how he died."

"Yes?" Paul pressed Clarence, feeling his patience completely deteriorating.

"He hanged himself."

"What?" the other three monks shouted again as one.

"He evidently found a rope somewhere, most probably from the stables, and he hanged himself from an upper birch-tree branch."

"God have mercy on us all!" Paul cried out with genuine grief. Pulling himself together as best he could, Father Abbot said to Brother Clarence, "Thank you for informing me. We will follow you immediately to bring Prior Thomas back to the monastery and prepare his body for burial."

Brother Clarence solemnly nodded, pulled back his head and closed the door. The three monks stared at one another in paralysed disbelief.

"We must go now," Abbot Paul announced. The other two monks nodded their agreement and followed him out of the meeting cell.

———◆•◆•◆———

Richard rode Orion as he left the monastery to head back south to Northumbria. With each step that the steed took, Richard's heart crumbled into more pieces as he moved further away from Peter.

"How will I ever recover from this?" he asked Orion. "I have lost him forever. He blames me for causing this, and he is right. I did lie. I did keep secrets and deceive him. I fell completely in love with him. He and I were one, but now we are nothing. How do I survive this?"

Orion could feel all the pain and anguish Richard was experiencing and wanted to help his grieving human. But how? Orion could only carry Richard to his destination and trust that the knight would find some hope there.

"What will I tell Anne? Do I say nothing and live yet another lie? Or do I tell her the truth and face the anger and hurt it will undoubtedly cause her? I am lost either way. *"Mi sono dannato per un'eternità dell'inferno."* {"I have damned myself to an eternity of hell."}

Step by step, Orion carried his miserable human forward and listened to his cries of loss and self-hatred.

"Ti amo. Ti amo per sempre." {"I love you. I will love you forever."}

"Sono molto dispiaciuto. Come vivo con questa culpa? Sono imperdonabile." {"I am very sorry. How do I live with this guilt? I am unforgivable."}

"Dannazione all'inferno! Sei il mio amato. Ma tu sei perso per me per sempre." {"Damn it to hell! You are my beloved. But you are lost to me forever."}

The heaviness of Richard's emotions made Orion feel as if his passenger had quadrupled in weight.

"Come posso vivere mai senza Peter? Non posso. Vorrei morire presto, quindi non devo sopportare questa infinita sofferenza." {"How can I ever live without Peter? I cannot. I want to die soon so I do not have to endure this endless misery."}

Orion understood Richard's every word and could also sense every emotion wracking the knight's body. This loving steed sent enormous compassion to Richard but felt unable to help him in any other way.

Richard constantly wiped tears from his cheeks as he continued to ride south. His heart felt broken and empty.

"Per favore lasciami morire presto." {"Please let me die soon."}

"Ti amo per sempre, Peter." {"I will love you forever, Peter."}

But then Richard instantly contradicted himself.

"Non amero mai più. Mai e poi mai. Non amero mai più. Mi sono perso." {"I will never love again. Never ever. I will never love again. I am lost."}

———•◦●◦•———

The cold lashing wind felt good on Peter's face as he forced himself to walk across the monastery's courtyard towards the arched entryway and then towards his Highland hills. He imagined each whip of the wind ripping away any remaining shreds of his pain – and his entire consciousness itself – bit by bit.

Patches of early March snow still lay upon the earth, but the pre-dawn fog had lifted. A tiny fragment of the sun courageously attempted to penetrate the heavy grey-slated sky.

Peter estimated that both Richard and the king's messenger must be well on their ways south by now. When another sharp pang of grief gripped his chest and stomach, Peter stopped walking in order to take several deep breaths. He repeatedly ordered the grief to disappear – like an endless mantra.

"God-damned feelings! Go bury yourself where I cannot find you!"

"And I will not think of him," Peter ordered himself. But even the vaguest thought of Richard resurfaced new waves of pain and grief, and then Peter had to start all over again to force himself to feel nothing.

Sitting in the cold wind on a rickety wooden bench near the monastery's arched entryway was a forlorn Brother Andrew. The young monk appeared lonely and fragile, his entire body sagging with sadness. Andrew was in pain to see Richard leave, to know it was over between Richard and Peter, and to realise that Peter would never be interested in him. After all, Andrew was no Richard. At this point, the youth was unaware of Prior Thomas' suicide.

Peter, also unaware of Prior Thomas' death, immediately felt irritated and impatient when he saw a crushed Andrew. Despite seeing Andrew's despair as he sat upon a bench that was as broken as the youthful monk himself felt, Peter could only focus on repressing all his own emotions. Andrew was too direct a mirror of what Peter was trying to avoid, deny and get rid of within himself.

Unfortunately for Peter, Brother Andrew looked up before Peter could pass him by unnoticed and escape out into the countryside.

"Good day, Brother Peter," Andrew said with the deepest pain.

"Yes, good day," Peter answered without directly looking at the young monk. He passed the youth, reached the archway, and then, suddenly and mysteriously, Peter stopped and stood dead still.

"What the hell?" he muttered.

His legs were completely locked, frozen in place. Peter could not take another step, no matter how hard he tried. He made a half dozen attempts to push himself forward, to force his body to move on, but nothing worked. Peter's legs had decided he would not take another step. They were rigid, and his feet were frozen to the spot.

"Get out of here before Brother Andrew notices I am just standing still here and then tries to start a conversation or ask to help. Get me out of here now!" Peter ordered his body.

But Peter's legs refused to listen. There would be no more steps at this time – which drove Peter into a silent panic. How long would this last? What if Andrew noticed?

Then Andrew DID notice, and he looked at Peter with teary eyes.

"You miss him too, do you not?"

"Damn, damn, double damn!" Peter thought angrily. *"Now I have lost control and must start all over again!"*

"Yes, I miss him," Peter responded to shut up Brother Andrew. An upheaval of pain wrenched Peter's stomach.

"Going for your walk into the hills, I suppose," Andrew said. "I know how important those walks are for you. So please do not let me stop you. I am sorry I detained you."

"Yes, well, that is good to hear. Thank you. Goodbye."

Brother Andrew curled up on the bench in a foetal position. Peter tried to walk again, but his legs refused to budge. Peter fought back tears that had begun to well in his eyes, foiling his attempt at total emotional repression.

"No!" Peter ordered himself silently. *"I will not cry. I will NOT feel this pain! I will feel NOTHING! I reject all my emotions, bury them as deeply as I can so I no longer see or feel them!"*

Peter wondered how to get his legs moving again. From the deepest source within himself he heard an answer, but Peter was aghast at what he heard.

"I WILL NOT!" he screamed with silent fury. *"I will NOT invite Brother Andrew to join me on my walk. It is an invasion of my privacy, a rejection of MY needs. I do not want any friendship with Brother Andrew. He does not interest me in the least. Because he gives me NOTHING! He is too*

young, immature, naïve, weak and cowardly. He is NOT what I want, and I will not be forced into any relationship with him. Absolutely NOT!"

As he screamed these inward thoughts, Peter somehow retrieved his will power and mobilised it to overcome the resistance in his legs. With the greatest exertion, Peter fought stubbornly until he finally forced his legs to move forward. Then he quickly walked through the archway, out of the monastery and towards his healing Highland hills.

Andrew watched sadly as Peter left the monastery. "I am nothing, unworthy of anything or anybody. Why do I even exist?"

It never occurred to Andrew to talk about his feelings with any other monk, not even to Father Abbot. And no one ever considered talking to Andrew about his obvious despair. This would lead to centuries of unhappy and self-destructive reincarnations.

Peter's legs ached with stiffness and occasional spasms, but he did not care. He was back in control of himself, he was finally walking again, and he was returning to his hills for solace and peace. The monk ordered himself to remain in control and never let his emotions take over again.

At one point, Peter dared to stop briefly and look to his left, knowing Richard was heading south, leaving Alba forever to cross the border back into Northumbria.

"I will never see you again, ever," he whispered to himself between tears. "I will be alone for the rest of my life, and I do not know how I will bear it."

Before facing forward again to continue his trek into the Highland hills, Peter uttered the only phrase he could remember in Richard's native tongue.

"Addio, amato fratello." {"Farewell, beloved brother."}

With each step forward, Peter repeated as a mantra his command to remain in control: "I will never love again. Never ever. I will never love again."

———•◆•———

It took two days to make the arrangements to bury Prior Thomas. After the burial ceremony, Father Abbot Paul and Brothers Clair and Bartholomew met once again in the monastery's meeting room.

"That was depressing," Bartholomew spoke in a barely audible whisper.

"We have much to take responsibility for," Clair said in agreement. "We were not there for Prior Thomas when he needed us the most."

"How were we to know?" Bartholomew asked. "He never shared anything with us. He only criticised and condemned."

"That in itself should have told us something," Paul said. And he knew it was not true that Prior Thomas never confided in anyone about his personal torment. But Paul felt it was not yet appropriate to bring that up.

"Did any of you notice Brother Peter was nowhere to be seen during the burial?" Clair asked.

"A deliberate rejection towards Prior Thomas?" Bartholomew conjectured.

"I am not sure Brother Peter even knows about Prior Thomas' death," Paul stated. "He has hardly been seen anywhere in the monastery since Richard's departure. It IS possible he still does not know."

The three men sat in silence, each brooding on their separate guilt-ridden doubts.

It was the monastery's healer who finally broke the silence.

"Why would Prior Thomas choose to kill himself, and by hanging?" Bartholomew asked.

"Perhaps," Clair suggested with a deep sigh, "Prior Thomas finally gave up all hope that Brother Andrew would ever respond positively to him." Clair shook his head sadly.

"Andrew?" Abbot Paul asked. "Do you think Prior Thomas was enamoured with Brother Andrew?"

"Of course," Clair replied. "It was obvious to all of us. Prior Thomas was always mooning over Brother Andrew and disappointed that Brother Andrew ignored him, which was mostly from fear of Prior Thomas. And remember how furious Prior Thomas was every time Brother Andrew had eyes only for Brother Peter? He was obviously jealous that Brother Peter got all of Brother Andrew's adoring attention instead of him."

"Oh my God," Father Abbot whispered. "All this time you have all thought that Prior Thomas was lusting for Brother Andrew?"

"Yes, of course," Clair replied as Bartholomew nodded in agreement.

Paul shook his head, understanding that now the time had come to share his secret regarding the dead prior. "Then I need to inform you that ALL of you were quite wrong. The truth is, Prior Thomas was not drawn to Brother Andrew at all. In fact, he was disgusted by our young monk, seeing Brother Andrew as useless, naïve, weak and immature – just as Brother Peter had also judged him to be. Prior Thomas also blamed Brother Andrew for constantly getting in the way of who he truly lusted after."

"What?" Clair exclaimed. "Brother Andrew was blocking Prior Thomas from whom?"

Paul took another deep breath. "From Brother Peter."

"Brother Peter?" Bartholomew and Clair exclaimed in unison. But it was Clair who continued aloud first.

"Brother Peter? Are you sure? Prior Thomas was forever complaining about Brother Peter, scathingly claiming Brother Peter was arrogant, heartless, selfish and every other damning word he could think of. Prior Thomas condemned Brother Peter whenever he could!"

"Exactly," Paul said, nodding his head. "Prior Thomas was so hurt by Brother Peter's constant rejections that the only way he could deal with that pain was by attacking Brother Peter whenever he could. But I know it was Brother Peter he was lusting after all along because he came to me and told me so."

Brothers Clair and Bartholomew stared at Father Abbot with dumbfounded expressions.

"We had several discussions about it," Paul continued. "I tried several times to warn Prior Thomas about Brother Peter, explaining that Brother Peter was far too shut down and emotionally unavailable to respond to any monk, let alone Prior Thomas with his constantly aggressive judgements."

"Oh Lord!" Bartholomew gasped. "And then Richard came along."

Paul nodded. "Exactly. And then Richard came along," he repeated.

"Brother Peter fell madly in love with Richard after I had told Prior Thomas that Brother Peter would forever be too emotionally unavailable to be attracted to anyone. But that turned out not to be the case. Poor Prior Thomas was forced to watch the man he most desired fall in love with the knight instead."

"The poor man," Clair sighed. "To be so constantly denied by Brother Peter who then fell in love with Richard – and so quickly. Prior Thomas must have felt this rejection was just too humiliating and beyond his capacity to accept."

"So he destroyed himself – and by hanging," said Paul, shaking his head with immense grief.

"Choking to death on his repressed emotions," Clair mumbled.

"I wonder," Bartholomew began but then hesitated.

"Yes?" Father Paul prompted.

"This is madness, and I apologise. We have just buried Prior Thomas after he killed himself by hanging, and here I am considering theories."

"Continue, Brother Bartholomew," Paul insisted. "Your theory may give us better understanding."

"Alright. So now we know that Prior Thomas actually lusted after Brother Peter but used aggressive accusations against him to cover up the pain of feeling rejected. I can see that now."

"Yes?" Paul prompted.

"But I wonder – was the prior's desire just for Brother Peter, or did he also want Richard because the knight looked so identical to Brother Peter? If that were true, was our prior therefore experiencing a DOUBLE rejection from BOTH men?"

Clair and Father Abbot Paul were stunned by Bartholomew's insight.

"A very interesting point, Brother Bartholomew," Paul said. "But I do not feel there is any way we can ever know the answer for certain. The tragedy did happen, and now nothing can be done about it. Poor, poor man."

"We were so focussed," Clair shared, "on trying to help Brother Peter that we totally ignored the needs and pain of Prior Thomas, and now he is dead and buried."

"We did this to him," Bartholomew agreed. "We drove Prior Thomas to his suicide through our neglect. This will take LIFETIMES to clear, if that is even possible. But at least we can all learn something from this."

"We have made grievous errors," Paul stated flatly. "We have much to atone for, much to take responsibility for, much to straighten out. I have a horrible feeling deep in my gut that the work we have to carry out to try to heal these errors and bring some semblance of healing peace to all of us involved will take us a long, long time."

Clair nodded his head. "Lifetimes and lifetimes upon lifetimes." For once, there was no jovial smile on his face.

They stared at one another grimly.

"Crap," Bartholomew muttered.

"Another problem, Brother Bartholomew?" Father Abbot asked.

"I was just thinking," Bartholomew began.

"Have you ever thought about NOT thinking?" Clair asked. "Your theories are wearing me out!"

"Brother Clair!" Paul admonished the chubby monk.

"Sorry," Clair replied with a sheepish grin.

"Please proceed, Brother Bartholomew. Every one of your insights has given us a lot to think about."

"Well," Bartholomew began again. "I am now feeling a theory about Richard."

"Go on," Paul encouraged.

"We have discussed before how Peter may have, on a deeper spiritual level but not in his conscious awareness, co-created this tragic ending so that he would have an escape from his relationship with Richard because he fears that love always and automatically ends in rejection, abandonment and pain."

"Yes," Paul prompted with a nod.

"Now I wonder about Richard."

"And?" Paul prompted again.

"BOTH men may be acting on fears deep within themselves unknown to their conscious awareness."

"This is what usually happens in life, so we can see exactly what we are doing and why," Paul answered. "So Brother Bartholomew, what do you feel is Richard's unconscious issue?"

"What if Richard had the same rejection fears as Brother Peter? I remember us theorising at some point that Richard might have used his knighthood duties as a way to avoid intimacy and commitment."

———————————

"What does he mean that THEY discussed that possibility?" one raven asked the other as both birds perched atop the monastery roof above the meeting cell, telepathically listening in on the monks' discussion. *"WE were the ones who had that conversation!"*

"And then I passed our conversation on to the three men in their dreams so when they woke up they would have the same discussion and come to their own conclusions."

"But —"

"Shh! I want to hear what they are saying."

———————————

Bartholomew continued speaking.

"Even though we now know that Richard is married, he might be apart from his wife the majority of the time. His lifestyle requires a lot of travel and that could be the way he has escaped commitment to his wife."

"I see. And?" Paul asked.

"Did Richard unconsciously fail to tell Brother Peter he was married because he was so thoroughly consumed by his affair with our fellow monk? Or did Richard deliberately keep the truth from him, hoping it would eventually come out and then use that as the way to escape from any commitment to Brother Peter?"

The other two monks stared blankly again at Bartholomew with his channelled theorising.

"The first possibility does not exclude the second one," Clair offered.

"Brother Clair makes a good point," Paul said. "These are all possibilities we should meditate on. What a mess! But in the end, I fear we may never know the answers to ANY of our questions."

"Crap!" the three monks muttered simultaneously.

"Uh oh," Bartholomew muttered.

"Heaven save us all! He is thinking again!" Clair complained.

"Brother Clair!" Paul admonished with a glare.

"Sorry."

"Continue, Brother Bartholomew."

"Another thought just hit me. But once more this is not about Prior Thomas, who we must really focus on today as we just buried him."

"Please continue anyway," Paul insisted. "Any insights will help us meditate on these events."

"I always thought how extraordinary it was that Brother Peter and Richard look so much alike but are not related and were born in different countries."

"Yes," Paul agreed.

"But now it all makes sense to me," Bartholomew said with wonder. "Of course the two men looked alike – so that Brother Peter could see himself in Richard's face and thereby finally learn to love HIMSELF as much as he loved Richard."

Paul and Clair nodded their agreement.

"But it seems to me that Brother Peter did NOT learn that lesson," Paul said. "Therefore, this process will continue for him into his future lifetimes, and we will follow him each time to do our best to help him."

What none of the monks at Saint James Monastery would ever learn about was the "chance" meeting that had taken place between Prior Thomas and Richard when Thomas had mistaken Richard for Peter.

Because Thomas was accustomed to being constantly criticised and ridiculed, he therefore developed aggressive avoidance tactics to protect himself against the negative reactions of others. Pity and compassion Thomas could neither understand nor tolerate. So Richard's compassion had completely thrown Thomas off guard.

But no one at the monastery would ever realise that Richard's COMPASSION had been the "straw that broke the camel's back," leading to Thomas' decision to commit suicide by hanging.

Seventeen

BEFORE THE DISCOVERY of Prior Thomas' death and before his burial three days later, there was the departure of Richard from the monastery and the escaping of Peter into his beloved Highland hills.

"*I was right!*" the first raven spat triumphantly, as the two birds flew circles around each other.

"*Shove it up your feathery ass,*" the second raven retorted, trembling with anguish for Richard and Peter – and even for Prior Thomas as well. The two ravens conversed telepathically as they spiralled high in the sky.

"*Humans always screw everything up,*" the first raven continued. "*They destroy everything in their paths. They cannot help it. They are too ignorant to realise how ignorant they are.*"

"*You forever judge them too severely.*"

"*And as for all this importance that you place on humans recognising what they feel and FEELING what they feel and then being HONEST about what they feel –*"

"*Will you shut up!*" the second raven cawed angrily. "*You do not get it at all.*"

"*Get what?*"

"*The importance of emotions.*"

"*Here we go again with THAT lecture.*"

"*No lecture. Just the most basic truth in this Universe. EMOTIONS ARE THE ONLY FACTS. Everything else is just caw-caw.*"

"*And yet,*" said the first raven, "*everyone did as they did, emotions or* no emotions. *The knight deceived the monk. The monk hated the prior and then shut down his emotions – entirely. The prior hated everybody but secretly lusted after your monk and then hanged himself. The youngest monk remains irritatingly self-deprecating. What else do you expect from humans? You are just being a sore loser."*

"By the Cosmos, what is happening?"

"What?" The bitching raven scanned himself nervously. *"What is wrong? What do you see?"*

"I cannot believe it! Are your tiny, skinny little raven legs transforming into human legs, and your claws manifesting into tiny human toes? And oh – your wings are sprouting arms!"

The other raven cawed in panic and flew away.

"You stupid, naïve little twerp. Good riddance!" the other raven replied defiantly.

The remaining raven continued his wide spiralling. Down below, the black bird could see Richard upon his white steed heading south, with the Northumbrian king's messenger on his horse far ahead of the knight. Veering west, the raven watched Peter, the bird's personal human, as the monk plodded towards the Highland hills.

"The two of you have missed the point once again, just like all your lifetimes before," the raven sighed. *"When will you humans learn that it is not WHAT happens that is most important but rather the lessons beneath the actions? The two of you remain stuck in WHAT has happened, and in JUDGING what has happened and in REACTING to your judgements. All that only carries you further and further away from the real meaning that the experience was meant to teach you about yourselves. Neither of you sees how or why you two co-created your relationship to end the way it did.*

"What untransformed fears and negative expectations did both of you fail to recognise in yourselves? What self-sabotage still runs wild in your unconscious minds? How can you both learn to see these fear-based patterns, heal them and no longer need to repeat them?"

The bird continued his circling. *"I will stay with you,"* he called out telepathically to Peter. *"I will come back in each of your lifetimes as a guiding spirit to help you find your way home – just as I have done in almost all of your previous lifetimes."*

The raven watched Peter from above as the monk walked towards his beloved hills. *"Your fears, judgements, expectations and attitudes still dominate and limit your lifetimes – until you are finally ready to see what is really happening inside you. Someday both you and Richard will choose to see and heal your patterns. First change your attitudes and then your life experiences will change. Shift your focus. Look for deeper meanings inside yourself and others, instead of just reacting to surface-level events. Stop imprisoning yourself by reacting to your judgements. How can I help you to understand this? It remains a mystery to me. And maybe that is MY lesson to learn."*

Peter's mentor raven continued to circle high above, looking down upon the grieving Peter and Richard as they moved further apart in their different directions. Then the raven telepathically called down to both of them.

"Coraggio! Dove c'è amore, c'è sempre speranza." {"Have courage! Where there is love, there is always hope."}

Neither the knight nor the monk was ready to hear the raven's wise and supporting words – but someday they would, the raven prayed.

"Non amero mai più. Mai e poi mai. Non amero mai più," cried the broken-hearted knight riding south upon Orion. And as Peter continued to walk westward, he repeated Richard's lament in his own language.

"I will never love again. Never ever. I will never love again."

The saga continues into their following reincarnations.
An Ending to the Next Beginning.

Author's Afterword

The original and much shorter version of this past-life memory novel was written back in 1984. Then in early March of 2019, I went into a diabetic coma for three days and lost all conscious memory of an entire week. When I was finally coherent and back in this earthly here-and-now, the very first thing I felt and heard deep within me was firm guidance from my Higher Self to re-write and expand *Beloved Brother* with alterations that would be clearly channelled to me.

Okey-dokey, I thought – why not? As I re-wrote my past-life story, I relived all its emotionally intense memories and also made many textual changes and additions in order to more accurately depict the events that had been experienced and felt at that time.

As mentioned in the "Author's Foreword" at the beginning of this book, I added the fictional raven dialogues because they added so much depth and expansive clarity to the novel – and they were so much fun, too.

The other change was the ending. In the original 1984 manuscript, I gave a happier and more hopeful ending to the novel that did not accurately portray the truth of what had actually occurred. Thirty-five years ago, I had originally written this book to be conventionally published, and I thought the public would prefer a more uplifting ending.

But this time around, I knew it was more important for me to stick to my truth about that lifetime as I clearly remembered and "relived" it throughout this re-write. In addition, I am a (hopefully) wiser person now with a much deeper understanding of what "happy" and "hopeful" mean and how we humans can create those states of consciousness. So if anyone reading my revised book is saddened by or disappointed with its true ending, well deal with it yourself! That is YOUR process to learn and grow from.

I now understand that the main reason for me to re-write this book was to bring those severe emotional traumas from my seventh-century Alban (Scottish) lifetime into my here-and-now to be fully embraced on a much deeper level. I feel that the diabetic coma was my body's way to get me to "shut down" for a few days so I could then more clear-headedly revisit these urgent and unresolved emotional issues in order to create a fuller healing transformation within myself.

During my week's stay in the hospital, I was told by several nurses and doctors (because I had and still have no memory about it whatsoever) that I came out of the diabetic coma screaming hysterically, and that it took them a very long time to get me to stop screaming. When Peter and Richard were making their final farewell 1,300 years ago, Peter broke down into uncontrollable screaming until he managed to totally repress his emotions for the rest of his life. This made me wonder if I had already relived that particular emotional memory of Peter's farewell to Richard while I was in the coma, finally releasing what had been too successfully repressed 1,300 years before. If this is true, then my waking up from the coma screaming my guts out (so to speak) makes a lot of sense. *Oy vey!*

During the six intense months that it took me to re-write this book, I cried a lot because of both the physical and emotional pains that surged up to the surface of my consciousness to be accepted and healed. For example, after coming out of my diabetic coma, I developed a constant burning pain in my left nipple that vanished (the pain, not the nipple) when the re-writing was completed.

So what is it with me and nipples? It certainly was a big theme between Richard and Peter (with Brother Clair's inspiration). And if Clair were here with me now, what could he share with me about this?

——————◆◆◆——————

So far I have written seven novels based on my various past-life memories, which each time gave me a solid foundation for revisiting issues, memories and emotions that I let slip away from me in the past.

Okay, not slip away. I downright buried, ignored and denied them. However, all these issues now need to be readdressed and embraced. The diabetic coma prepared me mentally, emotionally and energetically for the subsequent roller-coaster ride I needed in order to remember, heal, transform and complete the Peter/Richard learning experience.

Also, I strongly believe that once past-life issues are worked through and their lessons fully absorbed within, it is vital to then release those past-life memories. Their purpose was to teach and transform. Once that is accomplished, the past must be released and stored only as unconscious memories – so that the conscious mind can be fully present in THIS here and now. Consciously and indefinitely holding on to past-life memories can become an all too easy ploy or safety net to escape being fully present with the emotional issues that we need to be experiencing NOW. I feel that this mental game is a karmic no-no.

———————•◦◉◦•———————

Re-writing *Beloved Brother* at this time in my life has also given me some deeper insights into my strong emotional relationship with VENICE – which I passionately love. It is the most beautiful and extraordinary city on the planet. Certainly, part of my love for Venice is about its architecture, art, food, culture and so on. But re-writing this novel made it clear to me that my deepest emotional love for Venice is not about Venice itself at all. Rather, it is because Venice is where Richard was born, and therefore this city has always unconsciously reminded me of HIM.

Now if I am not careful here, this "Author's Afterword" could end up being as long as the novel itself! Well, there it is.

Listening to Italian always gives me goose-bumps and sends chills up my spine. Of course it does. Let's look back at this lifetime that I just wrote about. When Richard was feeling his most passionate, he always reverted back to his native Venetian dialect of whatever was seventh-century Venetian-Italian. I can see why. Italian SOUNDS so sensuously rich and musical. If you curse someone with the rudest possible Italian words, you always end up sounding utterly romantic. Italian reminds me of Richard's verbal lovemaking to Peter (me!).

When I was very young, I thought the definition of oral sex was to talk about it. Older now, I know better. Now my definition of oral sex is to speak Italian. **Grazzi**, Richard – Riccardo.

————◆•◆•◆————

After our brief but passionate seventh-century love affair, it would be nearly one thousand years before reincarnations of Peter and Richard crossed paths again. And when they did reunite, it was at the very beginning of the seventeenth century – in Venice of course! In the near future, I plan to write my eighth past-life novel detailing this particular lifetime. I pray I won't need another diabetic coma (or any other kind of coma) to begin writing that book. And I hope I won't experience a painful nipple (or any other part of my body) like I did this time. Can we make that a deal, Universe?

For a long time, I debated whether or not in this "Author's Afterword" I should tell you how things ended up for Richard and Peter. I wasn't sure whether to end the story as I have done or to fill you in on what finally happened to each of them individually. In the end, after much inner debate, I felt not to divulge Peter and Richard's ultimate fates in that lifetime. Some of you may prefer this and thus leave Peter and Richard where they are at the end of the novel – both of them on the edge of their new but very uncertain futures.

HOWEVER, if any of you readers out there desperately want to know what finally happened to Richard and Peter (and even to some of the other monks), you can e-mail me at <u>william.shaffer52@outlook.com</u> – and I will respond and fill you in. But I warn you, have your hankies ready because it is not "good" news in the conventional sense. You have been warned.

I would also like to take a moment to mention the healer monk, Brother Bartholomew. In the original version of this book, he was hardly present at all. While rewriting this book, I realised how horribly under-valued Bartholomew was by Peter and ALL the monks. But Richard was the only one who did not fall into that trap. Instead, he recognised the enormous value of Bartholomew and made an effort to explore the monk's true soul-value.

In this version of my book, I wanted to develop Bartholomew much more and show some of his deeper qualities that were so unappreciated at the time.

I also discovered after rewriting this book that the present reincarnation of Brother Bartholomew is a very close, special and dear friend of mine whom I value and treasure tremendously. Bartholomew tended to hold himself back 1,300 years ago, afraid to show others the incredible depths, talents and gifts he so wondrously possessed. Now in this present lifetime, he is beginning to heal and transform that tendency, which I am very happy to see. There is much more to see of Bartholomew in this updated version. I want to celebrate the wisdom and special soul that he was back then and continues to be today.

And now I hope that this book that you have just read about one of my past-lives will trigger and accelerate a healing and transformational process of your own.

And to the man who is now living as the reincarnated Richard, I send you my total love and wish you a life full of healing, magical adventure, personal fulfilment and abundant huggy-love.

Oh, and one more thing, Mr. Reincarnated Richard. Did you manage to come back this time with those same pretty nipples? Or is that too personal a question to ask you since we haven't yet met (as of the time I am writing these words) and we may not ever meet in this lifetime? I kept my pretty nipples. Just thought you'd like to know. Wherever Brother Clair is now, he would be delighted if we BOTH came back with our pretty nipples. You can e-mail me, former Richard, if you feel to do so. But ONLY if you feel to. Otherwise, we will go our separate ways without meeting again in this lifetime. It's absolutely okay. But maybe next life? Because I still love you and miss you. That never ended, regardless of how it all ended 1,300 years ago.

Goodbye, Richard. *Addio, amato fratello*, and thank you for our past adventures together.

"You see," the first raven boasted. *"I told you that if I stuck with Peter and kept giving him my support, he would eventually grasp the real purpose of that life experience and use it for his growth and transformational healing."*

"Good for you!" said the second raven. *"But it took the human THIRTEEN HUNDRED YEARS to finally get it!"*

"Linear time is only a teaching illusion. All existence is NOW! You know that as well as I do. You complain just for the sake of complaining. The Hebrews have the perfect word to describe you – **KVETCH**! *So just stop it!"*

"What does **kvetch** *mean?"*

"Someone who incessantly complains just for the joy of complaining!"

"I still say you see in humans what is not there," the second raven insisted.

"And I tell you that you are blinder than a cockroach's butt."

"I will believe you when I see that humans can truly change, grow and heal – which will be an hour after NEVER!"

"I do not think you have the capacity to see anything at all."

"Bitch!"

"Good God – do not move!"

"Why? What is wrong?" the second raven asked with mounting terror. *"What is happening to me?"*

"I cannot believe it – but you are transforming into a human body right before my eyes!"

"Oh, you liar! You ARE lying, are you not? You have to be! You unsavoury pile of puppy poop!"

Let's show that second raven a thing or two and make him eat his own words, puppy poop and all! WOO-HOO!

Addio!

William L. Shaffer
Dinas Powys, Wales
3 September 2019